Best Hikes Rocky Mountain National Park

A Guide to the Park's Greatest Hiking Adventures

Kent Dannen

FALCONGUIDES

GUILFORD, CONNECTICUT
HELENA, MONTANA

FALCONGUIDES®

An imprint of Rowman & Littlefield
Falcon, FalconGuides, and Outfit Your Mind are registered trademarks of Rowman & Littlefield.

Distributed by NATIONAL BOOK NETWORK

Copyright © 2015 by Rowman & Littlefield

Maps by Melissa Baker and Alena Pearce © Rowman & Littlefield
All photos by Kent Dannen

British Library Cataloguing-in-Publication Information Available

Library of Congress Cataloging-in-Publication Data
Dannen, Kent.
  Best hikes Rocky Mountain National Park : a guide to the park's greatest hiking adventures/ Kent Dannen.
    pages cm
  Includes index.
  ISBN 978-1-4930-0813-1 (pbk.)—ISBN 978-1-4930-1477-4 (e-book) 1. Hiking—Colorado—Rocky Mountain National Park—Guidebooks. 2. Trails—Colorado—Rocky Mountain National Park—Guidebooks. 3. Rocky Mountain National Park (Colo.)—Guidebooks. I. Title.
  GV199.42.C62 R6224
  796.5109788'69—dc23

                          2015009922

Contents

The Hikes

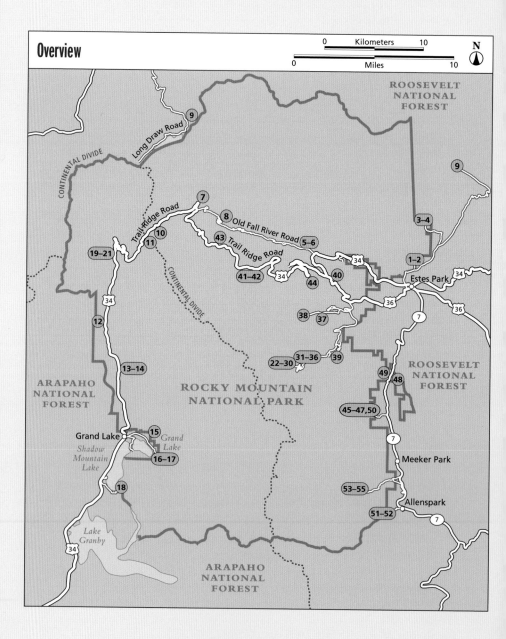

To my parents, who showed me ancient paths: Mary Ellen and Dwight Dannen

Ask for the ancient paths
where the good way is; and walk in it
and find rest for your souls.

—Jeremiah 6:16

Introduction

Although my guidebooks to trails in Rocky Mountain National Park have been widely read, I never have been asked, "What is the park's best trail?" I *have* been asked, however, "What's your favorite trail?" I suppose this is the same question.

I always answer, "My favorite trail is the one I hiked most recently." This answer is not flippant or evasive. The best hike is defined differently not only by the values and goals of each individual who steps on a trail but also by the infinite variety of experiences each hike can provide.

For instance, I once led the late, great authority on bird identification, Roger Tory Peterson, on a short walk from a parking lot on Trail Ridge Road up to the edge of Lava Cliffs and the perpetual snowbank there. He wanted to add the brown-capped rosy finch to the list of birds he had seen.

This may seem a rather odd goal, but to the constantly expanding population of people who watch birds, this is a very big deal. It likely was a bigger deal to the famous RTP than to anyone else. The rosy finches were there in ideal rosy finch habitat of snow and cliffs, unafraid in rosy finch fashion and very easy to see. Doctor Peterson did not need the high-powered binoculars that hung around his neck.

He was more than delighted and praised me to others in the world of natural history publishing, which boosted my career as an outdoor writer. To Roger Tory Peterson this short puff-and-pant above 12,000 feet to a somewhat hazardous cliff edge (other birders below did not focus their binoculars on rosy finches—they were concerned about their hero's safety) was the best hike in Rocky Mountain National Park.

I did not include Lava Cliffs in this collection of the best: too short, less opportunity for less-specific interests than rosy finches, not as varied as other tundra hikes originating from Trail Ridge Road. Yet, for perhaps one of history's most prominent naturalists, Lava Cliffs was the best.

Other factors influencing the best may include convenient access. It seems absurd that the size of a trailhead parking lot can affect the quality of the hike. But when hikers' cars on an August weekend line the roadside from the Longs Peak Trailhead parking area halfway down to CO 7, the climb up Longs can begin with a frantic attitude that leads to a fatal fall on the normally safe "Homestretch" below the summit. The National Park Service would be negligent in its preservation duty if it built parking lots big enough for the largest crowds on the busiest day. So on

◀ *The Bierstadt Lake Trail climbs amid quaking aspens in fall below silhouettes of Front Range peaks.*

that particular day, Longs Peak may not occupy its usual place among the best. At such times, hikers can restore Longs firmly to the best list simply by consciously choosing to leave the frustration behind and enjoy the climb that many climbers of all 14,000-foot peaks in Colorado leave until last because they believe Longs to be the best.

Also among the best hikes may be those that advance hikers to other goals. Longs Peak is the goal of some 15,000 mountaineers each year. Many of these hikers are, to be generous, inadequately conditioned to climb a 14,259-foot peak. Lack of adequate conditioning affects the mind first. The body is quite capable of moving on without any dictates from a brain shut down by weariness until some part of the body collides with something overly hard at an overly fast speed. Hopefully, the body part affected is a stubbed toe rather than a cracked skull.

Conditioning in a gym is not the best way to prevent such mishaps. The best way to get in shape for hiking is to hike. Therefore, this book describes some hikes that include off-trail sections in order to encourage those aspirants to the park's highest peak to work their way to proper conditioning by ascending some lower mountains before heading up Longs. Start with short hikes such as Ouzel Falls or Emerald Lake. Move on to a couple of longer lake hikes, such as Crystal or Black Lake. Then ascend an 11,000-foot peak such as Twin Sisters, followed another day by a 12,000-foot peak like Hallett. Head next for the top of a thirteener like Taylor Peak or Ypsilon Mountain. Finally, purchase a commemorative alarm clock and hit the Longs Peak Trail at 3 a.m.

Of course such pleasant preparation will take a couple of weeks. This may seem like a long time to get ready for Longs Peak. But, under the best circumstances, six weeks are required to heal a broken bone that might have been prevented by first doing fun hikes to achieve the best physical shape to ascend a challenging fourteener.

Season also helps define best. Woodlilies blooming along the Cub Lake Trail in early July put it among the best. The same is true of calypso orchids blooming at Calypso Cascades in Wild Basin a bit later in July. The tundra hikes from Trail Ridge Road are best when tiny floral jewels bloom in mid-July. But if you have an ornithological goal to see white-tailed ptarmigan in their mostly white feathers, tramp above tree line on Trail Ridge Road in December, the best time to hike there for ptarmigan despite 100-mile-per-hour winds.

Wildlife encounters define best for many hikers. Seeing a water ouzel is a common, entertaining experience that puts Ouzel Falls on many hikers' best lists.

But most wildlife encounters are much harder to predict. While revising the guidebook *Best Easy Day Hikes Rocky Mountain National Park*, I literally ran up the trail to The Pool to see for myself what damage some unknown fool had inflicted by forest fire. I had hiked this trail countless times and would not need my comparatively heavy camera. Not carrying a camera broke my decades-long policy, but

I was frantic about fire damage. Walking back after learning that the trail to The Pool still ranked among the best, I met a bear at trailside, sitting in a large creeping juniper patch happily gorging on berrylike blue juniper cones. Acting against experience by hiking without a camera, I missed a photo opportunity that would have made a best hike permanently "bester" for me.

You never know for certain what the best hike today will be. This book is my best guess.

How to Use This Guide

This guide describes 55 hikes ranging in distance from very short to my-feet-are-killing-me. The hikes are scattered across one of America's most popular national parks, averaging approximately 3 million visitors each year. (Do not despair; they do not all hike.)

The descriptions are organized by proximity of one trail to another. These 55 hikes usually follow trails, although there are many hiking destinations in Rocky Mountain National Park not reached all the way by trails. I have included a few of these to mountain summits primarily because Longs Peak is the inspiring goal for very many hikers, and they need to ascend some less high peaks to prepare for Longs (yes, really). The 12,000- and 13,000-foot peaks have trails only partway to the summits. Longs Peak, by contrast, has a very well-marked, if sometimes ignored, route to the top. (Hiking goals without trails all the way are included in my comprehensive guide, *Hiking Rocky Mountain National Park*.)

Each hike description begins with decision-making data to help you determine whether this hike is for you. Following a short overview, you'll find where the hike starts, distance, average hiking time, difficulty, trail surface, elevation, the best season to make the hike, other trail users, whether you can bring your pet, whether a fee or permit is required, trail contacts for additional information, useful topo maps (in addition to the maps provided in this book), trail highlights, and wildlife you may encounter along the way.

None of the hikes are necessarily better than the others on any particular day, but they do differ in difficulty and accessibility. Unsurprisingly, long hikes are harder than short hikes. If distances are similar, hikes that go to mountaintops are harder than those that do not. The Lulu City site and Cub Lake are similarly easy. But if you happen to be in Grand Lake on the west side of the park, easy access to the Colorado River Trailhead will make walking to the site of Lulu City infinitely easier than driving up and over to Cub Lake Trailhead on the east side, especially if Trail Ridge Road is closed by snow, which can happen any day of the year.

Following the at-a-glance information, you'll find directions to the trailhead.

The Hike describes why you would want to spend precious time on an even more precious experience. Following each hike description, the Miles and Directions section provides a mile-by-mile summary of junctions and major landmarks along the trail. These were determined by a national park volunteer pulling a wheeled measuring device. The distances are accurate, even if at times your feet may doubt them.

Sidebars throughout this guide highlight some of the people, places, and things that help (or helped) make Rocky Mountain National Park the wonder it is. Two of these sidebars deal with two different types of light: alpenglow and lightning. Alpenglow is gradual and benign; lightning is not.

Transportation

There is no public transportation to Rocky Mountain National Park from airports, bus, or train stations in the outside world removed from the mountains. There is public transportation to Estes Park. The town of Estes Park provides free bus transport to link with free shuttle buses that operate along Bear Lake Road. The bus ride is free, but hikers must pay a park entrance fee. Bear Lake Road runs past trailheads that begin many of the finest hikes in the national park, so all is not hopeless for hikers who do not use private vehicles.

For hikers with private vehicles, there are roads that easily reach trailheads over most of the park. There are, however, no gas stations within the park. Enter with a full tank and you will not be paying more attention to the gas gauge than the very scenic road.

History

People lose stuff. Subsequent people find that stuff and call it history.

Around 10,000 years ago, hunters on the plains 35 miles east of today's Rocky Mountain National Park killed a dozen mammoths, in the process losing some of their projectile points. (This was prior to the invention of the bow and arrow in the Americas. Hunters threw the points tied on short spears.) Archaeologists later found the mammoth bones and projectile points but not a clear reason why anyone would kill twelve mammoths when one or two would have filled their needs.

When mammoth hunters crossed the mountains over Trail Ridge, they lost some projectile points, which eventually turned up in present-day Rocky Mountain National Park. Perhaps the Clovis/Folsom Culture people, who chipped their points from rock not found in the area, were crossing to Middle Park to find mammoths, which had been wiped out east of the mountains. Did they realize before they found whatever prey was there that they had lost their killing tools?

Another hunter found his way into the future national park in 1843. Rufus Sage was the first to arrive toting a rifle. Other hunters followed, including in 1858 Joel Estes and his family, for whom the area soon would be named. Miners drawn to Colorado by an 1859 mineral boom were too busy to feed themselves, and commercial hunters soon wiped out Estes Park's previously abundant elk to feed the miners. Cattle grazing was more profitable down on the plains than in mountain meadows. There was not much mineral wealth this far north in the Colorado Rockies, so the Estes clan and their few neighbors turned to boarding the first tourists who showed up to wonder over this spectacular scene. As was the fate of many subsequent efforts in the tourist industry, serving visitors three months a year was inadequate to sustain the Estes family, and they left.

But the tourists still came. Explorer John Wesley Powell led the first documented ascent of Longs Peak in 1868. In 1871 Addie Alexander was the first woman to climb

Longs, followed in 1873 by other ladies, who lectured and wrote about their experiences. One of these, Anna Dickinson, left her tape measure, which she evidently thought might be useful for climbing a 14,259-foot peak—perhaps for determining that height, which was not yet known.

In 1874 Abner Sprague climbed Longs after homesteading in Moraine Park and saw the tape measure on top. He left it, and it was lost to history, perhaps found and removed by some unknown climber. Or perhaps a yellow-bellied marmot found it and hid it under some rock on the summit, where it remains today. Sprague made other climbs up Longs and most of the other peaks in the area. He also found success as an innkeeper, success lost by many others before and after. His name remains at Sprague Lake, his wife's at Alberta Falls; in this book's table of contents are many other names Sprague added to the map of Rocky Mountain National Park.

While Sprague was climbing Longs Peak and pioneering, miners attempted to find silver among volcanic peaks that would be added to the west side of the national park in 1929. By 1886 the mining town of Lulu City was a bust. But in 1895, in the Never Summer Range above Lulu City, other wealth-seekers found water and spent the next forty years digging the Grand Ditch to divert the vital liquid from the damp and thinly populated west side of the Continental Divide to the arid population centers on the east side.

In 1884 another future innkeeper showed up as a teenager below the East Face of Longs Peak. Enos Mills, who eventually became famous as the "Father of Rocky Mountain National Park," built a cabin in the Tahosa Valley. Mills spent his early years as a miner, but not below Longs Peak, the folly of which was proven between 1896 and 1902 by some of his neighbors at Eugenia Mine. Neither did Mills try to find silver in the mines dug in vain around Lulu City. In 1889 fire closed the copper mine where Mills worked in Butte, Montana, giving him time to vacation in California, where he happened to meet John Muir. This foremost of American naturalists mentored Mills, who thereafter devoted his life to the preservation of wilderness values. The center of his efforts was Longs Peak Inn, which he bought in 1902.

Inventor Freelan Stanley brought to Estes Park the income from his invention of a photographic process, purchased by Eastman Kodak, and from his less-influential but extremely colorful Stanley Steamer automobile. Stanley was searching for health, which mountain grandeur and purity supplied abundantly. He built the Stanley Hotel in 1905 and became, like Sprague and Mills, a leader in the tourist economy. Under Stanley's leadership, elk were transported from Montana to Estes Park to rebuild herds lost a half century earlier. Stanley, Mills, and other Colorado mountain enthusiasts eventually experienced success in providing a core of wildlife habitat when Rocky Mountain National Park was dedicated September 4, 1915, in a ceremony near Lawn Lake Trailhead.

Between 1913 and 1920, Fall River Road was built past the trail to Lawn and Ypsilon Lakes to link the towns of Estes Park and Grand Lake during the summer months. The transmountain route lost by the mammoth hunters and later by the Utes was found by motorists with the building of Trail Ridge Road between 1933 and 1942. Water moved across the park by a hidden route after tunnelers bored Adams Tunnel beneath the Continental Divide from near East Inlet Trailhead between 1937 and 1947.

Water disaster burst from Lawn Lake in 1982 with a dam break that killed three people and flooded Estes Park. In 1992 the National Park Service forestalled similar future disasters by purchasing and administering another potential flood source at Lily Lake and removing several dangerous dams from within the park. But no one could prevent flooding from massive rain in September 2013, which damaged many park trails east of the Continental Divide.

Over the century since Rocky Mountain National Park came to be, the park service, local residents, Colorado admirers of mountains, and visitors from around the world have expressed their love for the park in various, sometimes conflicting, ways. Annual park visitation now usually totals approximately 3 million. Sometimes these lovers of the park encounter lost and then found artifacts that preserve the park's history, such as Holzwarth Historic Site on the western edge or MacGregor Ranch on the eastern boundary near Gem Lake.

Motorists traveling over Trail Ridge, lost to time by the Utes who followed this trail, traverse three distinct natural environments, as though driving to the Arctic Circle in an hour. Hikers through Windy Gulch enjoy the same experience. They also find the historical inspiration of wilderness, mostly lost around their homes and found in Rocky Mountain National Park.

Geology

For geologists, 65 million years—when formation of the current Rockies began—is merely a long time ago. Four and a half billion years, the theoretical span of time, is a very much longer time ago.

In time, Rocky Mountain geology began 2.3 billion years ago, when the oldest Rocky Mountain rocks came to be. In space, the Rockies began a long distance away as the North American tectonic plate began to drift on convection currents within the earth's molten mantle layer, below the relatively thin crust. The North American plate crashed into the Pacific plate, which crashed back. At very roughly the same time, the dinosaurs became extinct (except for bird descendants). The two events likely were unconnected, but 65 million years ago was not a good time to be present.

"Tectonic" comes from the Greek word *tekton*, which means "carpenter" or "builder." *Tekton* is the word used in the Greek in which the New Testament originally was written to describe the profession of Joseph and then Jesus. All the tectonic crashing, crinkling, crushing, crumbling, crunching, and colliding built the mountains.

By 10 million years ago, the Rockies had risen remarkably high. Today, after considerable erosion, more than fifty peaks above 14,000 feet remain in Colorado. Longs Peak, the tallest in Rocky Mountain National Park (14,259 feet), is the farthest north of the "fourteeners."

The broad, flat summit of Longs is a remnant of previous mountain building and erosion to plains. At less high-altitude, broad expanses of alpine tundra above glacier-steepened valleys also are remnants of plains, defining features that cover one-third of Rocky Mountain National Park. Hiking trails cross tundra along Trail Ridge Road and above Bear Lake, as well as the flanks of Longs, Ypsilon Mountain, and Mount Ida.

Tearing down mountains is easier to understand than building them up. Gravity, of course, is the chief destroyer, using water as a tool. Water penetrates cracks in the rocks, freezes and expands, then melts and freezes again. All this freezing and thawing wedges rocks apart, eventually turning mountain-size rocks into grain-size rocks. Big and small, water carries away the broken bits of mountains, as liquid water washing the rock away and as a flexible solid conveying rock away on belts of ice.

The removal by liquid water continues as you read this; the removal by ice is more complex. Moving masses of ice and snow are glaciers, in our case alpine glaciers. Slight irregularities in the Earth's orbit cause varying amount of solar energy to reach the surface, resulting in changes in the average annual temperature. We call the colder times ice ages. Prevailing winds blow from the west due to the direction of the Earth's rotation. During ice ages, this causes much of the snow carried from the west to drop on the eastern flanks of high mountains, mostly out of reach of the wind. Very cold temperatures plus perhaps increased amounts of precipitation result in more snow accumulating on shaded eastern slopes than melts. When the accumulation reaches at least 250 feet thick, it is so heavy that it begins to flow down mountain valleys already carved by flowing water. The mass of ice freezes to the rock, plucking chunks as it moves, usually breaking the rock along preexisting cracks.

On a valley floor, the glacier plucks out basins that accumulate water after the glacier finally melts during alternating warm spells. Rock debris from all that ice wedging and glacial plucking freezes into the moving belt of ice like rasps on a file. The weight of the glacier applies pressure on the file, generating yet more excavation, mostly grinding along the base of a V-shaped river-cut valley, converting it to a U-shaped valley.

A glacier melts either because it slides down to warmer elevation or because the ice age ends as orbit changes cause the Earth's surface to receive increased solar heat. When this melting occurs at the lowest point of glacial descent, the rock debris carried on and within the conveyor belt of ice collects in a ridge along the downhill edge of the glacier. This ridge at the glacier's end is called a terminal moraine. Rock debris also accumulates along the sides of a glacier, creating lateral moraines. When a glacier melts back during a warm spell, it often pauses for some centuries; more ridges of rock pile up at the pause points, recessional moraines. After a glacier melts, the moraines become dams, creating lakes.

Moraine-dammed lakes together with basins plucked from valley floors combine to form a string of lakes along a connecting stream. Because these formations, when seen from peaks and passes above, resemble beads along a cord, they are called paternoster lakes. The name refers to the centuries-old use of beads as a memory aid for reciting the Roman Catholic Rosary prayers. The first words of the Lord's Prayer are "Our Father," or "*Pater noster*" in Latin, once the preferred language for reciting these prayers. Paternoster lakes in Rocky Mountain National Park include the Lake Verna string, Mill and Black Lakes with others above in Glacier Gorge, and Bear, Nymph, Dream, and Emerald Lakes.

Where a glacier originates, it plucks and grinds rock away from surrounding walls, forming a bowl-shaped cirque. Successive glaciers forming in the same place in successive ice ages deepen the cirque. Particularly when vertical cracks exist in the rock, precipitous cliffs form above the cirque. Cirque bowls often accumulate water, such as Chasm and Crystal Lakes and Lake of the Clouds.

Glaciers that cut more deeply into their valleys than glaciers in adjacent valleys can cut off the ends of valleys that have weaker (smaller) glaciers, leaving them suspended as hanging valleys above the floor of the valleys cut by larger glaciers. Glacier Gorge is a hanging valley above Loch Vale. Even more obvious is Windy Gulch, which never contained a glacier and was left hanging above the Big Thompson River by the passing of a glacier along today's path to The Pool.

Glaciers may continue to flow, grind, and pluck in Rocky Mountain National Park. But during the current warm spell between ice ages, what slight movement that remains is difficult to detect. Andrews Glacier below Taylor Peak seems the most likely candidate for continued glacial legitimacy, with icebergs floating in the lake, Andrews Tarn, at the lower end of the glacier. All the glaciers in the park are comparatively recent additions to the landscape, forming some 4,000 years ago after much larger glaciers had completely melted. The best guess may be that present-day glaciers are headed for the complete melting of their predecessors. But geological guesses are not rock solid.

Another form of mountain building that is less common in the park is exemplified by the Never Summer Range. About 27 million years ago, erupting lava and explosions of ash fueled by molten rock pluming to the surface from the mantle formed the distinctive rock of Little Yellowstone Canyon. Volcanic rock surrounds Lake of the Clouds. Such rock towers above the site of Lulu City and was responsible for the few concentrations of silver that created the town's brief boom.

Weather

Everyone who presumes to make pronouncements about the weather prefaces their predictions with pleas not to be trusted. The perils of weather predicting are proverbial.

Weather in Rocky Mountain National Park is no more certain than anywhere else. Even so, it is possible to present possibly useful weather comments about hiking in the national park.

During the summer hiking season, afternoon rain is common. Storms usually come from the west. Storms that come from the east often are particularly nasty.

You should assume that storms coming from any direction are malevolent. Lightning tries the hardest to kill you. But wind, wet, and cold are waiting to attack should lightning miss you. Lately, mountain pine beetles have brought death to uncountable lodgepole pines, which wind can blow onto the unwary or unlucky.

Despite the danger of falling trees during a storm, you are much safer below tree line than above. Besides lightning danger, you can face assault from falling snow at high altitude any day of the year. Precipitation might be only inconvenient if you carry warm clothing appropriate for snow. But wet rocks are slick, and gravity seems to work more perversely at cliff edges.

Some hikers decide not to be careful in difficult weather. But most would take care except for the fact that rain and snow tend to dissolve our thought processes. Failing to respect and retreat before bad weather is foolish—and possibly fatal.

Nonetheless, remember that explorer Stephen Long (of Longs Peak fame) called this "the great American desert." Residents never think it rains enough. So start hiking very early with sunny confidence and lots of sunscreen. (It works best when applied well before exposure to the sun's ultraviolet radiation.) Colorado's typical abundant sunshine and thin air give this state the nation's highest rate of skin cancer.

Flora

All high mountains are wrapped in bands of different communities of plants at different altitudes. Rocky Mountain National Park contains three such altitude-determined plant communities. The altitudes of these bands fluctuate somewhat, depending on whether they are growing on north- or south-facing slopes. Were you to travel to the Arctic Circle at the same altitude from the base of the mountains, you would encounter these same plant communities in bands hundreds of miles wide.

At the park's lowest elevation (and extending lower down to the plains) is the montane zone of plants. Most spectacular is the ponderosa pine, which matures over centuries to elegant red-barked beauty of various shapes. Full-grown ponderosas grow widely separated, with widespread roots to gather water.

Even more elegant along montane zone streams is the blue spruce, state tree of Colorado and transplanted as an ornamental tree to residential yards over much of the country. Willows of nearly indistinguishable species, mountain maple, water birch, alder, and quaking aspen join blue spruce along montane watercourses.

Two junipers, Rocky Mountain (a small, many-branched evergreen) and dwarf (a low, spreading shrub), prefer drier slopes. The flexible limber pine finds a home in the montane zone, as does Douglas-fir on shaded slopes. Lodgepole pine grows near the top of the montane zone where forest fire has raged.

Shrubs that lose their leaves in autumn include squaw current, the red berries of which are a favorite food of birds and which often grow at the base of ponderosas, where birds perch and defecate the seeds. Antelope bitterbrush, a favorite browse of mule deer, is very common; its fragrant yellow blossoms bloom in spring. The large white blooms of thimbleberry mark the rockiest areas of the montane zone in spring. The smell of sage may be the first thing park visitors notice when they exit their cars, although residents sadly no longer detect the smell.

Wildflowers of many colors decorate the montane zone, with the abundance of particular species changing from year to year. One year wallflowers may create yellow carpets that are remembered for a lifetime. The next year the blue of tall one-side penstemon may play the same role. A few dots of red paintbrush or pink wild geranium (much smaller than its domestic cousins) always provide striking highlights. Aptly named shooting star adds bright magenta to wet areas.

Above approximately 8,600 feet, the subalpine zone cloaks the mountains with deep forests of subalpine fir and Engelmann spruce. Limber pines find space in rocky areas. Dense stands of lodgepole pine mark the sites of forest fires, which can be caused naturally by lightning or unnaturally by people. The cause makes no difference, and there seem to be a lot of lodgepoles, although an explosion of mountain pine beetles due to global warming (the naturalness of which is much to be doubted) has ravaged lodgepole numbers, creating excellent fuel for future fires. Between roughly 10,500 feet and 11,500 feet, the subalpine zone transitions to the alpine zone, with many luxuriant, flower-filled meadows and lakes created by glaciers.

The alpine zone is the land above tree line—about one-third of the park's area—covered by ground-hugging plants of alpine tundra where it is not just bare rock. Fierce wind plus cold temperatures diminish the size of subalpine zone tree species to shrubby krummholz ("twisted wood") at tree line. The wind sculpts self-portraits in the heroic banner trees that lead the forest in its futile war to take over the heights. Although treeless tundra expanses look uniform, different types of plants divide up the terrain according to various wind conditions and microclimates. This bitter battle of life against wind is an interesting spectacle for hikers traveling through Timberline and Forest Canyon passes and climbing to the summits of Flattop, Longs, Ida, Ypsilon, and even Twin Sisters.

The hike from Trail Ridge Road down Windy Gulch to Upper Beaver Meadows takes hikers through classic examples of all three plant zones. The 9-mile stroll down Fall River Road from Fall River Pass to Horseshoe Park affords the same revelation.

Fauna

For humans, mountains are an acquired taste. We learn to see them as beautiful, as visually exciting, because the high regard for high places is so old in our culture, dating from the times of Bible composition. We usually fail to realize this taste is not natural.

We do have hints. My father told me of a flatlander who said that mountains just got in the way of the view. Some non-biblical literature dating from as far back as the Middle Ages refers to mountains as ugly blemishes on the otherwise smooth and gentle face of the land. Therefore, we have no way of knowing how the first humans who hiked through what's now Rocky Mountain National Park felt about these high places. Even the feelings of the first literate people here are not completely clear.

But we can be sure that the wild animals that lived in the mountains were well regarded by the people who hunted them for 10,000 years. We still hunt these animals today, although in different ways and for different reasons. To share the enjoyment of wild animals, we very strictly protect them from human harm (intentional or accidental) within the sacred sanctuary of a national park.

Wild animals are generally common and relatively easy to observe in Rocky Mountain National Park. The animals can thrive here because the variety created by different plants growing at different altitudes provides many conduits by which the sun's energy can flow to animals to keep them living. Most wildlife can move up and down the mountains, using different plant communities, or from one part of a plant community to another part of the same community to find food.

High mountains also snare water from passing air, which wildlife needs to survive. And the variety of mountain terrain provides different kinds of shelter for day-to-day protection from the weather and for places to breed and rear young.

These three essential elements of wildlife habitat—food, water, and shelter—the mountains supply well.

People tend to identify with and enjoy most of our fellow mammals, the bigger the better. Perhaps we have a genetic attraction to the elk, mule deer, moose, and bighorn sheep, even though they no longer feed us in the park. Perhaps we identify with our fellow predators—lions, bears, bobcats, coyotes, even badgers and little weasels—or value them because we see them much less often. Naturally, we hold the predators in less high regard when they seem to compete with us or even threaten those we love.

We admire beavers because, like us, they are builders. We like muskrats because they remind us of beavers. And the really small mammals—tree squirrels and ground squirrels—we enjoy as clowns that make us smile. Other small mammals, such as mice or pack rats, are interesting in some circumstances and irritating in others.

The mountains present us with birds, other warm bloods like ourselves. But the birds also are radically different. Their babies come from eggs outside their bodies. They have feathers of sometimes gaudily different colors, which our eyes too can perceive. (Male western tanagers are jaw-droppingly spectacular even to visitors from the East, who are used to cardinals.) Like us, birds are singers, although some (like Swainson's thrushes) are much more talented than people. And, inciting our envy, birds can fly. Watching birds is the most popular of outdoor recreations.

Wildlife photography also is popular, perhaps combining the interest of wildlife watching with the genetic drive of hunting. Park visitors must be careful not to harass wildlife by attempting to get too close for a photo.

Photography may hold a similar appeal to the catch-and-release fishing of greenback cutthroat or Colorado River cutthroat trout, species native to the national park's lakes and streams. National Park Service management has protected these fish species from extinction as a result of ill-advised introduction of alien fish species in unenlightened days.

Despite its fantastic display of many wildlife species, Rocky Mountain National Park is poor in reptiles and amphibians—one harmless (but unfriendly) garter snake, maybe a lizard near Gem Lake Trailhead, a flashy looking salamander, two dull frogs, and a toad. I think the NPS receives very few complaints about this lack and even fewer when these cold bloods eat mosquitoes, deerflies, or ticks. In happy contrast, the national park is home to an exceptional variety of butterflies and moths.

Wilderness

"Wilderness" was, in a sense, made a technical term by the federal Wilderness Act of 1964. This landmark law for preservation of a precious resource defines wilderness characteristics very specifically. Nine-five percent of Rocky Mountain National Park is overlain by official wilderness protection under the Wilderness Act.

The bulk of park visitors and all the animals living in the park do not recognize this wilderness definition, which leaves out roads, buildings, power lines, reservoirs, and campgrounds. Most creatures within the park do not perceive these wilderness encumbrances and ignore them. To them the whole park is wilderness untrammeled by humankind and part of a broader treasure spreading throughout much of the Rocky Mountain chain.

If you feel uncomfortable using the word "wilderness" to describe Moraine Park or Longs Peak Campground, maintain instead that you camp in the wilds. It is easier for labeling photographs. But be aware that the critters do not care.

Park Fees

In 1939 pioneer innkeeper Abner Sprague was delighted to buy the first entrance pass to Rocky Mountain National Park. At least he seemed to be delighted.

Today there are four entrance stations into Rocky Mountain National Park where entrance fees are collected or entrance passes examined. These are the Grand Lake entrance on the west side of the national park and the Fall River, Beaver Meadows, and Wild Basin entrances on the east side. The USDA Forest Service charges a fee to park at the Shadow Mountain Trailhead in Arapaho National Recreation Area. But there also is an annual pass good for both Rocky Mountain National Park and Arapaho National Recreation Area that costs the same as an annual pass for the national park alone.

Fees for the national park vary. There also are annual interagency passes that provide access to federal recreation sites that charge entrance fees all over the country, as well as one-time fee passes for a US citizen 62 years of age or older, good for life; free passes for active-duty military members and their families, good for a year; and free lifetime passes for US citizens with a permanent disability.

Perhaps Abner Sprague was delighted because NPS personnel at a visitor center or entrance station would figure out the fees for him. The rest of us can visit http:// rockymountainnationalpark.com/planning/fees-permits for current rates.

Pets

Pets in Rocky Mountain National Park are not permitted more than a few yards from roads or parking lots and must be kept on a leash no more than 6 feet long. Also, they must be supervised at all times to keep them from disturbing people without pets and to protect pets from injury inside an unattended vehicle, primarily from heat, which is surprisingly possible even in this haven of coolness.

Physical restraint and supervision of pets are important to keep them safe. Nothing throws gloom over a hike like seeing a note scrawled on whatever paper was available and affixed to a trailhead sign pleading for help in locating a lost pet. Fortunately, although I once became an instant hero to a cat owner whose pet I encountered and returned in Moraine Park Campground, my impression is that public adherence to pet regulations is widespread.

However, many pet owners who expected to escape to the glories of the wilderness in the company of much-loved family members who happen to have four feet can be deeply disappointed to be banned from national park trails. There are satisfactory alternatives. Fall River Road and the road into Upper Beaver Meadows provide trail-like experiences when closed to auto traffic in off-season (late May and June for Fall River and winter for Beaver Meadows). The trail in Roosevelt National Forest that winds up Lily Mountain from a short way down the road from Lily Lake is very popular (and easy) among canine-loving hikers. A trail named for former national park superintendent Homer Rouse and developed by Larimer County leads east from the Lily Lake parking area and descends by a closed historic toll road into the Estes Valley. Of course you must hike back up unless you have arranged for transport at the bottom of the road along Fish Creek. The trails of friendly-to-leashed-dogs Indian Peaks Wilderness (administered by the forest service) are south of Wild Basin and south of the Shadow Mountain Trailhead near Granby. Indian Peaks trails are without doubt equal in quality to national park trails.

Camping

Throughout this book I urge hikers to hit the trail early, often very early. But there are no commercial lodgings within the national park. Thousands of beds are for rent along the east and west park boundaries, but sleeping in park campgrounds or in backcountry campsites provides you with extra rest before rising to enjoy the best hikes in Rocky Mountain National Park.

There are five campgrounds within the park plus three forest service campgrounds near trailheads: Olive Ridge Campground near Wild Basin, Green Ridge Campground (little shade due to beetle attack of lodgepole pines) near the trail to Shadow Mountain Lookout, and Long Draw Campground near the Corral Creek Trailhead for Mirror Lake. On the west side of the national park is Timber Creek Campground, now deprived of almost all timber by pine beetle devastation. On the east side are Aspenglen near the Fall River Entrance Station and Longs Peak (tents only and a heavy favorite of hikers planning a 2 a.m. rising to ascend the park's highest mountain) plus Moraine Park and Glacier Basin campgrounds along Bear Lake Road in the heart of hiking country. Moraine Park Campground is open year-round (without water in the cold months). There are no showers, laundries, or hookups for water, sewer, or electricity in any Rocky Mountain National Park campground.

These campgrounds all are so popular that they fill each day in July through August and on weekends in June and September. Check out is at noon; check in is at 1 p.m. Campers can stay seven nights June through September, fourteen more during the rest of the year. NPS recommends making reservations six months in advance. Nonrefundable payment is due at the time the reservation is made. Call (877) 444-8777 or reserve online at www.reserveamerica.com.

To reserve sites at the forest service's Olive and Green Ridge Campgrounds, call (801) 226-3564 or visit www.americanll.com; Long Draw Campground sites cannot be reserved. The forest service campgrounds are open from early summer through fall. Reservations at Olive Ridge and Green Ridge must be made five days in advance and will be taken six months in advance.

In Rocky Mountain National Park, backpackers must reserve backcountry campsites at one of two backcountry offices. On the east side, the office is a short walk from the Park Headquarters (1000 US 36). On the west side, the backcountry office is at the Kawuneeche Visitor Center near Grand Lake. All backcountry campers must use commercially manufactured bear-proof containers to carry food in and out of the backcountry.

Trail Finder

Best Hikes for Great Views

11 Mount Ida
15 Lake Nanita
25 Hallett Peak
28 Dream Lake
31 Mills Lake
34 The Loch
39 Sprague Lake
41 Timberline Pass
46 Longs Peak
47 Chasm Lake

Best Hikes for Waterfalls

 3 Bridal Veil Falls
 4 West Creek Falls
16 Adams Falls
17 Lake Verna
35 Timberline Falls
53 Ouzel Falls

Best Hikes with Children

 1 Gem Lake
16 Adams Falls
22 Bear Lake Nature Trail
29 Emerald Lake
33 Alberta Falls
39 Sprague Lake
43 Toll Memorial
53 Ouzel Falls

Best Hikes for Wildlife

 3 Bridal Veil Falls
11 Mount Ida
37 Cub Lake
49 Lily Lake
55 Bluebird Lake

Best Hikes for Photographers

    1 Gem Lake
    5 Ypsilon Lake
   11 Mount Ida
   25 Hallett Peak
   29 Emerald Lake
   35 Timberline Falls
   39 Sprague Lake
   41 Timberline Pass
   46 Longs Peak
   47 Chasm Lake
   53 Ouzel Falls

Best Summit Hikes

    8 Ypsilon Mountain, Mounts Chiquita and Chapin
   11 Mount Ida
   25 Hallett Peak
   46 Longs Peak

Best Hikes for Solitude

    3 Bridal Veil Falls
    4 West Creek Falls
   14 Haynach Lakes
   15 Lake Nanita

Map Legend

Municipal

⊨{34}⊨	US Highway
⊨(7)⊨	State Road
━━━━	Local/County Road
═══:	Gravel Road
═══:	Dirt Road
┝━━┥	Railroad

Trails

-------	Featured Trail
------	Trail
··········	Off-Trail Hike

Water Features

⬭	Body of Water
∿	River/Creek
⌇	Intermittent Stream
≋	Waterfall
▨	Glacier

Symbols

⤻	Bridge
■	Building/Point of Interest
⛺	Campground
❗	Gate
🅿	Parking
⤸	Pass
▲	Peak/Elevation
⛬	Picnic Area
⛹	Ranger Station
🚻	Restrooms
⬒	Scenic View
○	Town
①	Trailhead
❓	Visitor Center

Land Management

▭	National Park/Forest
⬚	Ranch

Lumpy Ridge and Cow Creek

1 Gem Lake

This trail winds amid uncounted granite monoliths to a gem's setting on the east end of Lumpy Ridge.

Start: Gem Lake Trailhead
Distance: 4.6 miles out and back
Hiking time: About 3 hours
Difficulty: Moderately easy
Trail surface: Dirt
Elevation: Gem Lake Trailhead, 7,920 feet; Gem Lake, 8,830 feet
Best season: Spring
Other trail users: Equestrians
Canine compatibility: Dogs prohibited
Fees and permits: No fees or permits required

Trail contacts: Rocky Mountain National Park Backcountry Office, 1000 US 36, Estes Park 80517; (970) 586-1242; www.nps.gov/romo
Maps: USGS *Glen Haven* and *Estes Park*; Trails Illustrated *Rocky Mountain National Park*
Highlights: Unique rock formations, views of Longs Peak above Estes Valley, Gem Lake (1.8 miles)
Wildlife: Mule deer, Richardson's ground squirrels, golden-mantled ground squirrels, white-throated swifts

Finding the trailhead: From downtown Estes Park, drive north on MacGregor Avenue (which becomes Devils Gulch Road) about 2 miles to a well-marked left turn leading to the Gem Lake and Lumpy Ridge Trailheads. **GPS:** N40 23.57' / W105 30.75'

The Hike

Gem Lake nestles in a granite setting on the east end of Lumpy Ridge. When Arapaho horse nomads ventured from the plains, they called the uncounted rock domes along the ridge bounding the north edge of Estes Park the Little Lumps. Mapmakers adapted this name to Lumpy Ridge. In the 1870s bear hunter Israel Rowe discovered the lake and declared it to be a gem.

Some hikers may find Gem Lake to be a less-fitting name than Lumpy Ridge. Gem is small, shallow, and stagnant. Nonetheless, many hikers vote for its attraction with their feet, making Gem Lake one of the most frequently visited in the national park. Among its charms is easy access; its well-marked trailhead is closer to the throngs in Estes Park than any other trail in Rocky Mountain National Park. The granite lumps are fascinating abstract sculptures carved by natural elements. The plants are varied. The wildlife, such as white-throated swifts, is often different from animals seen along other park trails.

Glaciers formed most of the other lakes in the national park, but Lumpy Ridge was not glaciated. Gem Lake was etched from the rock when falling rain picked up carbon dioxide molecules from the air (blame volcanoes somewhere for that carbon footprint) and formed mild carbonic acid. The carbonic acid broke down some granitic minerals into erodible clays, especially where the surface rock was weaker than

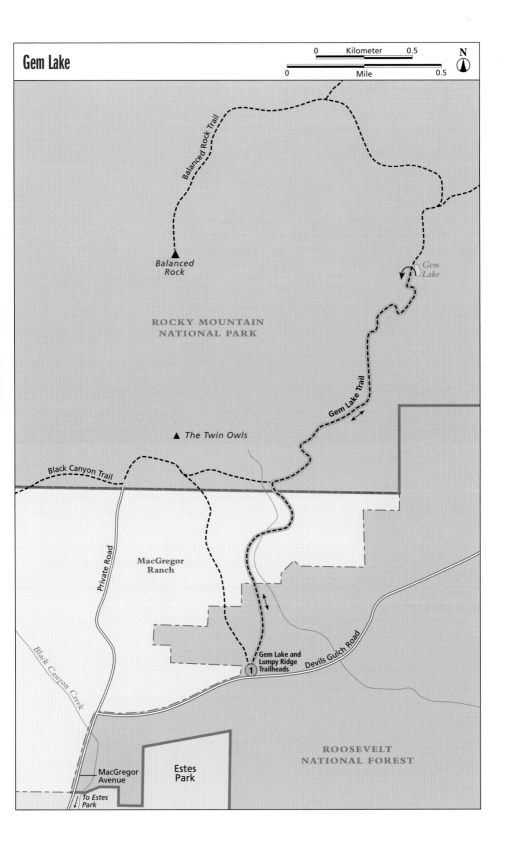

Gem Lake

0   Kilometer   0.5

0   Mile   0.5

N

Balanced Rock Trail

Balanced Rock

ROCKY MOUNTAIN NATIONAL PARK

Gem Lake

Gem Lake Trail

The Twin Owls

Black Canyon Trail

MacGregor Ranch

Private Road

Black Canyon Creek

Devils Gulch Road

Gem Lake and Lumpy Ridge Trailheads

1

ROOSEVELT NATIONAL FOREST

MacGregor Avenue

Estes Park

To Estes Park

Gem Lake is a large pothole on Lumpy Ridge.

surrounding rock and where the surface shape encouraged pooling of rainwater. The shape of the rock at Gem Lake created the pothole basin of the lake and the smaller, more-complex chemical erosion features atop the surrounding cliffs. Pooling acidic rain also created the hole in Paul Bunyan's Boot, an entertaining granite hunk obvious along the Gem Lake Trail.

Miles and Directions

0.0 Start at the Gem Lake Trailhead, and take the right of two trails leaving from the starting point.

2.3 Arrive at Gem Lake. Retrace your steps.

4.6 Arrive back at the trailhead.

2 Balanced Rock

Balanced Rock does not convey an impression of stability; run to see it before it becomes unbalanced.

Start: Gem Lake Trailhead
Distance: 7.8 miles out and back
Hiking time: About 4.5 hours
Difficulty: Moderate
Trail surface: Dirt
Elevation: Trailhead, 7,863 feet (according to Garmin); Gem Lake (highest point on trail), 8,830 feet
Best season: Spring
Other trail users: Equestrians
Canine compatibility: Dogs prohibited

Fees and permits: No fees or permits required
Trail contacts: Rocky Mountain National Park Backcountry Office, 1000 US 36, Estes Park 80517; (970) 586-1242; www.nps.gov/romo
Maps: USGS *Glen Haven* and *Estes Park*; Trails Illustrated *Rocky Mountain National Park*
Highlights: Gem Lake; giant abstract sculptures carved by natural elements, including Balanced Rock
Wildlife: Mule deer, chipmunks, golden-mantled ground squirrels, white-throated swifts

Finding the trailhead: From downtown Estes Park, drive north on MacGregor Ranch Avenue (which becomes Devils Gulch Road) about 2 miles to a well-marked left turn leading to the Gem Lake and Lumpy Ridge Trailheads. **GPS:** N40 23.57' / W105 30.75'

The Hike

Balanced Rock is one of the most remarkable of Lumpy Ridge lumps—an egg-shaped monolith perhaps 20 feet tall atop a relatively thin pillar of obviously less-substantial rock eroding from beneath it. Geologists describing time with numbers too long for anyone to really understand inform us that the balancing of Balanced Rock began some 40 million years ago when the top of Lumpy Ridge was a plain. Weather broke up rocks such as the base of Balanced Rock and decayed them into soil along deep fractures in the plain. Movement of the earth's crust raised the surface of the plain to the level of the tops of the lumps some 5 to 7 million years ago. (A million years here, a million years there—it all adds up to a fairly long time.)

This uplift empowered water to carry away much of the weathered rock and soil, leaving the unweathered granite cores isolated in place. Freed from the pressure of surrounding rock, internal pressure confined within the granite at the time of its conversion from liquid within the earth to solid as it rose to near the surface began to push outward. This outward pressure enabled the ongoing weathering to flake off granite plates in a curved pattern evident in the egg shape of Balanced Rock and in the shapes of the other lumps. Technically, these rounded rocks are called exfoliation domes.

I hope Balanced Rock remains balanced. In 2014 an analogous formation fell in Utah's Arches National Park, a short way west of Colorado. The crash crushed no

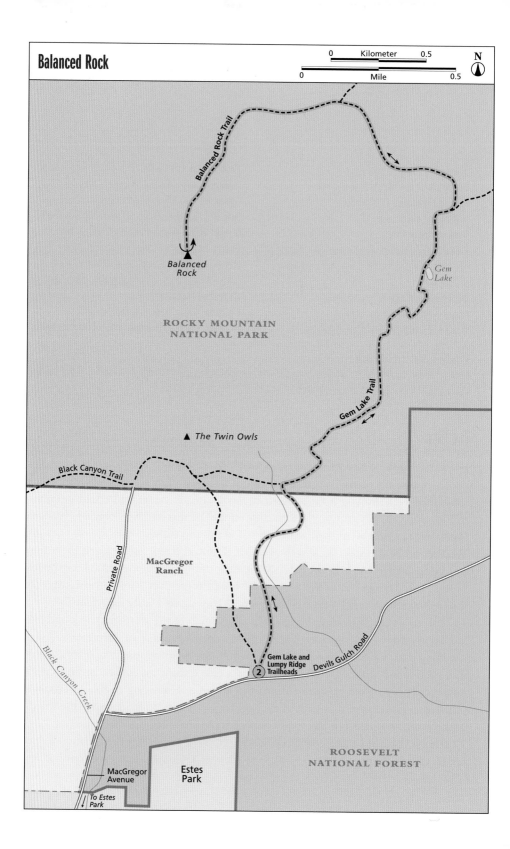

Balanced Rock

Balanced Rock remains balanced at present on Lumpy Ridge.

climber. Everyone knew it would fall someday. No one expected it to fall in his or her lifetime.

I don't have a counter's inclination, but you may wish to count the huge boulders you pass on the way back to the trailhead, itself surrounded by gigantic rocks, many displaying bowls dissolved in them by chemical weathering. I doubt that you will find your car smashed flat under such a stone, but most of the trailside boulders came to rest in their current place of temporary repose because the seemingly solid rock beneath them eroded away. Many once were balanced—or will be someday.

Miles and Directions

- **0.0** Start at the Gem Lake Trailhead and take the right of two trails leaving from the same starting point.
- **1.7** Pass Gem Lake on the trail that continues beyond the lake from the opposite end.
- **2.9** Turn left at the junction with the Balanced Rock Trail.
- **3.9** Reach Balanced Rock. Return to the trailhead by the same trails.
- **7.8** Arrive back at the trailhead.

3 Bridal Veil Falls

Meadows and aspen groves surround the way to a waterfall easy to imagine from its name. In spring, this may be the most interesting and spectacular waterfall in the national park.

Start: Cow Creek Trailhead
Distance: 6.0 miles out and back
Hiking time: About 4 hours
Difficulty: Moderately easy
Trail surface: Dirt
Elevation: Trailhead, 7,840 feet; Bridal Veil Falls, 8,900 feet
Best season: Fall
Other trail users: Equestrians as far as a hitch rail below the falls

Canine compatibility: Dogs prohibited
Fees and permits: No fees or permits required
Trail contacts: Rocky Mountain National Park Backcountry Office, 1000 US 36, Estes Park 80510; (970) 586-1242; www.nps.gov/romo
Maps: USGS *Estes Park*; Trails Illustrated *Rocky Mountain National Park*
Highlights: Aspen-lined Cow Creek, Bridal Veil Falls (3 miles)
Wildlife: Elk, mule deer

Finding the trailhead: From downtown Estes Park, follow Devils Gulch Road 3.9 miles to McGraw Ranch Road. Turn left and drive 2.3 miles to the Cow Creek Trailhead at the end of this unpaved road. Parking is only permitted in the parking area at the trailhead. Do not park along the road beyond the ranch boundary. **GPS:** N40 24.88' / W105 30.06'

The Hike

Waterfalls commonly have been named for a common item of wedding attire, so Rocky Mountain National Park also has its Bridal Veil Falls. It seems unfortunate that a name made mundane by overuse should label what may be the most unusual and interesting waterfall in the national park. No less dull would be The Falls or merely Waterfall.

Bridal Veil Falls is doubly cursed by being formed by Cow Creek, a name saved from equal dullness only by alliteration. When bolstered by melting snow, Cow Creek bursts over a ledge and crashes into a basin whose form throws the water back into the air. Hope to view the spectacle under overcast skies, which will reduce the contrast of Bridal Veil's white against its surroundings, making the falls even more impressive to view and photograph.

Because clouds typically gather in the afternoon, begin hiking from the Cow Creek Trailhead at McGraw Ranch during midmorning. Lunch at the falls, but be ready to drop your food and snatch your camera if the sunny glare fades.

Bridal Veil Falls in spring may be the most spectacular waterfall in the national park.

Bridal Veil Falls

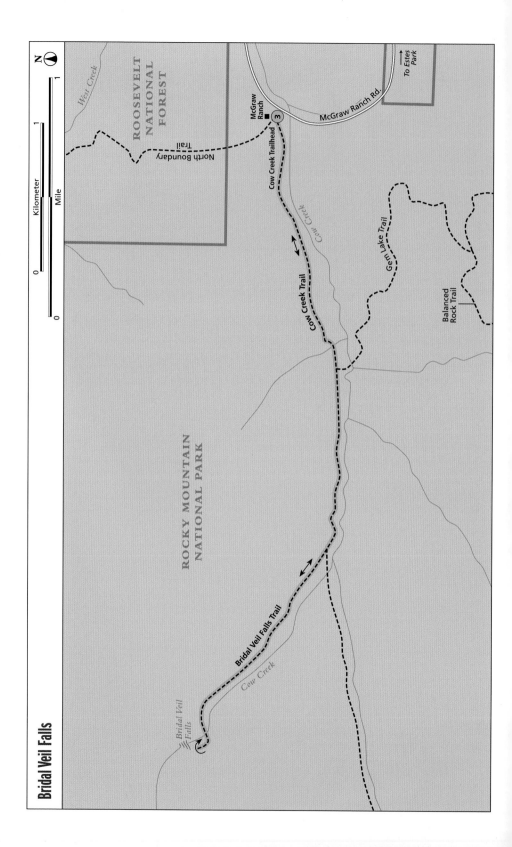

Miles and Directions

0.0 Start at the Cow Creek Trailhead.

0.1 The North Boundary Trail cuts steeply up to the right; continue straight along Cow Creek.

1.1 Bridal Veil Falls Trail branches to the right along Cow Creek, departing from the Cow Creek Trail, which swings away from its namesake.

3.0 Arrive at Bridal Veil Falls. Return the way you came.

6.0 Arrive back at the trailhead.

4 West Creek Falls

Beyond a steep ascent and steep descent, West Creek Falls tumbles over two tiers in a secluded setting.

Start: Cow Creek Trailhead
Distance: 4.0 miles out and back
Hiking time: About 3 hours
Difficulty: Moderate
Trail surface: Dirt
Elevation: Trailhead, 7,840 feet; West Creek Falls, 8,160 feet; high point, 8,440 feet
Best season: Summer
Other trail users: Equestrians
Canine compatibility: Dogs prohibited

Fees and permits: No fees or permits required
Trail contacts: Rocky Mountain National Park Backcountry Office, 1000 US 36, Estes Park 80510; (970) 586-1242; www.nps.gov/romo
Maps: USGS *Glen Haven* and *Estes Park*; Trails Illustrated *Rocky Mountain National Park*
Highlights: McGraw Ranch, West Creek Falls (2.0 miles)
Wildlife: Mule deer, elk, red squirrels

Finding the trailhead: From downtown Estes Park, follow Devils Gulch Road 3.9 miles to McGraw Ranch Road. Turn left and drive 2.3 miles to the Cow Creek Trailhead at the end of this unpaved road. Parking is only permitted in the parking area at the trailhead. Do not park along the road beyond the ranch boundary. **GPS:** N40 27.88' / W105 30.06'

The Hike

McGraw Ranch was pioneered in 1874, and Cow Creek, which flows near the ranch buildings, indicated its initial purpose. An 1882 map calls it Cow Creek Stock Ranch. But tourists paid better than cows, and West Creek Falls became a destination for horseback rides by ranch guests. The National Park Service bought the ranch in 1988, easing access for hikers to West Creek Falls.

The ranch buildings remain at the trailhead, providing interesting architectural background for photos. A short way from Cow Creek Trailhead, the North Boundary Trail to West Creek is another dude ranch reminder as it cuts straight uphill on a route that was tougher on horses than on the guests who rode them. On the north side of the ridge between Cow and West Creeks, the trail enters Roosevelt National Forest, pretty much as steep as the south side but benefitting from typical north slope—caused moisture and deeper shade, in this case mostly from Douglas-firs.

The grade gentles as the trail approaches West Creek. Beyond the creek, keep heading upstream at trail intersections to reenter the national park and reach West Creek Falls, tumbling in two steps through a rocky setting. The trail to the right after

The lower tier of West Creek Falls drops ▶
into a pool in autumn.

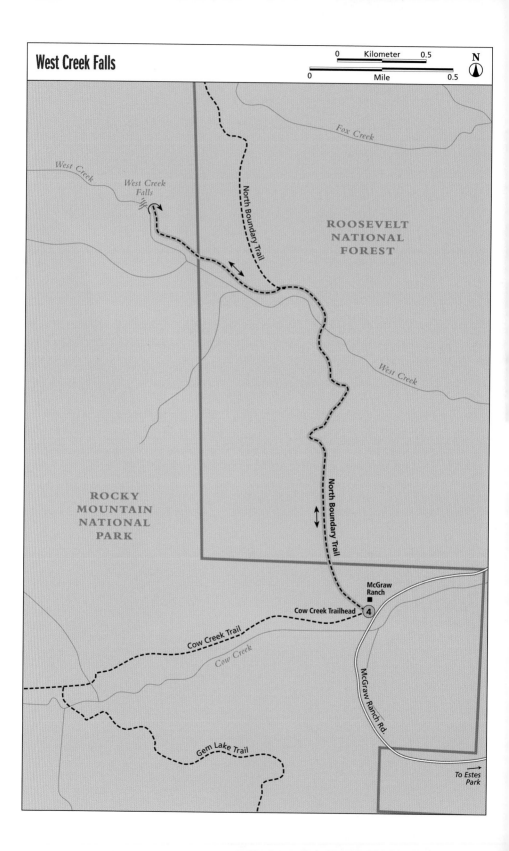

West Creek Falls

0 Kilometer 0.5
0 Mile 0.5

N

Fox Creek

West Creek

West Creek Falls

North Boundary Trail

ROOSEVELT NATIONAL FOREST

West Creek

North Boundary Trail

ROCKY MOUNTAIN NATIONAL PARK

McGraw Ranch

Cow Creek Trailhead 4

Cow Creek Trail

Cow Creek

McGraw Ranch Rd.

Gem Lake Trail

To Estes Park

Roaring River flows over "alluvial fan" of rock debris from 1982 flood caused by failure of Lawn Lake Dam.

the stream crossing eventually recrosses West Creek to circle back over the ridge to McGraw Ranch. The North Boundary Trail soon thereafter departs right from West Creek to rise and fall and rise and fall toward the park's north boundary, which it does not quite reach.

Miles and Directions

0.0 Start at the Cow Creek Trailhead.

0.1 Cut sharply up the North Boundary Trail.

1.4 Cross West Creek; head left on the trail up West Creek. (The trail to the right eventually circles back to the ranch.)

2.0 Arrive at West Creek Falls. Return the way you came.

4.0 Arrive back at the trailhead.

Mummy Range

5 Ypsilon Lake

Crossing the rubble left by the Lawn Lake flash flood, the trail to Ypsilon Lake passes Chipmunk Lake, a surprisingly dramatic mirror reflecting Ypsilon Mountain.

Start: Lawn Lake Trailhead
Distance: 9.0 miles out and back
Hiking time: About 7 hours
Difficulty: Moderate
Trail surface: Dirt
Elevation: Trailhead, 8,540 feet; Ypsilon Lake, 10,540 feet
Best season: Summer
Other trail users: Equestrians
Canine compatibility: Dogs prohibited
Fees and permits: National park entrance fee

Trail contacts: Rocky Mountain National Park Backcountry Office, 1000 US 36, Estes Park 80510; (970) 586-1242; www.nps.gov/romo
Maps: USGS *Trail Ridge*; Trails Illustrated *Rocky Mountain National Park*
Highlights: Alluvial deposits from the Lawn Lake Flood, views of Ypsilon Mountain, Chipmunk and Ypsilon Lakes
Wildlife: Mule deer, chipmunks, gray jays, mountain chickadees

Finding the trailhead: The Lawn Lake Trailhead is a parking lot on the north side of Fall River Road, shortly after it branches from US 34 in western Horseshoe Park, 2.1 miles west of the national park's Fall River entrance. **GPS:** N40 24.43' / W105 37.56'

The Hike

Ypsilon is the Greek letter corresponding to our letter Y. Very conspicuous Mount Ypsilon is named for the snow-filled gullies that form a Y across the huge bowl-shaped cirque cut by glaciers on the mountain's east face. Ypsilon Lake takes its name from the mountain against which it rests.

Switchbacks from the Lawn Lake Trailhead lift hikers through a ponderosa pine forest on the side of a steep slope laid down thousands of years ago by the icy conveyor belt of a glacier. The back-and-forth trail eases passage up and down this lateral moraine, but that is not the main virtue of switchbacks. They also eliminate erosion from hikers' or horses' feet by keeping this wear and tear on a less-steep slope, where it is less forceful and damaging than on a straight up-and-down path. Do *not* shortcut the switchbacks.

As you rise, damage from the 1982 flood is even more obvious below. Forest destruction has created a closer view of Ypsilon's face and a new perspective on Longs Peak. Through a scoured-sand landscape, you approach the trail that heads left to Ypsilon Lake. A bridge carries hikers across Roaring River, once shaded by delightful tall aspens. From there follow long stretches of lodgepole pine forest, varied now and then by views of the snow gullies on Ypsilon's face.

Chipmunk eats thistle seeds.

Never pass up a photograph, but the best view comes when the trail descends to Chipmunk Lake. From the trail (if a breeze does not ruffle the pond's surface), you can get a good photograph of bulky Fairchild Mountain reflected in the water. The tiny mirror often is still, good for pictures—and for mosquitoes. For a better view, sacrifice a little more blood and walk to the pond's eastern (right) shore for a great view of Ypsilon Mountain not visible from Ypsilon Lake. The trail terminates at the pleasant lake's western shore in subalpine forest growing among large boulders deposited by now-melted glacial ice.

◁ *Chipmunk Lake reflects Ypsilon Mountain along the Ypsilon Lake Trail.*

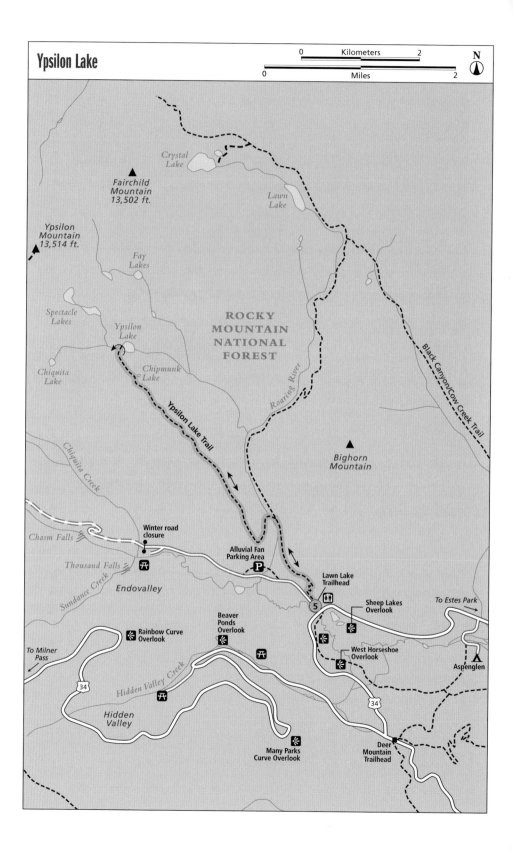

Ypsilon Lake

0 — Kilometers — 2
0 — Miles — 2

N

Crystal Lake

▲ Fairchild Mountain 13,502 ft.

Lawn Lake

Ypsilon Mountain 13,514 ft.

Fay Lakes

Spectacle Lakes

Ypsilon Lake

Chiquita Lake

Chipmunk Lake

ROCKY MOUNTAIN NATIONAL FOREST

Chiquita Creek

Ypsilon Lake Trail

Roaring River

Black Canyon/Cow Creek Trail

▲ Bighorn Mountain

Chasm Falls

Winter road closure

Thousand Falls

Sundance Creek

Endovalley

Alluvial Fan Parking Area

P

Lawn Lake Trailhead

Sheep Lakes Overlook

To Estes Park

5

To Milner Pass

Rainbow Curve Overlook

Beaver Ponds Overlook

West Horseshoe Overlook

Aspenglen

34

Hidden Valley Creek

Hidden Valley

34

Many Parks Curve Overlook

Deer Mountain Trailhead

CHIPMUNKS

"Chipmunk" is a name made from two Chippewa words meaning "mouth forward," indicating that this charming rodent's panhandling antics long preceded the arrival of Europeans. Where the range of least and eastern chipmunks crossed in the vicinity of the Great Lakes, Native Americans could distinguish the two species that ran through Chippewa villages. The least chipmunk is obviously smaller and more distinctly marked than the eastern variety most park visitors know. But the Arapaho, distant linguistic cousins of the Chippewa, likely had a tougher time telling apart the extremely similar least and Uinta chipmunks of the future Rocky Mountain National Park. If the Arapaho linguistically lumped all chipmunks together, park visitors would be wise to do the same. It is more fun to watch chipmunks tear around the forest edge with tail held perpendicular to the ground than to fuss over which exact species is on stage at the moment.

However, park visitors who cross the Great Plains from home can be forgiven for believing that they are seeing an eastern chipmunk, even though the nearest one is 600 miles to the east. The local golden-mantled ground squirrel does resemble the eastern chipmunk. The golden-mantled, named for the color of the hair over its shoulders, is larger than the local chipmunk species (except for those baby ground squirrels scampering around in June). The best identification is the face—stripped on chipmunks and not on ground squirrels.

All chipmunks and golden-mantled ground squirrels are eager to eat nearly anything. All have twenty-two teeth. So if you succumb to the great temptation to break park regulations and feed these cute beggars, counting the bloody puncture wounds on your hand will not inform you which stripped critter did the damage.

Miles and Directions

0.0 Start at the Lawn Lake Trailhead.

1.3 Follow the left trail through debris from the Lawn Lake Flood.

4.1 Pause at Chipmunk Lake to swat mosquitoes.

4.5 Arrive at Ypsilon Lake. Follow the same trail back to the Lawn Lake Trailhead.

9.0 Arrive back at the trailhead.

6 Crystal Lake

This lake carved into the flank of Fairchild Mountain jostles musical ice crystals when surrounding snow and ice fields melt in summer.

Start: Lawn Lake Trailhead
Distance: 15.4 miles out and back
Hiking time: About 12 hours
Difficulty: Difficult
Trail surface: Dirt
Elevation: Trailhead, 8,540 feet; Crystal Lake, 11,520 feet
Best season: Summer
Other trail users: Equestrians for all except the last 0.4 mile
Canine compatibility: Dogs prohibited
Fees and permits: National park entrance fee

Trail contacts: Rocky Mountain National Park Backcountry Office, 1000 US 36, Estes Park 80510; (970) 586-1242; www.nps.gov/romo
Maps: USGS *Trail Ridge*; Trails Illustrated *Rocky Mountain National Park*
Highlights: Views of alluvial deposits from the Lawn Lake Flood; Fairchild Mountain, Hagues Peak, Mummy Mountain, Lawn Lake, ice crystals on Crystal Lake
Wildlife: Mule deer, chipmunks, gray jays, water pipits, yellow-bellied marmots

Finding the trailhead: The Lawn Lake Trailhead is a parking lot on the north side of Fall River Road, shortly after it branches from US 34 in western Horseshoe Park, 2.1 miles west of the national park's Fall River entrance. **GPS:** N40 24.43' / W105 37.56'

The Hike

Standing on the shore of Crystal Lake, I have been delighted by the tinkling music of ice shards bumping against one another in the water, like crystals knocking together on a chandelier disturbed by wind through an open window. I do not know if something about the way glaciers plucked Crystal Lake's deep basin from the flank of Fairchild Mountain causes its ice to melt into natural music. Perhaps this magic music occurs in other tarns on some days. But in my experience, the sound created by ice crystals in Crystal Lake is unique.

I would like to believe that this wonderful phenomenon is the source of Crystal Lake's name. The visual beauty of the particularly scenic cirque in which the lake sits combined with its auditory wonder inspire hikers who venture above the flood damage below Lawn Lake.

The Lawn Lake Trail passes the turnoff to Ypsilon Lake and bypasses an area of obvious flood damage. The wall of water sliced a precipitous canyon through a glacial moraine. Because there remains no plant cover to stabilize the cliffy walls above Roaring River, precipitation will continue to cut the canyon farther into forest that the original flash flood did not touch. Earth slides will continue along the top of the

Crystal Lake may be the deepest tarn in the national park.

gorge until the walls are less steep and more stable. Unlucky hikers standing on the edge of the gorge when it falls could add to the total of flood-related fatalities. Stick to the portions of trail built to replace sections made unsafe or destroyed by the flood.

The trail steepens in two long switchbacks that take it east from the river. A good view of Mummy Mountain's cliffs rises to the north above a small basin. The upper end of the Cow Creek Trail heads right toward Black Canyon and Lumpy Ridge, a landmark notifying hikers that Lawn Lake is just 0.5 mile ahead. A barren, rocky "bathtub ring" surrounds the now-smaller lake. The former waterline is marked by lovely meadows where subalpine flowers blend their vibrant colors with tundra blooms.

Fairchild Mountain and Hagues Peak tower massively above Lawn Lake. The broad low spot between them is called The Saddle (although there are saddles between all adjoining peaks). This green swale lures hikers onto the trail that follows a rugged route above the trees. A half mile beyond Lawn Lake and 400 feet higher, the trail divides. The right branch heads toward The Saddle. The left climbs past an unnamed pond and Little Crystal Lake to the hopefully musical Crystal Lake.

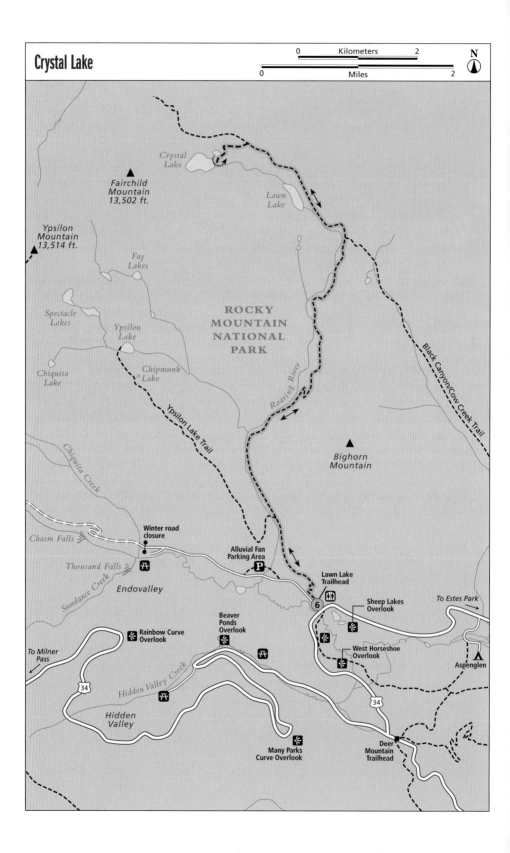

Crystal Lake

Kilometers 0 — 2
Miles 0 — 2

N

Crystal Lake

▲ Fairchild Mountain 13,502 ft.

Lawn Lake

Ypsilon Mountain 13,514 ft. ▲

Fay Lakes

Spectacle Lakes

ROCKY MOUNTAIN NATIONAL PARK

Ypsilon Lake

Chipmunk Lake

Chiquita Lake

Black Canyon/Cow Creek Trail

Ypsilon Lake Trail

Roaring River

▲ Bighorn Mountain

Chiquita Creek

Chasm Falls

Winter road closure

Alluvial Fan Parking Area

P

Thousand Falls

⛺

Sundance Creek

Endovalley

Lawn Lake Trailhead

🚻

6

To Estes Park

Sheep Lakes Overlook

Rainbow Curve Overlook

Beaver Ponds Overlook

West Horseshoe Overlook

To Milner Pass

34

Hidden Valley Creek

⛺

Aspenglen

34

Hidden Valley

Many Parks Curve Overlook

Deer Mountain Trailhead

0.0 Start at the Lawn Lake Trailhead and begin to ascend.

1.3 Keep right where the trail to Ypsilon Lake branches left.

4.9 Continue left where Black Canyon/Cow Creek Trail branches right.

6.2 Pass Lawn Lake.

7.7 Reach Crystal Lake. Return by the same trail to the Lawn Lake Trailhead.

15.4 Arrive back at the trailhead.

LAWN LAKE FLOOD

Early in the morning of July 15, 1982, I called the national park headquarters to discuss some hiking matter. I was told that the discussion would have to wait because Lawn Lake had "sprung a leak." In light of the incalculable devastation caused thereafter by the Lawn Lake Flood, "sprung a leak" seems a grimly humorous, albeit accurate, description.

In 1911, prior to the national park's 1915 establishment, a water company built an earthen dam to enlarge the natural Lawn Lake to store water for use on the plains. The company failed to maintain the dam properly, and a weld in a pipe leaked, permitting the dam to erode unabated until it failed catastrophically. A wall of water between 25 and 30 feet high roared down Roaring River, scouring away everything in its path. The flash flood eventually was stopped by the dam at Lake Estes after having killed at least three people, destroying $26 million in property in Estes Park, and requiring $5 million in repairs in the national park. An obscure Colorado law protected the water company from financial responsibility for this disaster, which had to be borne by its innocent victims and by the National Park Service. Multiple nonfinancial losses were beyond repair.

Thereafter, the NPS began acquiring rights to old reservoirs within the park and removing dams. An exception is the very popular Lily Lake on the park's eastern boundary, whose dam the NPS itself maintains with extreme diligence. This dam survived the awesome rain-caused flash flood of September 2013.

Warning of the Lawn Lake Flood came from an NPS contractor, Stephen Gillette, who heard the roar of the descending floodwaters from Horseshoe Park and rushed to the emergency telephone at Lawn Lake Trailhead to warn park personnel. This early alert allowed park rangers, sheriff's deputies, and Estes Park police to clear hundreds of potential casualties from the flood's path (a task that had killed two law enforcement personnel east of Estes Park in a flash flood in 1976).

7 Fall River Road

This one-lane byway drops through three life zones and is closed to vehicles during much of the year, when it makes an excellent route for hikers.

Start: Fall River Pass
Distance: 9.0-mile shuttle (5.2 miles out and back to Chasm Falls)
Hiking time: About 8 hours
Difficulty: Moderately easy
Trail surface: Dirt
Elevation: West Alluvial Fan parking lot, 8,250 feet; Chasm Falls, 9,060 feet; Fall River Pass, 11,796 feet
Best season: Early summer
Other trail users: Bicycles in early spring through late fall; cars after snow is removed at top of the road

Canine compatibility: Dogs permitted to hike the road after Trail Ridge opens in late May, as indicated by signs
Fees and permits: National park entrance fee
Trail contacts: Rocky Mountain National Park Backcountry Office; 1000 US 36, Estes Park 80517; (970) 586-1242; www.nps.gov/romo
Maps: USGS *Fall River Pass* and *Trail Ridge*; Trails Illustrated *Rocky Mountain National Park*
Highlights: Chasm Falls (2.6 miles in winter), avalanche site (4.8 miles)
Wildlife: Mule deer, elk

Finding the trailhead: In the spring, when Trail Ridge Road reopens (probably sometime in late May), hikers can leave one car at Fall River Pass on Trail Ridge Road and another near the bottom of Old Fall River Road at the West Alluvial Fan parking area, if a closer spot is unavailable.

From the park's Fall River entrance, follow US 34 for 2.1 miles to the Fall River Road turnoff. The West Alluvial Fan parking area is 0.8 mile along Fall River Road (past the first parking area labeled "Alluvial Fan"). **GPS:** N40 24.62' / W105 38.27' (GPS for Fall River Pass on Trail Ridge Road: N40 26.44' / W105 45.26'; base of Old Fall River Road: N40 24.85' / W105 39.31')

Note: The nearest parking lot to the base of Old Fall River Road is 1.2 miles east at the West Alluvial Fan parking area. Parking in the Endovalley Picnic Area or in roadside turnouts east of Old Fall River Road is closer.

The Hike

Opening in 1920, Old Fall River Road was the first motorized route to transect Rocky Mountain National Park. Many centuries earlier, however, Arapaho travelers called this the Dog Trail because their dogs pulled travois bearing the Native Americans' burdens over this route to the other side of the mountains.

Today, from the first Saturday in April (when there is access to the bottom of the road) until road crews reopen Fall River Road after winter closure (probably early July), it is one of the few places in this national park where hikers can re-create this human-canine partnership with dog packs. To preserve this opportunity for everyone, hikers absolutely must keep their dogs leashed per park regulations.

A rainbow arches over Fall River Valley east of Fall River Store at Fall River Pass. The store, formerly called the Shelter House, is at the intersection of Fall River and Trail Ridge Roads.

In winter, Chasm Falls, a 2.6-mile walk (one-way) along closed paved and unpaved roads, is a good safe hike. The nearest winter trailhead is 1.2 miles from the old road at the West Alluvial Fan parking lot. Exactly when winter ends is hard to determine. Absence of road closure may enable you to park closer (in small roadside parking spots) in spring and early summer.

This is one of the park's best areas to see elk, as indicated by the heavy black scarring of aspen trunks along the paved road that runs along the Fall River valley floor. Elk strip off the bark for winter food.

The right turn up unpaved Old Fall River Road is obvious. From the start of the unpaved road, it is another 1.4 miles to Chasm Falls, where potholes at the base of the falls were scoured out thousands of years ago by glacial meltwater dropping through ice cracks and swirling rocks. Fall River continues the same process at the base of the 25-foot-high falls. Be very careful of steep, slick surfaces when you are near the falls.

Care also is needed when hiking beyond the falls after heavy snows, which can occur well into May. In winter 1985–86 a major avalanche snapped off many large

Fall River Road

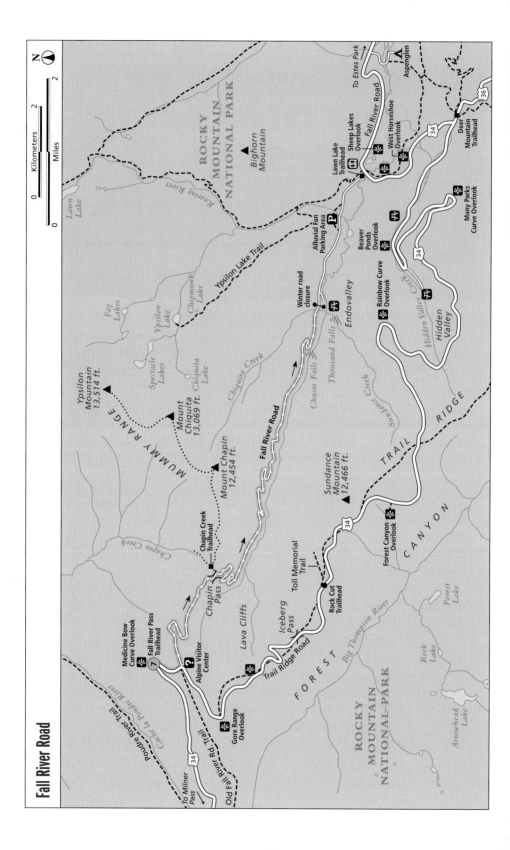

trees, visible in a jumbled mass as you look right up the slope of Mount Chapin, 2.3 miles beyond the falls. This avalanche had not run for many decades. No one knows when or where the next unpleasant surprise may roar across the road, but particular care is necessary after heavy snows. Avalanche danger probably increases with altitude as far as Chapin Creek Trailhead, 8.0 miles from the alluvial fan.

Above Chasm Falls, watch for bighorn sheep on rock outcrops north of the road. Elk often appear on the road itself and across the valley on the side of Sundance Mountain.

After Trail Ridge Road reopens, probably in late May, hikers have access to Fall River Pass and can hike downhill all the way to Horseshoe Park. This is a great hike in June, passing through all the national park's life zones, but requires arranging transportation at both ends of Old Fall River Road.

Fall River cuts through a narrow gorge at Chasm Falls near Fall River Road.

Miles and Directions

0.0 Start at Fall River Pass, where Old Fall River Road descends north (left) of the Fall River Pass Store.

2.5 Pass Chapin Creek Trailhead.

7.6 Chasm Falls is on the south (right) side of the road.

9.0 Arrive at the base of the road in the upper reaches of Horseshoe Park.

8 Ypsilon Mountain, Mounts Chiquita and Chapin

The very dramatic, glacier-carved east face of Ypsilon Mountain cannot be seen by climbers as they head up the much easier to ascend west slope.

Start: Chapin Creek Trailhead if Fall River Road is open; otherwise, Fall River Pass
Distance: 7.0 miles out and back
Hiking time: About 6 hours
Difficulty: Difficult
Trail surface: Dirt
Elevation: Chapin Creek Trailhead, 10,640 feet; Ypsilon Mountain, 13,514 feet
Best season: Summer
Other trail users: Human foot traffic only
Canine compatibility: Dogs prohibited
Fees and permits: National park entrance fee

Trail contacts: Rocky Mountain National Park Backcountry Office, 1000 US 36, Estes Park 80517; (970) 586-1242; www.nps.gov/romo
Maps: USGS *Trail Ridge*; Trails Illustrated *Rocky Mountain National Park*
Highlights: Views of the Mummy Range, view of spires on south side of Mount Chapin, view of Spectacle Lakes and tops of Y couloirs on Ypsilon's east face
Wildlife: Mule deer, elk, bighorn sheep, pikas, gray jays, mountain chickadees, white-tailed ptarmigan, water pipits

Finding the trailhead: Fall River Road is one-way uphill from its branching off US 34 at the western end of Horseshoe Park, 2.1 miles from the park's Fall River entrance. The Chapin Creek Trailhead is about 6.5 miles up Old Fall River Road from its base in western Horseshoe Park. **GPS:** N40.434' / W105 43.31'

If Fall River Road is not open, hikers must walk down Fall River Road toward Chapin Creek Trail from Fall River Pass (**GPS:** N40 26.08' / W105 43.80'). Leaving from Fall River Pass adds about 5 miles to the hike and necessitates walking back up to the pass above tree line at a time when lightning storms threaten.

The Hike

A short, steep trudge though pleasant subalpine forest from the trailhead leads to a branch to the right from the Chapin Creek Trail. Follow this branch toward the top of Mount Chapin. At best, 1.5 miles from the trailhead, this branch fades to trackless tundra where your route is a hiker's choice, influenced by whether or not you are peak-bagging Mounts Chapin and Chiquita in addition to Ypsilon Mountain. Climbing all three is easier walking but of course requires more time—and likely more effort.

These three peaks buttress the south end of the Mummy Range above Fall River. Mount Ypsilon was carved by glaciers more extensively than the others. These glaciers formed on the east side of the mountains because snow was dumped there by

Mounts Chapin and Chiquita are more dramatic when viewed ▶
from the east than from hikers' western approach.

winds coming mostly from the west. Chapin's southern slopes were steepened by the Fall River Glacier, which formed on the east side of Fall River Pass. The glacier plucked rock from the east faces, resulting in precipices not seen on the west-facing slopes, which are less scenic but much easier to climb.

Access to these steep but walkable approaches from the west is from Chapin Pass, a short way above Fall River Road. If Fall River Road is not open to auto traffic, the closest approach is from Fall River Pass. Starting the hike downhill from Fall River Pass in the early morning is pleasant. Less pleasant is pushing back up to the pass in the afternoon, urged along by the sound of thunder.

Some hikers head straight up to the summit of Mount Chapin, beginning along the branch trail from Chapin Pass. This gives them a striking view down to the spires rising above Fall River Road from the south side of Chapin. Other hikers skip Chapin and slant toward taller Mount Chiquita, to the left. Chiquita is a variant spelling of the name of the wife of Ouray, a famous Ute chief. Other hikers slant even farther left to head for the saddle between Chiquita and Ypsilon in order to reach the heights of dramatic Mount Ypsilon faster.

Traversing steep slopes directly to Chiquita or Ypsilon is faster than including Chapin, but the direct route to the higher peaks involves much walking with one foot higher than the other. It is not a comfortable gait, but one that many hikers select for the return trip down to Chapin Pass.

However you chose to get there, the view from atop Mount Ypsilon is very impressive. On the way, look down a snow-filled gully forming one branch of the Y carved by glaciers on the mountain's face. The view down to the Spectacle Lakes, in basins plucked by the glaciers, is also very interesting. The lakes were named for their resemblance to eyeglasses.

Do not become so carried away by the scenery that NPS rangers end up having to carry away your body from the snow at the base of the Y. Do not become a victim of the fable of "solid" rock. Although the rock that makes up these mountains is more substantial than most, it is solid only by comparison with our heads when they strike it.

These peaks look like they did thousands of years ago, when the Psalmist wrote, ". . . we will not fear though the earth be removed and the mountains be carried into the midst of the sea." But looks are deceiving, and deception can kill you. I have not counted the boulders surrounding Spectacle Lakes, but each of them used to be solid rock on the mountains. As the Psalmist points out, they now are being carried gradually to the sea. If you are unlucky enough to get in the way of this excavation, you could die. It has happened here previously. If the rock under your feet or that you grasp with your hand happens in that second among millennia to come loose, you could join the detritus at the bottom of the precipice. Heed the Psalmist (always a good idea): Do not fear the edge, but do respect it, because the edge is aged and may not be there tomorrow.

Ypsilon Mountain, Mounts Chiquita and Chapin

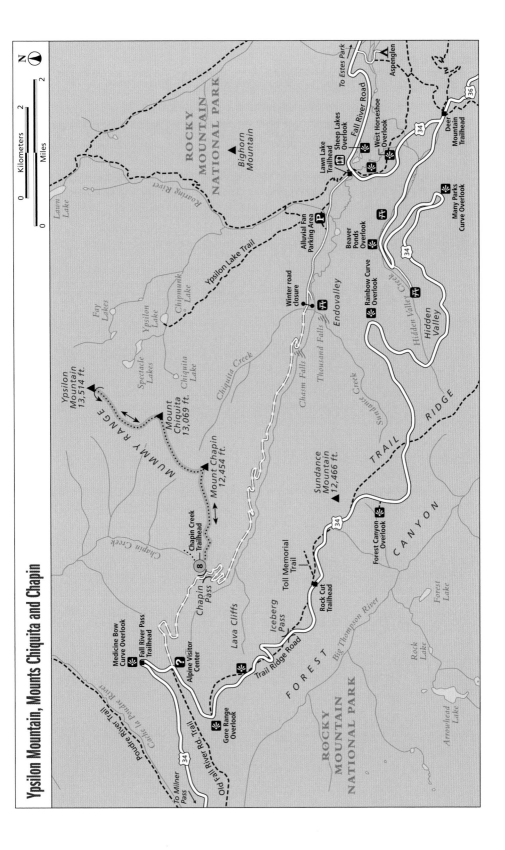

Miles and Directions

0.0 Start at the Chapin Creek Trailhead and begin ascending.

0.1 Come to Chapin Pass and take the branch trail to right toward Mount Chapin.

1.5 Reach the summit of Mount Chapin; then skirt cliffs toward the summit of Mount Chiquita.

2.1 Reach the summit of Mount Chiquita.

3.5 Arrive at the summit of Ypsilon Mountain. You can return via the top of Chapin, but you likely will be lured into following some trackless, rock-strewn route slanting down the tundra from the saddle between Ypsilon and Chiquita to Chapin Pass. This exploration avoids reclimbing Chiquita and Chapin, but be sure to keep far enough left to avoid having to climb up to Chapin Pass.

7.0 Arrive back at the trailhead.

9 Mirror Lake

After you reach the somewhat remote trailhead in the less-visited northwest corner of the national park, the path to this lovely lake is very pleasant.

Start: Corral Creek Trailhead
Distance: 14.2 miles out and back
Hiking time: About 8 hours
Difficulty: Moderate
Trail surface: Dirt
Elevation: Trailhead, 10,000 feet; Mirror Lake, 11,020 feet
Best season: Summer
Other trail users: Equestrians within the national park
Canine compatibility: Dogs prohibited on national park trails but permitted on USDA Forest Service Trails (not to Mirror Lake)

Fees and permits: No fees or permits required
Trail contacts: Rocky Mountain National Park Backcountry Office, 1000 US 36, Estes Park 80517; (970) 586-1242; www.nps.gov/romo
Maps: USGS *Comanche Peak*; Trails Illustrated *Rocky Mountain National Park*
Highlights: Riparian environment along Hague Creek, Mirror Lake
Wildlife: Elk, mule deer, gray jays, juncos, mountain chickadees

Finding the trailhead: From CO 14, about 4 miles north of Cameron Pass or 2 miles south of Chambers Lake, turn southeast onto two-lane, gravel Long Draw Road (FR 156), which travels through Box Canyon and Corral Park toward Long Draw Reservoir. Follow this road for about 8 miles to the Corral Creek Trailhead. Long Draw Campground is about 0.25 mile south of the trailhead. **GPS:** N40 31.078' / W105 46.236'

The Hike

Mirror Lake competes with Bridal Veil Falls for the title of most trite name for a hiking destination. Fortunately, this triteness certainly does not extend to the destinations themselves, which are exceptionally wonderful.

Mirror Lake is somewhat remote, on the northwest boundary of the national park. Remoteness is due to a long drive from the hiking hub of Estes Park to the Corral Creek Trailhead in Roosevelt National Forest. The trail itself is a moderate 7.1 miles, with just over 1,000 feet of elevation gain (much of it within a mile), a typically lovely lake hike to fill a summer day. The Mummy Pass Trail (named for a feature beyond Mirror Lake) begins as a stroll on an old road along Corral Creek. The road shrinks to a path that reaches the national park boundary and a bridge over the Cache la Poudre River.

Following the Mummy Pass Trail east beyond its junction with the Poudre River Trail takes hikers along a gentle valley floor containing Hague Creek. When the trail climbs left into thick forest, the grade steepens markedly. On top of a ridge, the path becomes less laborious to its junction with the Mirror Lake Trail.

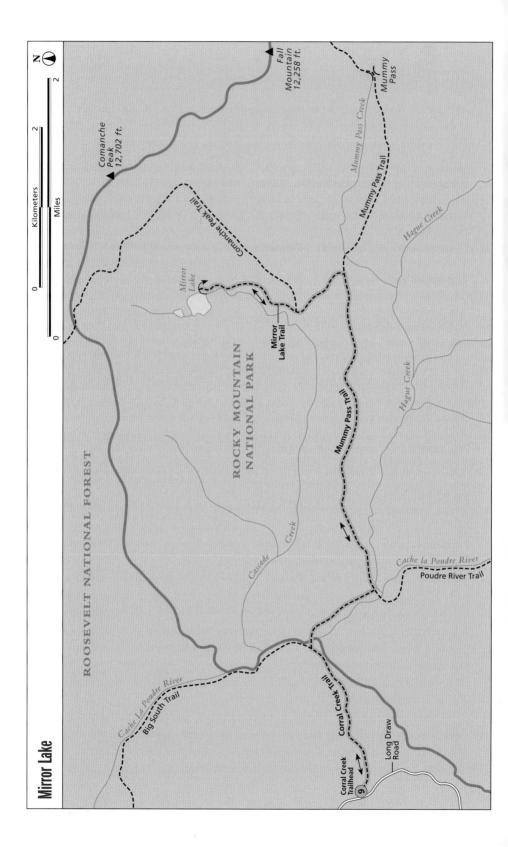

Mirror Lake

Mirror Lake nestles in a cirque along the national park's northern boundary.

A pleasant variety of subalpine forest and wet meadows lines the trail to the dramatic setting of Mirror Lake at tree line. Unnamed cliffy spires soar above the lake, with its banks covered by both subalpine and tundra plants. And, yes, when I was there, Mirror Lake did indeed reflect the surrounding grandeur.

Miles and Directions

0.0 Start at the Corral Creek Trailhead.

0.9 Reach the Rocky Mountain National Park boundary at the bridge over the Cache la Poudre River.

1.5 The Poudre River Trail heads south; keep heading east on the Mummy Pass Trail.

5.6 The Mirror Lake Trail leaves left from the Mummy Pass Trail.

6.3 The path heads right toward Comanche Peak. Continue left (north) along Cascade Creek to Mirror Lake.

7.1 Arrive at Mirror Lake. Return to Corral Creek Trailhead along the same trails.

14.2 Arrive back at the trailhead.

West Side

10 Fall River Pass to Milner Pass

If you manage to arrange transportation at both ends, this tundra/subalpine forest hike is a gentle, mostly downhill trail.

Start: Fall River Pass
Distance: 4.0-mile shuttle
Hiking time: About 3 hours
Difficulty: Moderately easy
Trail surface: Dirt
Elevation: Fall River Pass, 11,796 feet; Milner Pass, 10,758 feet
Best season: Summer
Other trail users: Human foot traffic only
Canine compatibility: Dogs prohibited

Fees and permits: National park entrance fee
Trail contacts: Rocky Mountain National Park Backcountry Office, 1000 US 36, Estes Park 80517; (970) 586-1242; www.nps.gov/romo
Maps: USGS *Fall River Pass*; Trails Illustrated *Rocky Mountain National Park*
Highlights: Alpine tundra, easy downhill hike, good views of the Never Summer Range
Wildlife: Mule deer, elk, ptarmigan, white-crowned sparrows

Finding the trailhead: Fall River Pass is located along Trail Ridge Road about midway between Estes Park and Grand Lake. **GPS:** N40 26.49' / W105 45.26'
Milner Pass is 4.2 miles west of Fall River Pass on Trail Ridge Road. **GPS:** N40 25.22' / W105 48.70'

The Hike

If you place a car at Milner Pass along Trail Ridge Road and another 4 miles up the road at Fall River Pass, the hike between these two passes via Forest Canyon Pass is mostly downhill, one of the easiest and most pleasant in the national park. Beginning across the road from the Fall River Pass parking area, the grade is gentle on joints, with interesting beauty anywhere you look—at your feet, down to the Cache la Poudre River, or across to the Never Summer Range. Lacking a car at Milner Pass, you can turn back at Forest Canyon and enjoy the alpine tundra while returning to Fall River Pass, not an overwhelmingly steep ascent. However, if you're climbing back to Fall River Pass, beware of afternoon lightning storms.

The primary tundra flowers here are cushion plants, such as moss campion, revegetating barren ground. It is a tough task when the plants are under frequent assault by wind and cold. Their rounded shapes and ground-hugging stature help shed the wind and protect much of their structure from cold. Their shape, however, provides no protection from pounding feet, so step carefully.

The Cache la Poudre River, winding through many curves on the valley floor, was named by trappers of French descent during the prosperous fur trade of the 1830s. Furs injected important capital into the American economy, which was otherwise mostly subsistence agriculture. The trappers dug a hole along the river to store and hide important supplies, including gunpowder. The river's name means "a storage place for powder."

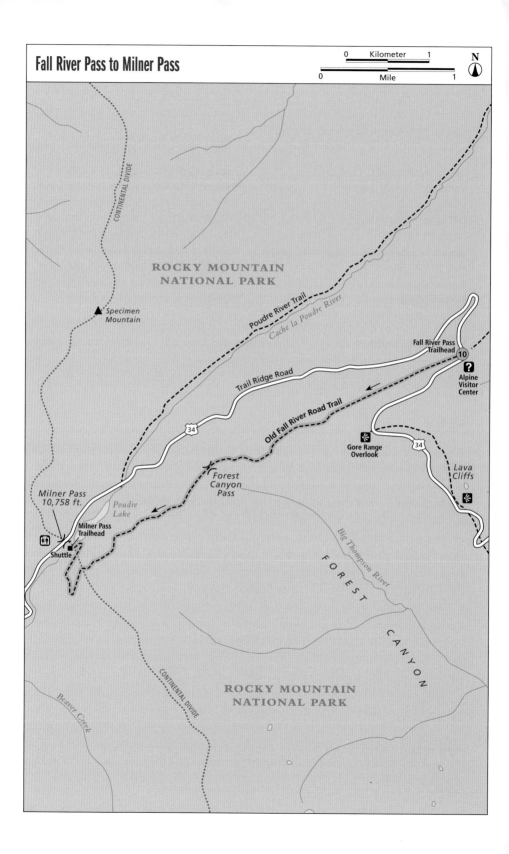

0   Kilometer   1

0   Mile   1

N

CONTINENTAL DIVIDE

ROCKY MOUNTAIN
NATIONAL PARK

▲ Specimen
Mountain

Poudre River Trail

Cache la Poudre River

Fall River Pass
Trailhead
10

Alpine
Visitor
Center

Trail Ridge Road

Old Fall River Road Trail

34

Gore Range
Overlook

34

Lava
Cliffs

Forest
Canyon
Pass

Milner Pass
10,758 ft.

Poudre
Lake

Milner Pass
Trailhead

Shuttle

Big Thompson River

F O R E S T

Beaver Creek

CONTINENTAL DIVIDE

ROCKY MOUNTAIN
NATIONAL PARK

C A N Y O N

Disputes about who gets to use the Poudre's water have been almost as explosive as the gunpowder. The barren slash across the side of the Never Summer Range indicates the Grand Ditch, some 14 miles long, which dumps precipitation falling on the Pacific-bound side of the Continental Divide into the east-flowing Poudre drainage. Allowing such a devastating diversion inside a national park would be unlikely today, but during the first part of the twentieth century it received congressional sanction.

The Grand Ditch was named for the Grand River, from which it diverted the water. The Grand River was renamed the Colorado River in 1921 after work already had begun on the ditch. The ditch kept its name, as did Grand Lake, Grand County, and Grand Junction, where the Gunnison River flows into the formerly Grand, now Colorado, River. Farther

Cushion plants, such as moss campion, pioneer recovery of life in tundra areas disturbed by road building along Trail Ridge.

west, in Utah, the former Grand River meets the Green River below Grand View Point in Canyonlands National Park before flowing through Grand Canyon in Arizona.

The east–west natural parting of precipitation along the Continental Divide prior to alteration by the Grand Ditch runs along the ridge of the Never Summers, looking pretty much how you would expect the coincidental shape of the land to divide the waters. However, the Divide also drops down to Milner Pass, from which the Colorado River flows west and the Cache la Poudre River flows east. Height of the land has little effect on Continental Divide location. Of Colorado's fifty-some 14,000-foot peaks, only two, Grays and Torreys, sit on the Divide. All water falling on Longs Peak flows toward the Atlantic.

At tree line, dwarf willows border the trail together with wind-distorted subalpine fir and Engelmann spruce. Then erect and majestic specimens of the same species make up woods punctuated by flowery bogs and avalanche clearings. Beyond a trail ascending toward Mount Ida, the path follows downward switchbacks for easy descent to the parking lot at the south end of Poudre Lake at a Continental Divide explanatory sign.

Miles and Directions

0.0 Start across Trail Ridge Road from the entrance to the Fall River Pass parking lot.

2.5 The route levels in Forest Canyon Pass.

4.0 Arrive at Milner Pass.

11 Mount Ida

The route up Mount Ida breaks out of magnificent subalpine forest onto wide-open alpine tundra, following the Continental Divide to gaze down ragged cliffs to Gorge Lakes.

Start: Milner Pass
Distance: 9.0 miles out and back
Hiking time: About 8 hours
Difficulty: Moderate
Trail surface: Dirt and alpine tundra
Elevation: Milner Pass, 10,758 feet; Mount Ida, 12,880 feet
Best season: Summer
Other trail users: Human foot traffic only
Canine compatibility: Dogs prohibited
Fees and permits: National park entrance fee

Trail contacts: Rocky Mountain National Park Backcountry Office, 1000 US 36, Estes Park 80517; (970) 586-1242; www.nps.gov/romo
Maps: USGS *Fall River Pass*; Trails Illustrated *Rocky Mountain National Park*
Highlights: Subalpine forest, alpine plants, good views of the Never Summer Range, dramatic cliffs above Gorge Lakes
Wildlife: Mule deer, elk, bighorn sheep, white-tailed ptarmigan, white-crowned sparrows

Finding the trailhead: Milner Pass is 4.2 miles west of Fall River Pass on Trail Ridge Road, at the Continental Divide sign at the southwestern end of Poudre Lake. **GPS:** N40 25.22' / W105 48.70'

The Hike

Along the Continental Divide in Milner Pass, a roadside sign at the southwest end of Poudre Lake explains the Divide. A few yards away, the trail up Mount Ida begins a twisting climb, never straying far from the Divide on the way to the summit. Magnificent subalpine forest carpeted with frequent patches of light blue Jacob's ladder lines the trail as it twists and turns to meet the trail coming down from Fall River Pass. Subalpine Jacob's ladder is a bit smaller than its counterpart seen along trails in the East. The wildflower was named for the pairs of leaflets that resemble rungs along the midrib. The blue blossoms may be reminiscent of heaven. Jacob was a biblical patriarch who, while on a journey to find a wife, camped in the wilds with a stone for a pillow, despite being normally crafty. Thus his sleep likely was not comfortable or sound when he dreamed of God standing at the top of a ladder rising from earth to heaven. God promised Jacob that his many descendents would cover the earth (Genesis 28:11–14), which may explain why so many hikers inhabit modern trails. At the junction, the trail up Ida turns right; along its rising way, tree size diminishes until trees disappear altogether along with well-made trail.

Above tree line the route is beaten by hooves of wildlife with little concern for grade or preservation of the landscape. To avoid a twisted ankle on ball bearing–like pebbles, tread carefully along the narrow route, created mostly by elk, likely with

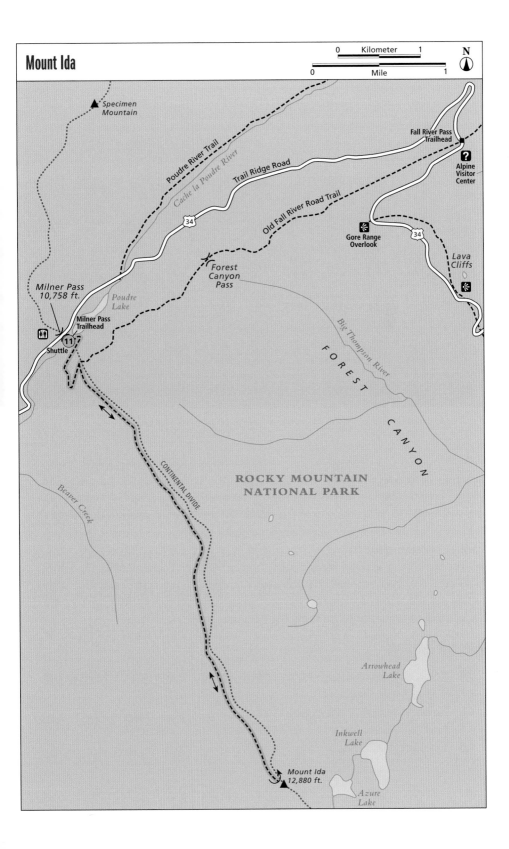

Mount Ida

0 Kilometer 1
0 Mile 1

N

▲ Specimen
Mountain

Poudre River Trail

Cache la Poudre River

Trail Ridge Road

Fall River Pass
Trailhead

Alpine
Visitor
Center

Old Fall River Road Trail

34

Gore Range
Overlook

Lava
Cliffs

34

Milner Pass
10,758 ft.

Poudre
Lake

Forest
Canyon
Pass

Milner Pass
Trailhead

11

Shuttle

Big Thompson River

F O R E S T

CONTINENTAL DIVIDE

Beaver Creek

C A N Y O N

ROCKY MOUNTAIN
NATIONAL PARK

Arrowhead
Lake

Inkwell
Lake

Mount Ida
12,880 ft.

Azure
Lake

The Never Summer Range reflects alpenglow as seen from Mt. Ida at sunrise.

help from mule deer and bighorn sheep. Eventually, even wildlife trails fade away, and you proceed to the true summit by not going downhill. The terrain falls off on both sides—not enough to generate fear, but enough to guide you ever up to the top. Just below the top, a false summit may disappoint, but it is not far to the true top, with its startling unobstructed views.

You have been looking across to the Never Summer Range during the entire hike, but it is not only the altitude that takes your breath away where cliffs drop away to Gorge Lakes. Do not allow this view to distract you completely from the scene in the opposite direction to Julian Lake, Big Meadows, and Lake Granby.

Miles and Directions

0.0 Start at the Continental Divide sign on the southwest end of Poudre Lake in Milner Pass.

0.7 Head right at the junction with the trail coming down from Fall River Pass.

1.5 The forest transitions to alpine tundra.

4.5 Reach Ida's summit. Turn around and retrace your route back to Milner Pass.

9.0 Arrive back at Milner Pass.

12 Coyote Valley

Short and flat, this easy trail follows the Colorado River, allowing even wheelchair-bound wilderness enthusiasts to enjoy trail experiences.

Start: Coyote Valley Trailhead
Distance: 1.6 miles out and back
Hiking time: About 2 hours
Difficulty: Easy
Trail surface: Packed dirt
Elevation: Trailhead 8,846 feet
Best season: Summer
Other trail users: Wheelchairs
Canine compatibility: Dogs prohibited
Fees and permits: National park entrance fee

Trail contacts: Rocky Mountain National Park Backcountry Office, 1000 US 36, Estes Park 80517; (970) 586-1242; www.nps.gov/romo
Maps: USGS *Grand Lake*; Trails Illustrated *Rocky Mountain National Park*
Highlights: Colorado River, views of the Never Summer Range
Wildlife: Elk, mule deer, moose, coyotes, black-billed magpies

Finding the trailhead: The Coyote Valley Trailhead is on the west side of Trail Ridge Road, 6.1 miles north of the Grand Lake entrance to Rocky Mountain National Park and 14.2 miles southwest of Fall River Pass. **GPS:** N40 20.67' / W105 51.50'

The Hike

This wheelchair-accessible trail—bolstered by benches, cul-de-sacs, and explanatory signs—along a short stretch of the Kawuneeche Valley does not indicate that coyotes are more likely to be seen here than anywhere else in the national park and surrounding country. Rather, "Kawuneeche" (Ka wu NEE chee) is an Arapaho word for coyote. The Colorado Geographic Board selected this name as an alternative for an even less-pronounceable Arapaho name. And the National Park Service imaginatively picked Coyote Valley as a synonym for Kawuneeche Valley.

Among a large segment of park visitors, coyotes are very popular because they seem like dogs. Other folks despise coyotes as killers of livestock and even inadequately supervised pets. Of course most livestock is produced to be killed for human food, so humans and coyotes are competitors for the same nutrition. Coyotes are even more omnivorous than humans, eating plants as well as rodents and rabbits that otherwise would be competing with livestock for grass. Therefore, by reducing small grazers, perhaps coyotes actually boost livestock production more than they decrease it. For many centuries, astute livestock producers have used guard dogs effectively to protect their flocks from predators such as coyotes. However, this solution is not without risk for the guard dogs (valued as part of the family by their human masters), and some livestock businesses consider the guard dogs to be just one more bother. Coyote booby traps sometimes set out on public land (presumably not in Rocky Mountain

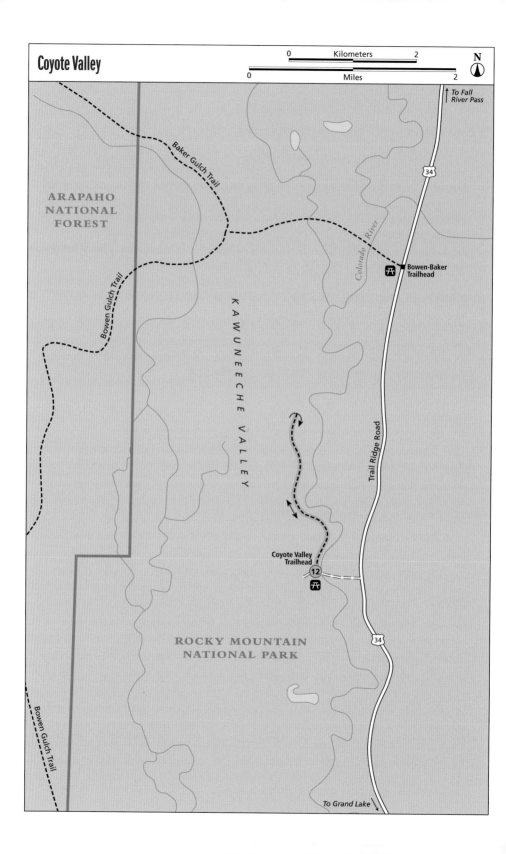

Coyote Valley

To Fall
River Pass

Baker Gulch Trail

34

ARAPAHO
NATIONAL
FOREST

Colorado River

Bowen-Baker
Trailhead

Bowen Gulch Trail

K
A
W
U
N
E
E
C
H
E

V
A
L
L
E
Y

Trail Ridge Road

Coyote Valley
Trailhead

12

ROCKY MOUNTAIN
NATIONAL PARK

34

Bowen Gulch Trail

To Grand Lake

A singing coyote symbolizes Coyote Valley, an English translation of the Arapaho Kawuneeche Valley.

National Park) are as likely to kill domestic pets and endanger humans as to kill coyotes. Be careful, and use a short leash if you pull over along a broad shoulder to walk your dog while on your way home from the national park.

Partly because coyotes have canine-loving allies among humans, and partly because coyotes define the term "wily," these very clever "song dogs" continue to thrive despite misguided attempts to kill them off, dating from the beginnings of European settlement in the Western Hemisphere. Non-European predecessors told admiring tales of coyotes, and a substantial number of such stories accumulate in the literature of subsequent American peoples. Perhaps singing coyotes convey through their howls their own stories about the two-legged omnivores and singers and find some of us to be amusing.

Miles and Directions

0.0 Start at the Coyote Valley Trailhead.

0.8 Come to trail's end. Turn around and retrace your route.

1.6 Arrive back at the trailhead.

13 Big Meadows

A lush trail passes the remains of historic structures while providing the variety of a loop hike.

Start: Green Mountain Trailhead
Distance: 7.0-mile loop
Hiking time: About 6 hours
Trail surface: Dirt
Elevation: Trailhead, 8,794 feet; Big Meadows, 9,400 feet
Best season: Summer
Other trail users: Equestrians
Canine compatibility: Dogs prohibited
Fees and permits: National park entrance fee

Trail contacts: Rocky Mountain National Park Backcountry Office, 1000 US 36, Estes Park 80517; (970) 586-1242; www.nps.gov/romo
Maps: USGS *Grand Lake*; Trails Illustrated *Rocky Mountain National Park*
Highlights: Circle hike, Big Meadows, log building ruins
Wildlife: Mule deer, elk, moose, red squirrels, mountain chickadees

Finding the trailhead: The Green Mountain and Onahu Creek Trailheads are 0.7 mile apart and are well marked along Trail Ridge Road, about 3 miles north of the Grand Lake entrance to Rocky Mountain National Park and 17 miles southwest of Fall River Pass. **GPS:** N40 18.45' / W105 50.49' (Green Mountain Trailhead); N40 18.97' / W105 50.61' (Onahu Creek Trailhead)

The Hike

Big Meadows is fairly well named. There is a meadow; it is big. There is, however, only one meadow, not two or more. It is puzzling why the singular noun "meadow" often is used as a plural when there is only one meadow present, which has been the practice at Big Meadows for more than a century. Similarly, there is one Long Meadows nearby and one Beaver Meadows on the east edge of the national park.

Maybe a thousand years ago, grassy fields were not used for grazing only one herd or flock of livestock. Maybe different herds belonging to different people were grazed simultaneously and had to be kept separate. Or perhaps the same flock was allowed to graze only in a particular part of the pasture at a time. Hence, maybe a single meadow was a conceptually rare occurrence. Just my guess.

There is a Ute Meadow in Windy Gulch, but that is a new name dreamed up by the National Park Service because they had to have some name for the designated campsite they established along the Ute Trail. There was a meadow nearby (camping in actual meadows is very actively discouraged in order to reduce wear and tear), so Ute Meadow appeared in its logically singular form.

It seems unlikely that Sam Stone cared about proper plurals around the turn of the twentieth century when he built a road to Big Meadows and began to mow

Sam Stone built substantial log structures that remind hikers of his hay-making efforts in Big Meadows a century ago.

grass there to produce hay to sell to nearby ranches. Remains of his cabin and barn still exist alongside the Tonahutu Creek Trail. You can guess that "Tonahutu" is an Arapaho word meaning "Big Meadows" (or "meadow"; my Arapaho is fuzzy).

It is hard to say if Sam's mowing enterprise in Big Meadows would have paid off. He abandoned it to follow a lady spiritualist who divined there was gold where there was none. But his hay road remains, now as the extremely pleasant Green Mountain Trail—wide, gentle of grade, and relatively clear of rocks. Because no one mows Big Meadows today, little red elephants have been able to replace Sam's livestock. These wildflower spikes display the aptness of their name if you crouch low to examine the individual blooms.

Beyond the log ruins of Sam's operation, Mount Ida is obvious to the north. Its left slope seems gentle; the right a sudden drop-off. Marshes and beaver ponds fill the sunny foreground. The trail stays just within the forest edge, avoiding the wet areas. In winter, reliable snow accumulation and a gentler than normal grade make this an outstanding trail for skiing and snowshoeing.

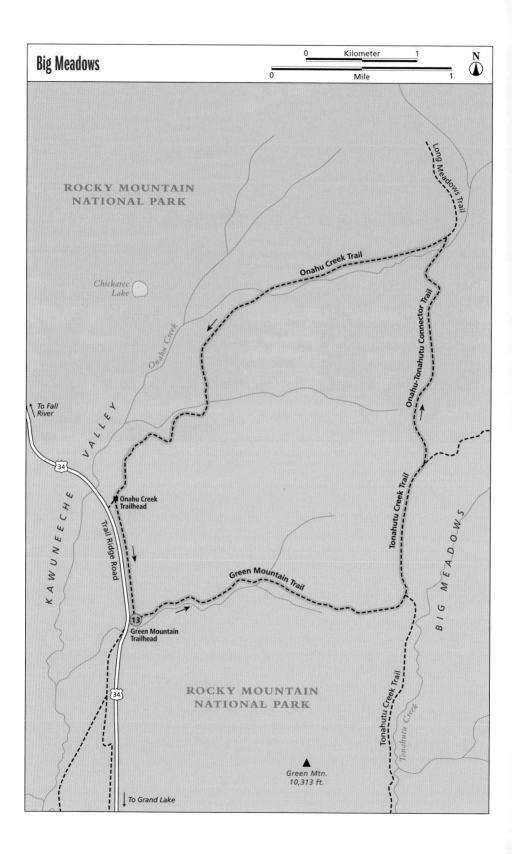

Winter travelers may appreciate the Onahu Creek branch trail that climbs left from the Tonahutu Trail nearly 1.0 mile north of the Green Mountain Trail. "Onahu" (ON a HU) is an Arapaho word meaning "warms himself." This happens to apply to hikers surmounting the ridge into the Onahu Creek drainage, but the Arapaho referred to one of their race horses, which on cold evenings (nearly all evenings) came up to the campfires to warm himself. This horse happened to die along what Euro-Americans usually called Fish Creek. Happily, the Colorado Geographic Board changed the too-common name Fish Creek to Onahu Creek.

The trail crosses Onahu Creek on a bridge to head southwest along the creek through spruce, fir, pine, aspen, and willows, descending to Onahu Creek Trailhead along Trail Ridge Road. A 0.7-mile trail parallels the road and takes hikers back to the Green Mountain Trailhead without having to dodge heavy vehicular traffic. In late August, watch the ground for tiny wild strawberries—just as tasty if less conspicuous than their domestic cousins.

Little red elephants have replaced Sam Stone's hay fields in Big Meadows.

Miles and Directions

0.0 Start at the Green Mountain Trailhead.

1.8 Arrive at Big Meadows; turn left onto the Tonahutu Creek Trail. (A right turn leads eventually to the park's west-side headquarters and visitor center.)

2.7 Turn left at a fork and ascend the Onahu-Tonahutu Connector Trail over the ridge; then descend to Onahu Creek, crossed by a bridge.

3.7 Turn left on Onahu Creek Trail.

6.3 Reach Trail Ridge Road and the Onahu Creek Trailhead. Find the path on the left side of the parking lot, and continue south to the Green Mountain Trailhead.

7.0 Arrive back at Green Mountain Trailhead.

PARKS

Big Meadows is what's often called a park in Colorado. "Park" is used to designate a grassy area surrounded by forested mountains. Hence, on the east side of Rocky Mountain National Park are Estes Park, Meeker Park, and Allenspark. Within the national park are Horseshoe, Moraine, and Tuxedo Parks. Between Horseshoe and Moraine Parks is Beaver Meadows, which used to be called Beaver Park. I cannot account for the name change, because Beaver Meadows also is a park, although I never have seen any sign of beaver there.

In central Colorado are very big parks: North, Middle, and South Parks and the San Luis Valley. (This southernmost of the big parks was named by Spanish speakers who did not use the park designation.) On the other hand, English speakers are far from consistent about their use of "park." The Kawuneeche Valley west of the Green Mountain and Onahu Creek Trailheads is a park, as is the Tahosa Valley east of Longs Peak.

Parks are nice places to live, and human settlements developed in some of them. For instance, Estes Park Village came to be in Estes Park, and today the town is always called Estes Park. Within Estes Park is Bond Park, a grassy area used for contemplation, recreation, and outdoor gatherings. The purpose of Bond Park and similar spaces within Estes Park is significantly different from the purpose of Rocky Mountain National Park, which is not only much bigger but also primarily intended to preserve the natural beauty of this very scenic area. Lawn mowers are much more appropriate in the small municipal parks than in the large national park. As indicated below, mowing is a relevant practice.

To recap: Bond Park is within Estes Park (Village), which is within Estes Park, which is adjacent to Rocky Mountain National Park, which contains many parks, including Big Meadows. Amazingly, most residents are not confused by this multiple usage of "park." The same cannot be said of visitors, especially when residents habitually refer to Rocky Mountain National Park as "the park," which simplifies nothing. So perhaps it is fortunate that Grand Lake residents long ago described part of the route from Flattop Mountain down to Grand Lake as Big Meadows.

Unlike "park," which has multiple meanings, the definition of "meadow" is fairly simple: a grassy field. It is derived from an Old English word meaning "a place where grass is mowed" (to produce hay). Not even Scrabble fans would immediately perceive the connection between "meadow" and "mow," but it seems obvious when pointed out. "Meadow" even can be used correctly as a verb meaning "to cut down a bunch of trees to artificially create a meadow." Logically, "park" also could be used in this way as a verb, but the word already has multiple additional meanings as a verb. Another would be counterproductive.

14 Haynach Lakes

Isolated by distance, these ponds and a lovely lake below dramatic peaks justify the trail pounding required to get there.

Start: Green Mountain Trailhead
Distance: 16.5 miles out and back
Hiking time: About 12 hours
Difficulty: Moderately difficult
Trail surface: Dirt
Elevation: Trailhead, 8,794 feet; Upper Haynach Lake, 11,080 feet
Best season: Summer
Other trail users: Equestrians on Tonahutu Creek Trail, human foot traffic only on branch to Haynach Lakes
Canine compatibility: Dogs prohibited

Fees and permits: National park entrance fee
Trail contacts: Rocky Mountain National Park Backcountry Office, 1000 US 36, Estes Park 80517; (970) 586-1242; www.nps.gov/romo
Maps: Trails Illustrated *Rocky Mountain National Park*; USGS *Grand Lake* and *McHenrys Peak*
Highlights: Granite Falls, Haynach Lakes, Nakai Peak
Wildlife: Mule deer, elk, moose, red squirrel, mountain chickadee

Finding the trailhead: Green Mountain Trailhead is well marked on the east side of Trail Ridge Road, about 3 miles north of the Grand Lake entrance to the national park and 17 miles southwest of Fall River Pass. **GPS:** N40 18.45' / W105 50.49'

The Hike

The Arapaho called these lakes *haa' nach* ("snow water"), which got anglicized to their current name. It is a truly charming name, but it does not differentiate these lakes from nearly all other lakes in the national park. Nonetheless, it is appropriate that such a beautiful name end up somewhere on the park map, and these bodies of water certainly merit the honor.

Haynach Lakes can be reached as a very lengthy extension of the Big Meadows loop hike, but perhaps the longer route down Onahu Creek may be more than you want to add to that already long hike. Bypassing the Onahu Creek connecting trail takes you farther along the very well constructed Tonahutu Creek Trail, which borders seemingly interminable Big Meadows. Along the way you will notice many lodgepole pine killed by beetles, making them fuel for wildfires, such as the summer 2013 fire that burned the forest through which the trail passes as it bends east around the north end of Big Meadows. By the time you pass Granite Falls and reach the path branching left up a pleasant stream, your eagerness to see the lakes may be devolving into impatience. You discover that the long trip was worthwhile after you pass various marshy ponds and view at last the magnificent Upper Haynach Lake. Nakai Peak rising above is spectacular.

Nakai is a prominent family name among the Navajo where Colorado, New Mexico, Arizona, and Utah meet at the only four-way right-angle state boundary

Haynach Lakes

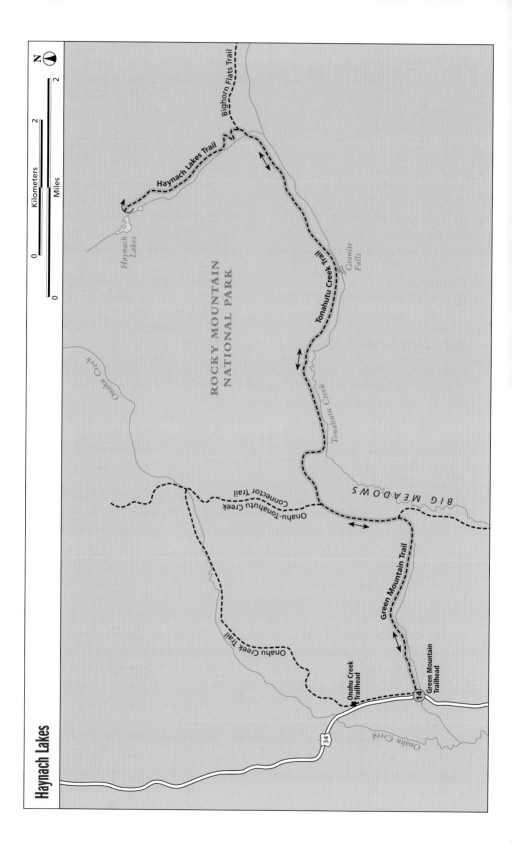

Haynach Lakes carry an Arapaho name aptly translated in English as "Snow Water."

in the United States, reasonably enough called the Four Corners. Although uncon-nected either linguistically or culturally, the combination of Navajo and Arapaho names seems to work well at Haynach Lakes.

On the return, a right turn at the Onahu Creek connecting trail will take you back to your starting point by a different route than the Green Mountain Trail. But returning the way you came is 2.8 miles shorter, which may be welcome after a wonderful but tiring exploration of Haynach Lakes.

Miles and Directions

0.0 Start at the Green Mountain Trailhead.

1.8 Reach Big Meadows; turn left onto Tonahutu Creek Trail. (A right turn leads eventually to the park's west-side headquarters and visitor center.)

2.7 Junction with Onahu-Tonahutu Creek Connector Trail. Continue right along Big Meadows.

5.2 Tonahutu Creek tumbles over Granite Falls, to the right of the trail. Continue past the falls.

6.7 After crossing the creek, head left on the Haynach Lakes Trail.

8.25 Arrive at Upper Haynach Lake. Return to the Tonahutu Creek Trail and turn right.

13.8 Pass junction with the Onahu-Tonahutu Creek Connector Trail. (**Option:** Decide if you want to add 2.8 miles to the hike by taking the Connector and Onahu Creek Trails.)

14.7 Reach the Green Mountain Trail and descend to the trailhead.

16.5 Arrive back at the trailhead.

15 Lake Nanita

There may be other lakes in the national park that rank with Nanita for beauty, but none surpass it.

Start: North Inlet Trailhead
Distance: 22.0 miles out and back
Hiking time: About 2 days
Difficulty: Difficult
Trail surface: Dirt
Elevation: Trailhead: 8,545 feet; Lake Nanita, 10,789 feet
Best season: Summer
Other trail users: Equestrians
Canine compatibility: Dogs prohibited
Fees and permits: Fee for backcountry campsite

Trail contacts: Rocky Mountain National Park Backcountry Office, 1000 US 36, Estes Park 80517; (970) 586-1242; www.nps.gov/romo
Maps: USGS *Grand Lake* and *McHenrys Peak*; Trails Illustrated *Rocky Mountain National Park*
Highlights: Cascade Falls, North Inlet Falls, Lake Nokoni, Ptarmigan Mountain, Andrews Peak, Lake Nanita
Wildlife: Mule deer, moose, red squirrels, mountain chickadees

Finding the trailhead: Drive east from US 34 toward Grand Lake on CO 278 (Tunnel Road). One-third mile from US 34, CO 278 forks. Take the left-hand fork, which bypasses the village of Grand Lake and leads eventually to the West Portal of the Adams Tunnel of the Big Thompson Irrigation Project. Leave CO 278 at 0.8 mile from the fork, turning left along a narrow unpaved road. After a short distance, a parking area on the left provides parking for the Tonahutu Creek Trail. Keep going over a hill, turn right, and cross Tonahutu Creek on a bridge uncomfortably narrow for most cars. Just past the bridge is a parking lot for the North Inlet Trail. **GPS:** N40 15.39' / W105 48.87'

The Hike

The trek to Lake Nanita winds gently through mostly lodgepole pine forest beset by beetles and varied by North Inlet, a creek that flows into the north side of Grand Lake. Where beleaguered forest opens to meadows, watch for moose. A worthwhile, less-ambitious hike culminates at redundantly named Cascade Falls. The falls present themselves to photographers most attractively from the bottom. This is not surprising, but the steep climb downstream demands care. The wet rocks are slick, and a slip could smash a camera (or a body) before it reaches one of the most photogenic lakes in Rocky Mountain National Park.

A little less than 1.5 miles beyond Cascade Falls, North Inlet gushes through a rockbound chute at Big Pool. The water slows in the pool, reminiscent of The Pool along the Fern Lake Trail on the east side of the national park. The water here operates under the physical constraints of the Venturi effect. This phenomenon occurs when a fluid (air counts, as does water of course) must flow through a constricted

Lake Nanita reflects Andrews Peak.

space. Because the same volume must get through as in the spaces above and below the constriction, the speed of the flow must increase within and then diminish below the constriction.

The trail remains easy until switchbacks announce a grade that grows gradually steeper. When you finally reach a right turn at the Lake Nanita Trail, take a few steps to celebrate the event with a view from a bridge of North Inlet Falls. Beyond the falls, an obviously steeper climb is made a bit easier by the shade of heavy subalpine forest. The view broadens after more switchbacks to reveal marshes and Lake Solitude on the North Inlet valley floor. Chiefs Head Peak is interesting above but does not reveal from this angle the distinctive outline that gave the peak its name.

After yet more switchbacks ease the ascent, an outlet stream from Lake Nokoni waters a magnificent display of subalpine flowers. Farther along, Nokoni itself is a textbook tarn scooped from a rock basin by glaciers. (Nokoni was the name of a prominent Comanche.) Do not be content with the views from Nokoni—an even greater spectacle awaits after more climbing and descending to Lake Nanita. (Nanita was either a Navajo name applied to Plains Indians meaning "aliens" or a term used by the small Kichai tribe of Texas for the much more powerful Comanches; in neither

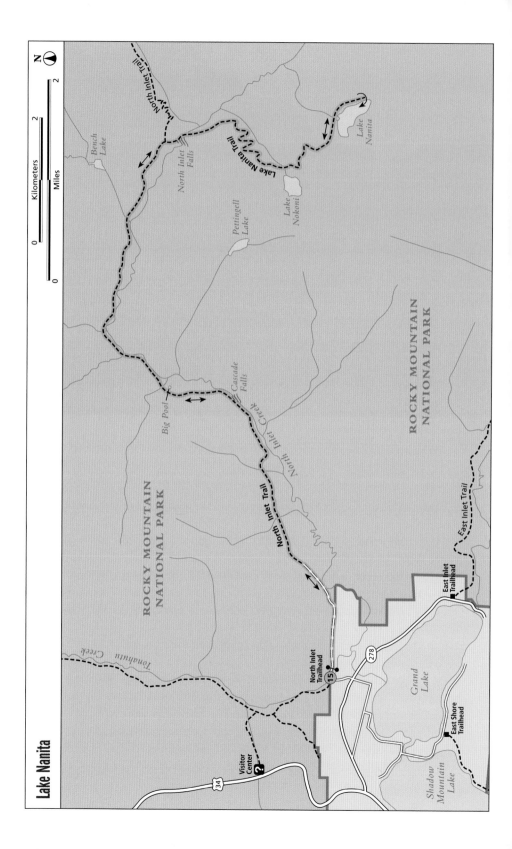

Lake Nanita

N

Kilometers
0   2

Miles
0   2

ROCKY MOUNTAIN
NATIONAL PARK

North Inlet Trail

Bench
Lake

North Inlet
Falls

Lake Nanita Trail

Pettingell
Lake

Lake
Nokoni

Lake
Nanita

Cascade
Falls

Big Pool

North Inlet Creek

North Inlet Trail

ROCKY MOUNTAIN
NATIONAL PARK

East Inlet Trail

East Inlet
Trailhead

Tonahutu Creek

North Inlet
Trailhead

15

278

Grand
Lake

East Shore
Trailhead

Shadow
Mountain
Lake

Visitor
Center

34

case was the name likely to be complimentary.) The drama of jagged spires on Ptarmigan Mountain (alliteratively called Ptarmigan Towers) and the classic mountain shape of Andrews Peak afford good light for photos of some gorgeous scenes, likely no matter what time of day you finally trudge to the shore of Lake Nanita. It is a rare hiker who will deny that the glory is worth the effort.

Miles and Directions

0.0 Start at the North Inlet Trailhead and follow a flat, unpaved road across private land.

1.2 At Summerland Park the trail narrows amid beetle-ravaged lodgepole pine. Watch for moose in the meadows.

3.5 Arrive at Cascade Falls.

4.8 North Inlet squeezes through a granite-confined slot at Big Pool.

6.65 Cross Ptarmigan Creek on a bridge.

7.45 The Lake Nanita Trail climbs to the right.

7.6 North Inlet Falls announces a steepening of the trail ahead.

9.9 Lake Nokoni tempts hikers to halt; resist the temptation.

11.0 Lake Nanita rewards a long hike. Return by the same trails.

22.0 Arrive back at the trailhead.

16 Adams Falls

This is likely the most popular hike in the Grand Lake vicinity.

Start: East Inlet Trailhead
Distance: 0.6 mile out and back
Hiking time: A leisurely 90 minutes
Difficulty: Easy
Trail surface: Dirt
Elevation: Trailhead, 8,391 feet; Adams Falls, 8,470 feet
Best season: Summer
Other trail users: Equestrians
Canine compatibility: Dogs prohibited

Fees and permits: No fees or permits required
Trail contacts: Rocky Mountain National Park Backcountry Office, 1000 US 36, Estes Park 80517; (970) 586-1242, www.nps.gov/romo
Maps: USGS *Shadow Mountain*; Trails Illustrated *Rocky Mountain National Park*
Highlights: Adams Falls
Wildlife: Gray jays, water ouzels (dippers), mountain chickadees

Finding the trailhead: East Inlet Trailhead is at the end of Tunnel Road (CO 278). Take CO 278 east from US 34 at the village of Grand Lake. After 0.3 mile, take the left fork to bypass the town and head directly to Adams Tunnel, a link in the Colorado–Big Thompson Irrigation Project. Follow more than 2 miles of paved road to the West Portal of Adams Tunnel. (The west end of the tunnel is at the East Inlet to Grand Lake, a minor point of confusion.) At the West Portal bear left on the unpaved road to the trailhead parking area. **GPS:** N40 14.39' / W105 48.02'

The Hike

Note: East Inlet is at the West Portal, confusing to those uninitiated to water demands in Colorado. The inlet is where a creek enters the east side of Grand Lake; the West Portal of Adams Tunnel reverses the flow to east of the Continental Divide. You will not encounter this confusion again, so just ignore it.

Adams Falls is an easy stroll along the initial stretch of the East Inlet Trail. It is so easy that repeated visits to view and photograph the falls in different moods are worthwhile.

Lucky coincidence oriented the falls so that the spray of falling water often refracts rainbows in sunny weather. To see a rainbow, orient yourself to view the falls with the sun at your back.

Under overcast skies, the contrast between white water and surrounding dark rocks and forest is diminished by diffused light. This permits a better recording of all elements of the view. Under less-bright light, photos may be made at 1/15th second or slower to cause the moving water to blur through the photo, conveying a veil of motion while the surrounding land remains sharp.

Adams Falls is an easy, hence popular, hike near Grand Lake.

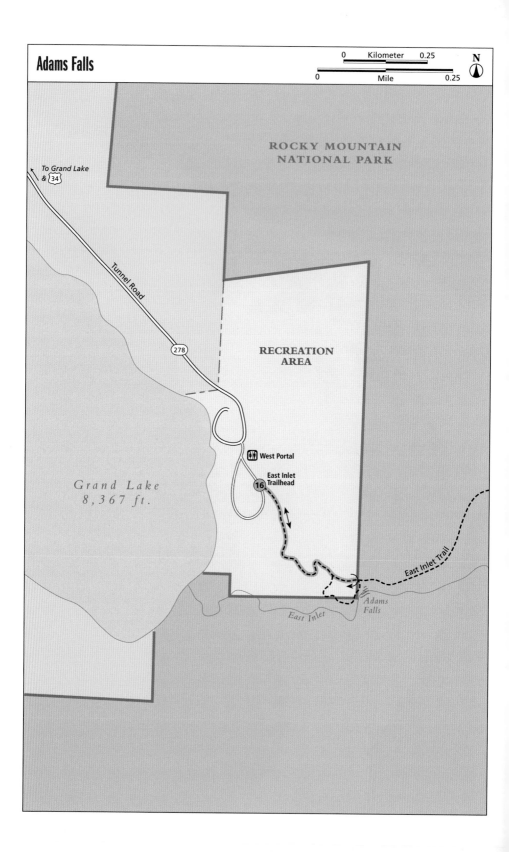

Adams Falls

0   Kilometer   0.25

0   Mile   0.25

N

ROCKY MOUNTAIN
NATIONAL PARK

To Grand Lake
& 34

Tunnel Road

278

RECREATION
AREA

West Portal

East Inlet
Trailhead

16

Grand Lake
8,367 ft.

East Inlet

Adams
Falls

East Inlet Trail

Adams Falls was named in 1917 for Jay Adams, a prominent Grand Lake resident who threw a big party for the community on the nearby eastern shore of the lake. All the happy attendees agreed that the falls should be named for their host. By good fortune, this prevented acceptance of its previous name of Ouzel Falls from causing confusion with a popular hiking destination on the east side of the national park.

Miles and Directions

0.0 Start at the East Inlet Trailhead.

0.3 Reach Adams Falls. Return the way you came.

0.6 Arrive back at the trailhead.

17 Lake Verna

The journey to Lake Verna is a prayer.

Start: East Inlet Trailhead

Distance: 13.8 miles out and back

Hiking time: About 12 hours

Difficulty: Moderately difficult

Trail surface: Dirt

Elevation: Trailhead, 8,391 feet; Lake Verna, 10,200 feet

Best season: Summer

Other trail users: Equestrians

Canine compatibility: Dogs prohibited

Fees and permits: No fees or permits required

Trail contacts: Rocky Mountain National Park Backcountry Office, 1000 US 36, Estes Park 80517; (970) 586-1242; www.nps.gov/romo

Maps: USGS *Shadow Mountain* and *Isolation Peak*; Trails Illustrated *Rocky Mountain National Park*

Highlights: Adams Falls, Lone Pine Lake, Lake Verna

Wildlife: Moose, gray jays

Finding the trailhead: East Inlet Trailhead is at the end of Tunnel Road (CO 278). Take CO 278 east from US 34 at the village of Grand Lake. After 0.3 mile, take the left fork to bypass the town and head directly to Adams Tunnel, a link in the Colorado–Big Thompson Irrigation Project. Follow more than 2 miles of paved road to the West Portal of Adams Tunnel. (The west end of the tunnel is at the East Inlet to Grand Lake, a minor point of confusion.) At the West Portal bear left on the unpaved road to the trailhead parking area. **GPS:** N40 14.39' / W105 48.02'

The Hike

The East Inlet Trail to Lake Verna is a prayer because it follows paternoster lakes. Roman Catholics for centuries have used a string of beads to recite the Rosary, each bead leading the worshipper to the next section of prayer. The first words of the Lord's Prayer, "Our Father," is "Pater Noster" in Latin. Because prior to the Second Vatican Council in 1962, Latin was the preferred language of this prayer, "pater noster" became another term for Rosary beads. From peaks and passes high above mountain valleys, the glacier-created lakes dotted along a watercourse suggested a string of beads. This typical geological formation came to be called paternoster lakes.

Alpine glaciers flowing in mountain valleys form lakes both as the conveyor belts of ice advance and as the glaciers melt. When gravity pulls build-ups of ice down the valleys, rocks from the surrounding valley walls fall onto the glaciers. The moving ice both carries this debris and freezes it into the ice mass, where rocks become like rasps on a file. As the glaciers flow down the valley, this rough surface eats away the bottom of the valley walls, which water erosion originally cut in a V-shaped profile. Removing the point of the V, glaciers steepen the valley walls, converting the profile from a V to a U. Most of the valleys in Rocky Mountain National Park display this classic glaciated U, visible when hikers pass into unforested open spots and can gaze upstream.

Fireweed pioneers soil in rock crack above Lake Verna.

The moving ice also scrapes away at the valley floor and freezes to the rocks, gouging and excavating basins in the valley's base rock. These basins form the type of paternoster lakes most prominent along East Inlet, including Lake Verna.

Eventually mountain glaciers melt, either because the flowing ice descends to a lower, warmer elevation or because climate becomes periodically warmer. The rock debris carried by the conveyor belt of ice accumulates where the glaciers succumb to heat. When the melting occurs at the same spot over centuries, the rock detritus accumulates in a ridge called a moraine.

Moraines that form at the lower ends of glaciers are called terminal moraines; moraines that accumulate along the sides of glaciers are called lateral moraines. Because climate tends to warm in a jerking pattern of rising average temperature, glaciers melt back at an inconsistent rate. The lower end of a glacier may sit in the same place for centuries before the retreat resumes, pulling the lower end up the valley until it pauses at a higher, colder elevation. This jerky pattern of retreat drops successive recessional moraines on the valley floor.

These recessional moraines become dams, behind which water from melting glacial ice and precipitation accumulates. The melting also exposes the basins plucked

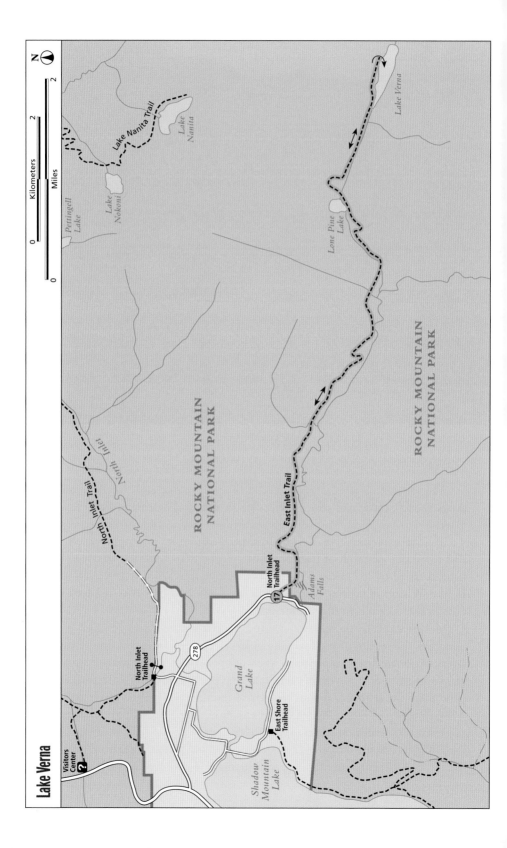

Lake Verna

0   Kilometers   2

0   Miles   2

ROCKY MOUNTAIN
NATIONAL PARK

ROCKY MOUNTAIN
NATIONAL PARK

Lake Verna

Lone Pine
Lake

Lake Nanita Trail

Pettingell
Lake

Lake
Nokoni

Lake
Nanita

North Inlet Trail

North Inlet

East Inlet Trail

Visitors
Center

2

North Inlet
Trailhead

278

North Inlet
Trailhead

17

Adams
Falls

East Shore
Trailhead

Grand
Lake

Shadow
Mountain
Lake

and scraped in the bedrock of the valley floor, which also accumulate water. Together moraines and basins create a line of paternoster lakes along the string of a connecting water course on the U-shaped valley floor.

The floor of East Inlet's valley displays five main paternoster lakes. Verna is the second bead from the bottom. The lowest bead in the line is Lone Pine Lake, named for a now-dead pine growing from a crack in a large rock left in the lake by the last glacier. That pine pioneer has been succeeded by several younger lodgepoles and an Engelmann spruce. Along East Inlet, occasional meadows are home to mosquitoes, whose vicious attacks may distract hikers from watching for moose. Likely the mosquitoes bug the moose as well, at which point perhaps they should be termed "moosquitoes."

Miles and Directions

0.0 Start at the East Inlet Trailhead.

0.3 Arrive at Adams Falls.

5.5 Reach Lone Pine Lake.

6.9 Arrive at Lake Verna. Return the way you came.

13.8 Arrive back at the trailhead.

18 Shadow Mountain Fire Lookout

This historic tower is built of unshaped stone, causing it to seem to grow from the rocks that surround it.

Start: East Shore Trailhead at Shadow Mountain Dam

Distance: 9.6 miles out and back

Hiking time: About 7 hours

Difficulty: Moderate

Trail surface: Dirt

Elevation: Trailhead, 8,390 feet; Shadow Mountain Fire Lookout, 9,923 feet

Best season: Summer

Other trail users: Equestrians

Canine compatibility: Dogs prohibited

Fees and permits: Arapaho National Recreation Area use fee (permit left on dashboard)

Trail contacts: Rocky Mountain National Park Backcountry Office, 1000 US 36, Estes Park 80517; (970) 586-1242; www.nps.gov/romo

Maps: USGS *Shadow Mountain*; Trails Illustrated *Rocky Mountain National Park*

Highlights: 360-degree view from fire lookout

Wildlife: Red squirrels, mountain chickadees, ospreys fishing in Shadow Mountain Lake

Finding the trailhead: Turn left off US 34 about 12 miles northwest of Granby at the southern end of Shadow Mountain Lake where a sign indicates "Green Ridge Complex." This turn is a few miles southwest of Grand Lake, but deciding where Grand Lake ends is problematic. Drive through the USDA Forest Service Green Ridge Campground in Arapaho National Recreation Area about 2 miles east on CR 66 and FR 274. There is a parking area at the dam, on the right side of the road. **GPS:** N40 12.25' / W105 50.27'

The Hike

Shadow Mountain has been called so many different names that the Colorado Geographic Board arbitrated its current name with the goal of offending no one (or everyone). At various times of day it shadows Grand and Shadow Mountain Lakes.

Formed by a glacial moraine dam, Grand Lake is the largest natural lake in Colorado. Shadow Mountain Lake is formed by a human-built dam a short way north of the farthest extent of glacial action. Shadow Mountain Lake was built between 1944 and 1946, when the United States, emerging from the Great Depression, was fighting two major wars simultaneously and nonetheless undertook major internal improvements such as the Colorado–Big Thompson Irrigation Project. Also a human-built lake, adjacent Lake Granby dwarfs both Grand and Shadow Mountain Lakes in size. When much water is pumped from Lake Granby up to Shadow Mountain Lake, the Granby shoreline broadens to mudflats so drastically as to cause doubt about the extent of open water. Meanwhile, Shadow Mountain Lake and Grand Lake, into which it flows via a canal, remain at a consistent level. All these lakes spread widely below the fire lookout tower on Shadow Mountain. The water in the lakes is directed

Listed on the National Register of Historic Places, the Shadow Mountain Fire Lookout lifts hikers above the forest for a view of the valley of East Inlet.

via a 17-mile tunnel below the national park and the Continental Divide to the thirsty plains east of the mountains.

While flowing east, this water generates electricity for various communities, with enough power remaining to flow via wires back through the tunnel to run the pumps that lift water from Lake Granby into Shadow Mountain Lake, then Grand Lake, then under the mountains to generate more electricity and water for the populous east slope of the Rockies. Physics informs us that a perpetual motion machine is impossible, but this seems close. Of course the original power comes from the sun, which lifts water to fall into mountain streams that flow into Lake Granby.

Towers to lift resident lookouts above trees to spot forest fires and direct firefighters to extinguish them have declined in usefulness, if not in romance, since the Shadow Mountain Lookout was built in 1932–1933. Indeed, the fighting of forest fire, although still a major task for various government agencies, has been reconsidered in light of research that points out the virtues of fire for the natural health of the land. Of course when that land is close to private land containing homes and other useful structures, the virtues of wildfires fall quickly into disrepute and controversy. Then aircraft begin to bomb the flames with retardant and firefighters rush in to battle the conflagration—and sometimes to die.

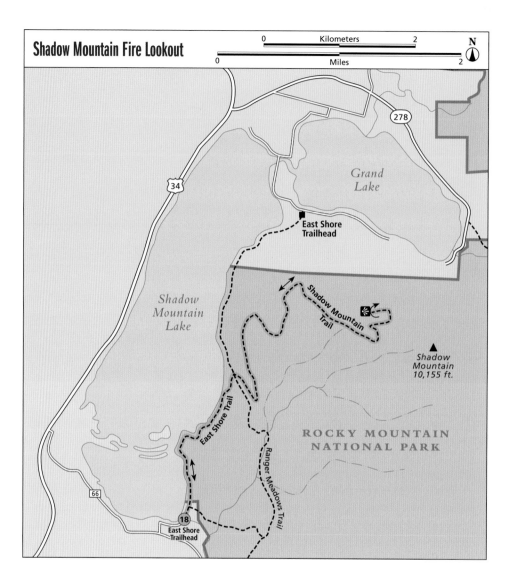

From Shadow Mountain Dam, follow the East Shore Trail into Rocky Mountain National Park and walk along the lake. Keep an eye out to the left for ospreys, or fish hawks, diving for fish in the reservoir. Keep an eye out to the right for a falling lodgepole pine killed by beetles, which might kill *you* if the tree falls in a particularly unlucky direction. Because the wind normally is from the west, the danger is relatively mild along the lake. The hike along the shore is restricted to pedestrians because a horse trail runs inland. The two meet where the ascent begins on the Shadow Mountain Trail.

After a sharp switchback, the trail climbs at a steady trudge up the side of a lateral moraine to the moraine's ridgeline. At this point the trail follows the rather narrow ridgeline until it meets the bulk of Shadow Mountain. The path bends right around the end of the gully between moraine and mountain. Circling below a prominence on Shadow Mountain, the trail enters a level area above another gully below the fire lookout tower. The grade steepens again as it switchbacks up to the tower, which is on a promontory lower than the true summit of Shadow Mountain but evidently affording a wider view of country endangered by fire.

Looking rather like a stone fortress surmounted by a wooden lookout structure, the tower rises three stories, providing a 360-degree view above surrounding pines and fir. Stairs climb the outside of the tower, and a walkway leads around the top. Directly below to the west is Grand Lake; to the east is the valley of East Inlet. Mount Craig forms the south wall, and the higher slopes of Ptarmigan Mountain and Andrews Peak to the north are covered by alpine tundra. Southwest is Shadow Mountain Lake, beyond what is left of the lodgepole forest beleaguered by beetles. Large islands in the lake are high points along a lateral moraine dumped by one of the series of glaciers that flowed from 20 miles north in the Never Summer Range. Lake Granby is huge to the south.

Miles and Directions

0.0 Start at the East Shore Trailhead at Shadow Mountain Dam.

1.3 Turn right on the Shadow Mountain Trail.

4.8 Reach the Shadow Mountain Fire Lookout. Return by the same route.

9.6 Arrive back at the trailhead.

Never Summers

19 Lulu City Site

Faint remnants of failed dreams of mining fortunes rest along the peaceful headwaters of the Colorado River.

Start: Colorado River Trailhead
Distance: 7.4 miles out and back
Hiking time: About 7 hours
Difficulty: Moderately easy
Trail surface: Dirt
Elevation: Trailhead, 9,010 feet; Lulu City site, 9,360 feet
Best season: Summer
Other trail users: Equestrians
Canine compatibility: Dogs prohibited

Fees and permits: National park entrance fee
Trail contacts: Rocky Mountain National Park Backcountry Office, 1000 US 36, Estes Park 80517; (970) 586-1242; www/nps.gov/romo
Maps: USGS *Fall River Pass*; Trails Illustrated *Rocky Mountain National Park*
Highlights: Shipler Mine, Lulu City site
Wildlife: Elk, mule deer, moose, red squirrels, beavers, gray jays

Finding the trailhead: The Colorado River Trailhead is on the west side of Trail Ridge Road, 9.6 miles north of the Grand Lake entrance to Rocky Mountain National Park and 10.7 miles southwest of Fall River Pass. **GPS:** N40 24.06' / W105 50.92'

The Hike

Colorado contains many history fanatics eager to explore the state's mining past. But even this mining multitude finds few structural remnants of the search for silver at the site of Lulu City, which disappointed humans abandoned in the 1880s, about ten years after it was founded. Even before Lulu City was founded, Joe Shipler pecked a living from a trailside mine. He stuck it out until 1914—like so many Grand County residents, reluctant to leave despite lack of riches. (Do not explore his workings; mines are not safe.)

Very common, however, along the Colorado River Trail through the long-ago hopes of seekers of riches are structures built by even older contributors to American capital: the nation's largest rodent, the beaver. In the 1830s, when most of the American economy depended on agriculture, bold mountain men of European ancestry ventured into the Rocky Mountains to kill beavers and peel their hides, which had miniscule barbs on their hairs. Thus beaver pelts were particularly suited for felting to make water-repellent hats.

Beaver trapping by both Europeans and Native Americans extended far back in colonial times, with many interesting implications. For instance, when diseases to which Europeans had ancestral resistance hit America's original human settlers from Asia, who had no natural immunity, the native populations in the East were decimated (as eventually were those in the West). No one knew to blame germs, and the surviving disease victims got the idea that the beavers were making war on

them. They responded by killing beavers with genocidal enthusiasm, boosted by the fact that Europeans were willing to pay for beaver pelts with manufactured goods.

Within a few human generations, this war on the beaver had changed Native American material culture so drastically that many of them could not survive without trading furs, primarily beaver, to the Euro-Americans. Unsurprisingly, the anti-beaver fur trade drastically reduced beaver numbers (now restored by government wildlife agencies). In 1803 President Thomas Jefferson sent Lewis and Clark into western lands newly purchased from France to determine if fur riches were there. The explorers reported much potential wealth.

The exceedingly colorful era of the mountain man resulted, particularly active in the 1830s and 1840s. Beavers survived in the Rockies because nutria pelts from South America were more easily obtained and therefore cheaper, greatly reducing the demand for beaver.

Beaver ponds along the Colorado River Trail remind hikers to the Lulu City site that wealth in furs preceded wealth from the mining camp's silver.

Until mineral wealth and manufacturing began injecting capital into the American economy, the fur trade, primarily the beaver trade, provided most of America's spending money. Now the mineral wealth is gone from the Never Summer Range. But the beaver remain—their dams, ponds, and lodges and the conical stumps showcasing their industry obvious along the Colorado River Trail through disappeared Lulu City.

Miles and Directions

- **0.0** Start at the Colorado River Trailhead.
- **0.6** The Red Mountain Trail heads left. Continue right on the Colorado River Trail.
- **2.5** Shipler Mine is not particularly obvious on the right.
- **3.5** The trail splits; take the left fork and head downhill.
- **3.7** Reach the Lulu City site. Turn around and retrace your steps.
- **7.4** Arrive back at the trailhead.

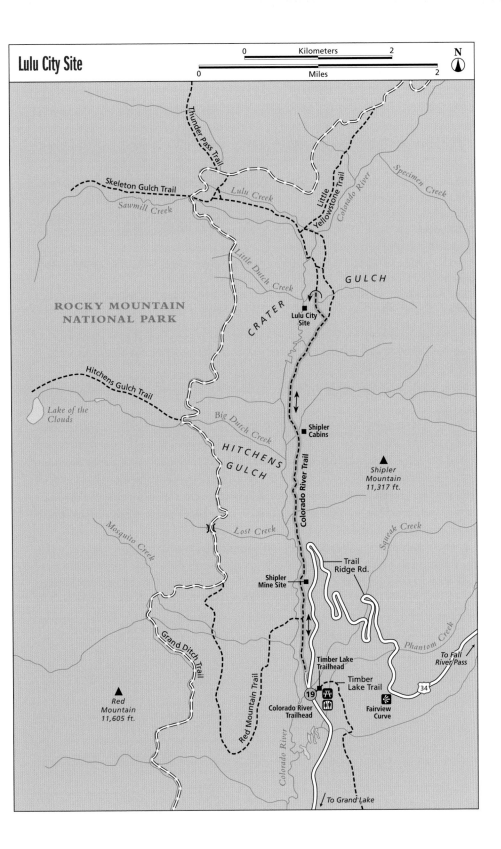

20 Little Yellowstone Canyon

Little Yellowstone Canyon is a worthwhile goal for those who desire to hike beyond the Lulu City site.

Start: Colorado River Trailhead
Distance: 9.2 miles out and back
Hiking time: About 8 hours
Difficulty: Moderately easy
Trail surface: Dirt
Elevation: Trailhead, 9,010 feet; Little Yellowstone Canyon, 10,000 feet
Best season: Summer
Other trail users: Equestrians
Canine compatibility: Dogs prohibited

Fees and permits: National park entrance fee
Trail contacts: Rocky Mountain National Park Backcountry Office, 1000 US 36, Estes Park 80517; (970) 586-1242; www.nps.gov/romo
Maps: USGS *Fall River Pass*; Trails Illustrated *Rocky Mountain National Park*
Highlights: Shipler Mine, Lulu City site, Little Yellowstone Canyon
Wildlife: Mule deer, elk, moose, red squirrels, beavers, gray jays

Finding the trailhead: The Colorado River Trailhead is on the west side of Trail Ridge Road, 9.6 miles north of the Grand Lake entrance to Rocky Mountain National Park and 10.7 miles southwest of Fall River Pass. **GPS:** N40 24.06' / W105 50.92'

The Hike

National Park Service Ranger Winnie Winston came from Kelly, Wyoming, in Grand Teton National Park, in the neighborhood of the Grand Canyon of the Yellowstone River in Yellowstone National Park. He saw a similarity between the yellow rock of Yellowstone and the eroded volcanic rock exposed near the headwaters of the Colorado River. It was an apt comparison, but do not expect to see mighty waterfalls or nesting ospreys in Little Yellowstone Canyon.

These volcanics exploded from Lulu Mountain some 28 million years ago. The canyon carving began about 26 million years ago. Beyond the Lulu City site there are two semi-parallel trails toward the canyon. The lower path that follows an old stage road through the Lulu City site and over Thunder Pass seems more interesting, but you can return by the higher path that looks down on the Lulu City site but bypasses it. The distances are about the same.

The Never Summer Range soars above the Little Yellowstone Canyon. ▶

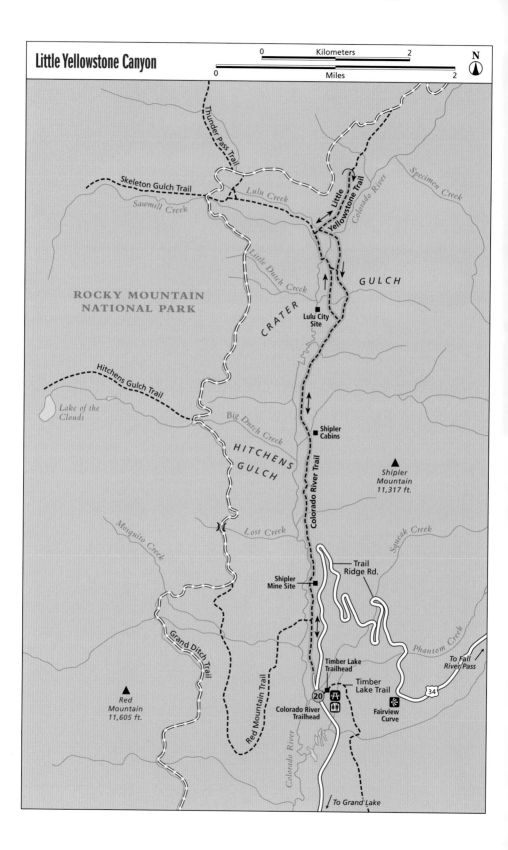

Little Yellowstone Canyon

Kilometers
0   2
0   2
Miles

N

Thunder Pass Trail

Skeleton Gulch Trail

Lulu Creek

Sawmill Creek

Little Yellowstone Trail

Colorado River

Specimen Creek

Little Dutch Creek

ROCKY MOUNTAIN
NATIONAL PARK

CRATER   GULCH

Lulu City
Site

Hitchens Gulch Trail

Lake of the
Clouds

Big Dutch Creek

HITCHENS
GULCH

Shipler
Cabins

Shipler
Mountain
11,317 ft.

Colorado River Trail

Mosquito Creek

Lost Creek

Squeak Creek

Shipler
Mine Site

Trail
Ridge Rd.

Grand Ditch Trail

Red Mountain Trail

Red
Mountain
11,605 ft.

Timber Lake
Trailhead

Timber Lake Trail

20

Colorado River
Trailhead

Phantom Creek

To Fall
River Pass

34

Fairview
Curve

Colorado River

To Grand Lake

Eroded towers of volcanic rock towers in Little Yellowstone Canyon along the Colorado River remind hikers of the much larger Grand Canyon of the Yellowstone in the first national park.

Miles and Directions

0.0   Start at the Colorado River Trailhead.

0.6   The Red Mountain Trail departs to the left. Continue right on the Colorado River Trail.

2.5   Shipler Mine is not particularly obvious to the right.

3.5   The trail splits. The left fork descends to the Lulu City site; the right stays high within the forest. Both go to Little Yellowstone Canyon with equal ease. Head left to the Lulu City site.

3.7   Arrive at the Lulu City site. Continue along an old stage road.

4.0   The trail heads directly uphill to the right for a short distance to rejoin the upper trail. I think staying on the stage road is preferable.

4.5   Head right, away from the stage road, to cross Lulu Creek toward Little Yellowstone and eventually La Poudre Pass.

4.6   Arrive at the Little Yellowstone Canyon rim. Where you arrive is as good a spot as any for photos. Follow the trail that follows Lulu Creek down to the crossing of the Colorado River to return via the upper trail, which bypasses the Lulu City site.

9.2   Arrive back at the trailhead.

21 Lake of the Clouds

Lake of the Clouds is the only large lake in the Never Summer Range.

Start: Colorado River Trailhead
Distance: 13.8 miles out and back
Hiking time: About 12 hours
Difficulty: Moderate
Trail surface: Dirt and large rocks
Elevation: Trailhead, 9,010 feet; Lake of the Clouds, 11,432 feet
Best season: Summer
Other trail users: The end of the trail is unmarked boulder hopping for human hikers only.
Canine compatibility: Dogs prohibited

Fees and permits: National park entrance fee
Trail contacts: Rocky Mountain National Park Backcountry Office, 1000 US 36, Estes Park 80517; (970) 586-1242; www.nps.gov/romo
Maps: USGS *Fall River Pass* and *Mount Richthofen*; Trails Illustrated *Rocky Mountain National Park*
Highlights: Grand Ditch, rock glacier, Lake of the Clouds
Wildlife: Elk, mule deer, red squirrels, gray jays, black spiders

Finding the trailhead: The Colorado River Trailhead is on the west side of Trail Ridge Road, 9.6 miles north of the Grand Lake entrance to Rocky Mountain National Park and 10.7 miles southwest of Fall River Pass. **GPS:** N40 24.06' / W105 50.92'

The Hike

Four peaks in the Never Summer Range are named for types of clouds. Lake of the Clouds fits right in with this happy system. Somewhat surprisingly given the many glacier-carved lakes to the east in the national park, Lake of the Clouds is the only analogous large body of water in the Never Summers.

The Red Mountain Trail below the Grand Ditch crosses Opposition Creek twice in a long switchback. The creek was named for a very large rock that delayed progress of Grand Ditch construction until workers could dig around this opposition. The Ditch is part of a water diversion project to take water from the relatively damp western slope of the Continental Divide to the parched eastern slope, where most of Colorado's population resides. After climbing to the service road that runs alongside the Ditch, turn right. The road, not open to public vehicles, is part of the trail to Lake of the Clouds.

After easy walking along the Grand Ditch, the route to Lake of the Clouds crosses the Ditch at Hitchens Gulch. In their brilliantly researched *High Country Names*, Louisa Arps and Elinor Kingery recount the story of a prospector in the 1890s who tried to find mineral wealth in the gulch that came to be named for him, although misspelled from Hichens. Over his mine he built a shaft house and other structures. He lived and mined in the gulch until he was an old man, showing up in Grand Lake

Lake of the Clouds is the only substantial tarn in the Never Summer Range.

from time to time to get supplies. On these trips he would ask the folks he encountered what he should say to his three dogs when he met them in Heaven because "Each of them thought he was my best friend."

Below Lake of the Clouds extends one of the national park's best examples of a rock glacier. Atop a core of ice, this massive accumulation of large angular rocks (plus one of my lost lens caps) moves in a fashion similar to ice glaciers, which in these warm times is very little or not at all. Something about this rock glacier makes it a habitat favored by large, black spiders. The rock glacier is a barrier to continuance of the trail, and the best route across the often-shaky river of stone is an equally shaky guess. Look for a waterfall that flows from the hidden lake. To the right of the falls is a ridge; set a course toward the lowest point in the ridge.

From atop the ridge, ascend left around snowbanks, rocks, and ledges into the basin containing the lake. On the floor of the basin, walk across tundra and bedrock to the shore. Conveniently, this brings you to the only solid rock at the lake; the other shores are steep loose rock and ice fields. Photos taken from the convenient solid rock

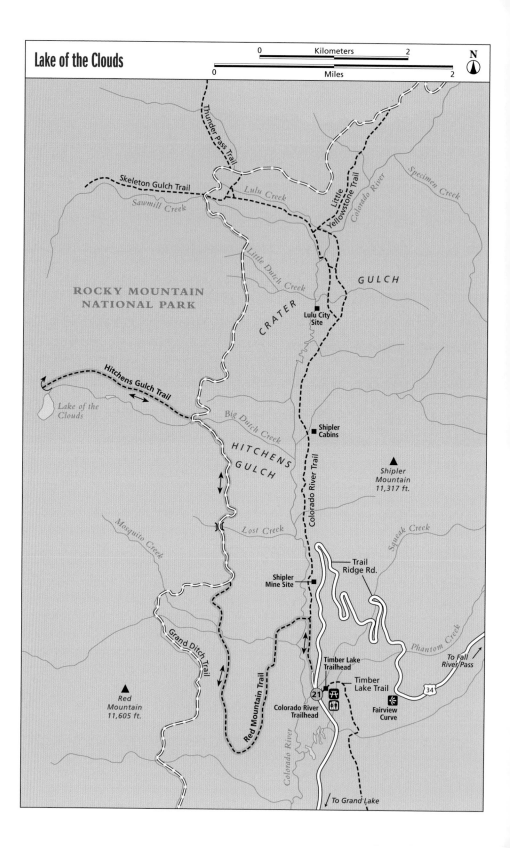

Lake of the Clouds

Kilometers
0 ———— 2

Miles
0 ———— 2

N

Thunder Pass Trail

Skeleton Gulch Trail

Sawmill Creek

Lulu Creek

Little Yellowstone Trail

Colorado River

Specimen Creek

Little Dutch Creek

ROCKY MOUNTAIN
NATIONAL PARK

CRATER

GULCH

Lulu City
Site

Hitchens Gulch Trail

Lake of the
Clouds

Big Dutch Creek

Shipler
Cabins

Shipler
Mountain
11,317 ft.

HITCHENS

GULCH

Colorado River Trail

Mosquito Creek

Lost Creek

Squeak Creek

Trail
Ridge Rd.

Shipler
Mine Site

Grand Ditch Trail

Red Mountain Trail

Red
Mountain
11,605 ft.

Phantom Creek

To Fall
River Pass

Timber Lake
Trailhead

Timber
Lake Trail

34

21

Fairview
Curve

Colorado River
Trailhead

Colorado River

To Grand Lake

are not visually stunning. Good shots can be had from the less-stable shores, but be very careful if you decide to make your way to a more photogenic position. A slip and uncontrolled slide could dump you in deep water, which you would share with chunks of ice. Less-threatening subjects for photography might be the yellow-bellied marmots and pikas that inhabit the rock piles. If they are not cooperative, move in close on the excellent examples of cushion plants.

Miles and Directions

0.0 Start at the Colorado River Trailhead.

0.5 Turn left at the Red Mountain Trail junction.

3.4 Reach the Grand Ditch and turn right (north).

5.6 Cross the Grand Ditch on a bridge at Hitchens Gulch. Ascend the gulch through switch-backs and impressive subalpine forest.

6.3 The trail ends atop a ridge overlooking a rock glacier. Look left (south) for a waterfall tumbling from the lip of a cirque within which hides Lake of the Clouds below Mount Cirrus. To the right of the falls is a ridge. Head for the lowest point on this ridge by whatever route across the rock glacier seems least bothersome.

6.9 Reach Lake of the Clouds. Return by the way you came, unless you can imagine a better way across the rock glacier.

13.8 Arrive back at the trailhead.

Bear Lake

22 Bear Lake Nature Trail

This path perambulates along the perimeter of the park's most popular lake.

Start: Bear Lake Trailhead, about 200 yards west of the parking area
Distance: 0.5-mile loop
Hiking time: About 1 hour
Difficulty: Easy
Trail surface: Dirt
Elevation: Trailhead/Bear Lake, 9,475 feet
Best season: Summer and fall
Other trail users: Human foot traffic only
Canine compatibility: Dogs prohibited
Fees and permits: National park entrance fee

Trail contacts: Rocky Mountain National Park Backcountry Office, 1000 US 36, Estes Park 80517; (970) 586-1242; www.nps.gov/romo
Maps: USGS *McHenrys Peak*; Trails Illustrated *Longs Peak*
Highlights: Views of Hallett Peak and Longs Peak, natural history points of interest
Wildlife: Red squirrels, golden-mantled ground squirrels, chipmunks, mountain chickadees, Steller's jays, gray jays, Clark's nutcrackers

Finding the trailhead: From the Beaver Meadows entrance to the national park, take US 36 a short distance west to Bear Lake Road. Turn left and drive 9 miles to the road's end at the large parking lot for Bear Lake. **GPS:** N40 18.698' / W105 38.674'

The Hike

Horace Ferguson, an early rancher and hotelkeeper near Marys Lake, saw a bear at Bear Lake, likely in the 1870s. It might have been a grizzly (now extinct in Colorado), but a better bet would be a black bear.

The National Park Service and Colorado Division of Parks and Wildlife go to great lengths to prevent negative interactions between bears and people. Bear-proof food containers are required of backcountry campers in the park. The accurate message conveyed to humans is that allowing bears (who will eat anything containing calories) to derive food from humans is very likely to result in bear behavior that will result in a dead bear.

Your chances of encountering a bear along the nature trail circling Bear Lake

Bear Lake was named by a pioneer Estes Park hotelkeeper after he saw a bear (likely a black bear) there.

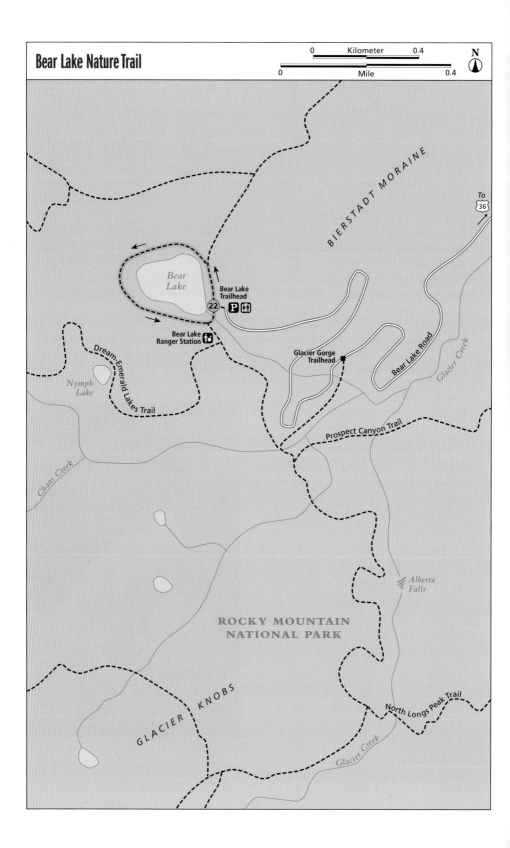

Bear Lake Nature Trail

Bierstadt Moraine

To 36

Bear Lake

Bear Lake Trailhead

22

P

Bear Lake Ranger Station

Dream-Emerald Lakes Trail

Nymph Lake

Glacier Gorge Trailhead

Bear Lake Road

Glacier Creek

Chaos Creek

Prospect Canyon Trail

Alberta Falls

ROCKY MOUNTAIN NATIONAL PARK

GLACIER KNOBS

Glacier Creek

North Longs Peak Trail

A quaking aspen grove that grew after a 1900 forest fire reflects autumn color in Bear Lake.

are similar to your chances of meeting a bear anywhere else: slim. But you might be lucky, in which case do not feed it, which could be very unlucky for the bear. Lacking a bear to photograph at Bear Lake, focus on landscapes while walking counterclockwise around the lake. There are numerous opportunities for prize-winning shots of patterns on tree trunks and boulders, wildlife portraits, and dramatic settings for people pictures. Morning is the best time for most photographs at Bear Lake, particularly of the sheer face of Hallett Peak rising directly above the water. But near stop 12 along the thirty-two-stop nature trail are excellent perspectives of Longs Peak and Glacier Gorge that are best shot in the late afternoon.

Miles and Directions

0.0   Start at the Bear Lake Trailhead and turn right on the nature trail Follow the numbered stakes counterclockwise around the lakeshore.

0.5   Complete the loop around Bear Lake. Walk back to the parking area.

23 Odessa Lake

Named for the daughter of a lodge owner at nearby Fern Lake, Odessa Lake gave its name to the gorge in which it lies.

Start: Bear Lake Trailhead, about 200 yards west of the parking area
Distance: 8.2 miles out and back
Hiking time: About 7 hours
Difficulty: Moderate
Trail surface: Dirt
Elevation: Trailhead, 9,475 feet; highpoint along trail, 10,000 feet
Best season: Summer
Other trail users: Equestrians
Canine compatibility: Dogs prohibited
Fees and permits: National park entrance fee

Trail contacts: Rocky Mountain National Park Backcountry Office, 1000 US 36, Estes Park 80517; (970) 586-1242; www.nps.gov/romo
Maps: USGS *McHenrys Peak*; Trails Illustrated *Longs Peak*
Highlights: Wildflowers, Notchtop Mountain above Lake Helene, Odessa Lake
Wildlife: Mule deer, chipmunks, golden-mantled ground squirrels, red squirrels, gray jays, mountain chickadees, Steller's jays, Clark's nutcrackers

Finding the trailhead: From the Beaver Meadows entrance to the national park, take US 36 a short distance west to Bear Lake Road. Turn left and drive 9 miles to the road's end at the large parking area for Bear Lake. **GPS:** N40 18.698' / W105 38.674'

The Hike

A pleasant stroll punctuated by exciting views, the hike to Odessa Lake also requires a bit of ascent and considerable descent. Assuming you ever desire to leave the wondrous spectacle of Odessa's shore, the way back is somewhat tougher than getting there.

The boot-pounded path from Bear Lake climbs for almost a mile to the trail leading up Flattop Mountain. Staying low and continuing right, the Odessa Lake Trail follows a gentle grade undulating through the upper reaches of Mill Creek Basin along the flank of Joe Mills Mountain in the vicinity of Marigold Pond and Two Rivers Lake.

Neither body of water is particularly obvious, but there are many trailside displays of marsh marigold, often mixed with masses of cream-colored globe flower. Two Rivers Lake may seem an exaggerated description of the un-river-like flow of Mill and Fern Creeks, which both trickle from the lake. Joe Mills, an early innkeeper in Estes Park, was both brother and competitor of Enos Mills, Father of Rocky Mountain National Park. Mill Creek is named for small lumber mills along its lower reaches in pre-park times, set up to salvage trees killed in a human-caused forest fire in 1900.

Where the Odessa Lake Trail switchbacks right and drops into Odessa Gorge, watch for a less-clear spur path that sneaks left to Lake Helene. For hikers short on time—or short on desire to hike back out of Odessa Gorge—Lake Helene is a

Aptly named Notchtop Mountain towers above Lake Helene.

worthwhile substitute for the descent to Odessa Lake. Perched at tree line, Helene sparkles beneath nearby Notchtop and Flattop Mountains, the latter appearing unflat from this perspective. Whatever the final goal, Lake Helene should not be bypassed. From Helene backtrack to the Odessa Lake Trail.

Across the valley from the trail dropping steeply down to Odessa Lake, Grace Falls is a lovely veil plunging into the gorge. The trail is not difficult but requires care to avoid an injurious fall when you're crossing snowfields that remain well into summer. The fairly easy progress toward Odessa Lake is encouraging until the path passes above the lake and keeps heading down as the lake drops behind. The *I am lost* thought likely will not have time to materialize before you reach the outlet stream from the lake and a sharp left turn along a narrow gorge back to Odessa.

Framed by forest leading up to dramatic peaks, Odessa certainly merits hikers' high regard. Notchtop by now is familiar, although somewhat less notchy than when viewed from Lake Helene. Descending between Helene and Odessa, hikers will not notice much resemblance between the Little Matterhorn ridge and its Swiss namesake.

Odessa Lake

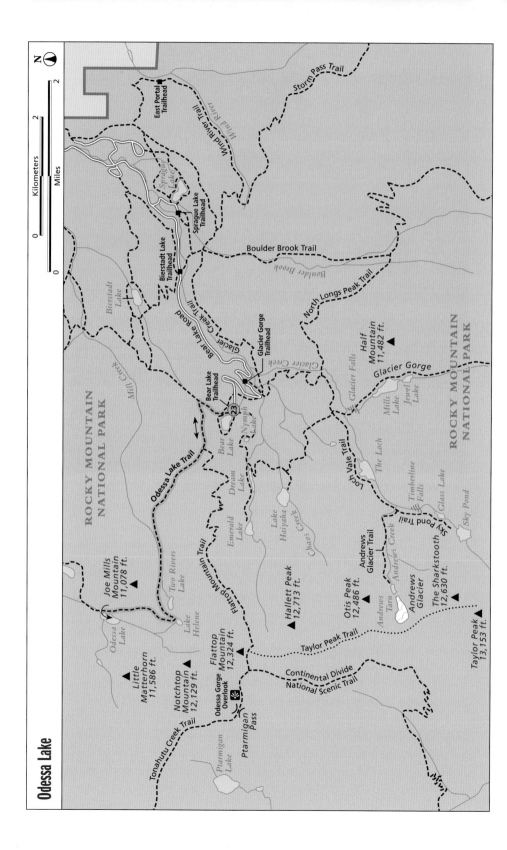

N

Kilometers
Miles

ROCKY MOUNTAIN
NATIONAL PARK

Storm Pass Trail

East Portal
Trailhead

Wind River Trail

Wind River

Sprague
Lake

Sprague Lake
Trailhead

Bierstadt Lake
Trailhead

Boulder Brook Trail

Boulder Brook

Bierstadt
Lake

North Longs Peak Trail

Mill Creek

Bear Lake Road

Glacier Creek Trail

Glacier Gorge
Trailhead

Bear Lake
Trailhead

Glacier Creek

Glacier Falls

Half
Mountain
11,482 ft.

Glacier Gorge

Odessa Lake Trail

Bear
Lake

Nymph
Lake

Mills
Lake

Jewel
Lake

ROCKY MOUNTAIN
NATIONAL PARK

Joe Mills
Mountain
11,078 ft.

Two Rivers
Lake

Dream
Lake

The Loch

Loch Vale Trail

Emerald
Lake

Lake
Haiyaha

Chaos Creek

Timberline
Falls

Little
Matterhorn
11,586 ft.

Lake
Helene

Flattop Mountain Trail

Hallett Peak
12,713 ft.

Otis Peak
12,486 ft.

Andrews
Glacier Trail

Andrews
Tarn

Andrews Creek

Glass Lake

Sky Pond Trail

Sky Pond

The Sharkstooth
12,630 ft.

Odessa
Lake

Notchtop
Mountain
12,129 ft.

Odessa Gorge
Overlook

Flattop
Mountain
12,324 ft.

Taylor Peak Trail

Andrews
Glacier

Taylor Peak
13,153 ft.

Tonahutu Creek Trail

Ptarmigan
Lake

Ptarmigan
Pass

Continental Divide
National Scenic Trail

Autumn colors the shore of Lake Helene at the head of Odessa Gorge.

The similarity is clearer from Odessa Lake's outlet. The best photography is handily right where you reach the lake. An easy exploration to the right along the shore leads to a delta at the upstream end where silt eroded from the steep peaks comes to rest.

Miles and Directions

0.0 Start at the Bear Lake Trailhead and go right on the Bear Lake Nature Trail.

0.1 Turn right up the Flattop Mountain Trail.

0.4 The trail divides; continue left on the Flattop Mountain Trail.

0.9 Where the Flattop Mountain Trail climbs left, stay low and head right on the Odessa Lake Trail.

3.0 An informal spur path heads left to Lake Helene. Do not skip this detour. After visiting the lake, return to the main trail.

4.0 A sharp left turn along Fern Creek heads up a narrow gorge to Odessa Lake.

4.1 Reach the outlet of Odessa Lake. Return by the same route to the Bear Lake Trailhead. (**Option:** An alternative route continues 4.5 miles down the trail to Fern Lake and through remnants of a 2012 forest fire to the Fern Lake Trailhead. In summer you can catch a free shuttle back to Bear Lake.)

8.2 Arrive back at the trailhead.

24 Flattop Mountain/Odessa Gorge Overlook

Despite its cliffy flanks, Flattop Mountain really is flat on top, at least as "flat" is defined in the Rockies.

Start: Bear Lake Trailhead, about 200 yards west of the parking area
Distance: 9.0 miles out and back
Hiking time: About 7 hours
Difficulty: Moderate
Trail surface: Dirt
Elevation: Trailhead, 9,475 feet; Flattop Mountain, 12,324 feet
Best season: Summer
Other trail users: Equestrians
Canine compatibility: Dogs prohibited
Fees and permits: National park entrance fee

Trail contacts: Rocky Mountain National Park Backcountry Office, 1000 US 36, Estes Park 80517; (970) 586-1242; www.nps.gov/romo
Maps: USGS *McHenrys Peak*; Trails Illustrated *Longs Peak*
Highlights: Tyndall Glacier, view of Hallett Peak, alpine tundra atop Flattop Mountain, view into Odessa Gorge
Wildlife: Pikas, yellow-bellied marmots, golden-mantled ground squirrels, chipmunks, mule deer, Clark's nutcrackers, gray jays, Steller's jays, white-tailed ptarmigan

Finding the trailhead: From the Beaver Meadows entrance to the national park, take US 36 a short distance west to Bear Lake Road. Turn left and drive 9 miles to the road's end at the large parking lot for Bear Lake. **GPS:** N40 18.698' / W105 38.674'

The Hike

Flattop Mountain is so flat on top that determining the exact location of the top is not worth the bother. However, proceeding to the unmarked overlook of Odessa Gorge is a dramatic way to assume you have encountered the top somewhere.

After a steady climb from Bear Lake, passing less-steep trails to Bierstadt and Odessa Lakes, the Flattop Trail enters deep subalpine forest before breaking out near the cliffs overlooking Dream and Emerald Lakes. The trail then cuts away from the precipices and passes a substantial sign bolted to a rock, warning of the dangers of storms and cliffs and that "Mountains don't care."

Winding back and forth across broad alpine tundra, the trail enters the habitat of the white-tailed ptarmigan. Much sought by birders, this small grouse looks like one of the rocks that pepper the tundra and is more often passed than seen by hikers. However, the fortunate few may find their hearts suddenly in their throats when a rock scurries from under a boot tread. A much smaller feathered rock or two may scurry after the mother ptarmigan. This magical act is always startling, even to mountaineers who have seen it often. Winter snows do nothing to diminish ptarmigan camouflage, for the grouse exchanges mottled feathers for white, even covering their feet, which double as snowshoes.

Flattop Mountain/Odessa Gorge Overlook

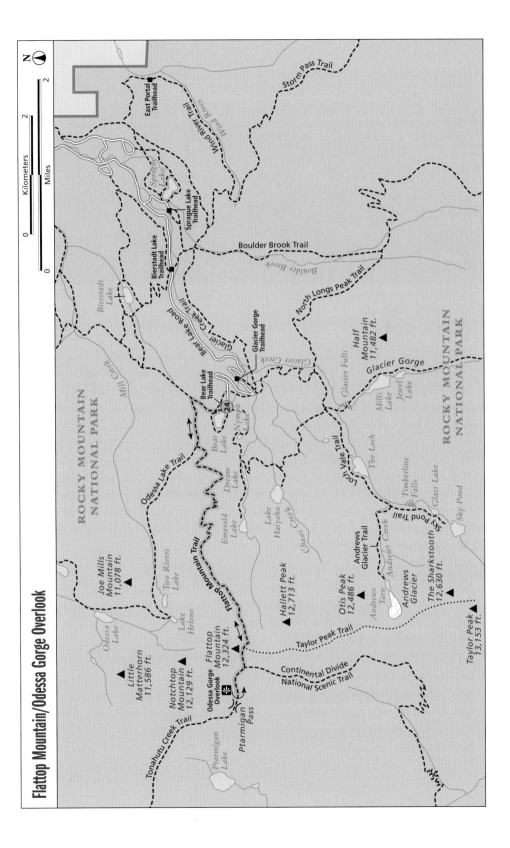

N

Kilometers
0   2

Miles
0   2

ROCKY MOUNTAIN
NATIONAL PARK

ROCKY MOUNTAIN
NATIONAL PARK

Storm Pass Trail

East Portal Trailhead

Wind River Trail

Wind River

Sprague Lake

Sprague Lake Trailhead

Boulder Brook Trail

Boulder Brook

Bierstadt Lake Trailhead

North Longs Peak Trail

Bierstadt Lake

Bear Lake Road

Glacier Creek Trail

Glacier Gorge Trailhead

Glacier Creek

Half Mountain 11,482 ft.

Glacier Falls

Glacier Gorge

Mill Creek

Bear Lake Trailhead

24

Mills Lake

Jewel Lake

Bear Lake

Nymph Lake

The Loch

Odessa Lake Trail

Dream Lake

Loch Vale Trail

Two Rivers Lake

Emerald Lake

Lake Haiyaha

Chaos Creek

Timberline Falls

Glass Lake

Sky Pond

Joe Mills Mountain 11,078 ft.

Flattop Mountain Trail

Hallett Peak 12,713 ft.

Sky Pond Trail

The Sharkstooth 12,630 ft.

Lake Helene

Otis Peak 12,486 ft.

Andrews Glacier Trail

Andrews Creek

Odessa Lake

Little Matterhorn 11,586 ft.

Notchtop Mountain 12,129 ft.

Flattop Mountain 12,324 ft.

Andrews Tarn

Andrews Glacier

Taylor Peak Trail

Taylor Peak 13,153 ft.

Tonahutu Creek Trail

Odessa Gorge Overlook

Continental Divide

National Scenic Trail

Ptarmigan Lake

Ptarmigan Pass

A white-tailed ptarmigan and her chick mimic the appearance of lichen-covered rocks atop Flattop Mountain.

When hikers quit staring down at ptarmigan, vibrant flowers, and rocks that reach up to trip the unwary, the summit of Hallett Peak rises above the snow and ice of Tyndall Glacier. Many hikers elect to head back down the trail after reaching Tyndall Glacier. But wherever the actual top of Flattop is, it sits a bit farther up the trail. At a pair of 8-foot-tall cairns, take the right branch along the Tonahutu Creek Trail. Pioneered centuries ago by ancestors of the Ute and Arapaho, this older of the two trails across Flattop follows the Continental Divide about 0.1 mile to the overlook of Odessa Gorge. The spot is not marked, but when you look to the right and gasp, you are there. Ptarmigan Point is only a short way farther along the trail at Ptarmigan Pass. Ptarmigan Lake is down in a cirque to the left. So your gasp could be either from being startled by a ptarmigan erupting from under your boot or from being stunned by the vista's beauty.

Miles and Directions

0.0 Start at the Bear Lake Trailhead and go right on the Bear Lake Nature Trail.

0.1 Turn right to ascend the Flattop Mountain Trail.

0.4 The trail divides; take the left branch up the Flattop Mountain Trail.

0.9 The Flattop Mountain Trail climbs left where the Odessa Lake Trail continues right.

1.6 Dream Lake Overlook presents a partial view of Dream Lake.

2.9 Rest at Emerald Lake Overlook to gaze down 1,300 feet to the lake.

4.4 Arrive at where the top of Flattop might be. Head right on the Tonahutu Creek Trail.

4.5 A view of Odessa Gorge opens to the right. Return by the same route.

9.0 Arrive back at the trailhead.

25 Hallett Peak

Hallett Peak is the most prominent pointy peak dominating the western skyline viewed from Estes Park.

Start: Bear Lake Trailhead, about 200 yards west of the parking area
Distance: 10.0 miles out and back
Hiking time: About 8 hours
Difficulty: Moderately difficult
Trail surface: Dirt and rock
Elevation: Trailhead, 9,475 feet; Hallett Peak, 12,713 feet
Other trail users: Equestrians as far as the top of Flattop Mountain
Canine compatibility: Dogs prohibited
Fees and permits: National park entrance fee

Trail contacts: Rocky Mountain National Park Backcountry Office, 1000 US 36, Estes Park 80517; (970) 586-1242; www.nps.gov/romo
Maps: USGS *McHenrys Peak*; Trails Illustrated *Longs Peak*
Highlights: Tyndall Glacier, view of Hallett Peak from Flattop Mountain, 360-degree view from atop Hallett Peak
Wildlife: Mule deer, pikas, yellow-bellied marmots, Clark's nutcrackers, gray jays, Steller's jays, white-tailed ptarmigan, water pipits

Finding the trailhead: From the Beaver Meadows entrance to the national park, take US 36 a short distance west to Bear Lake Road. Turn left and travel 9 miles to the road's end at the large Bear Lake parking lot. **GPS:** N40 18.698' / W105 38.674'

The Hike

The classic pointed summit of Hallett Peak is obvious from far away, but as you travel closer the peak appears even more pointed and very different in shape. The dramatic view from the Bear Lake area is of a false summit, which appears remarkably less spectacular when viewed from Hallett's actual top.

The climb up Hallett is very straightforward and simple. Starting at Bear Lake, follow the trail right around the lake, pausing occasionally to make what likely will be the best photos of the mountain; include glacially deposited boulders in the lake in the foreground. Turn right to head uphill when a sign indicates, followed soon by a signed turn left, followed 0.5 mile later by another left to Flattop Mountain. Your only question is why you bought this book to get you to so simple, albeit strenuous, a destination.

After a couple of hours of fun, you are looking up from Flattop to the true summit of Hallett. Flattop used to be called Table Top for good reason. The walk around the upper edge of Tyndall Glacier to the base of the final stretch up Hallett is easy enough to encourage stepping from rock to rock when possible to avoid damaging tundra plants.

Scrambling up the large rocks that cover the entire vague route to the top is tiring but still simple. Then you are there, enjoying a fantastic 360-degree view while taking lunch from your pack. Hallett is not easy, but it *is* uncomplicated.

Hallett Peak

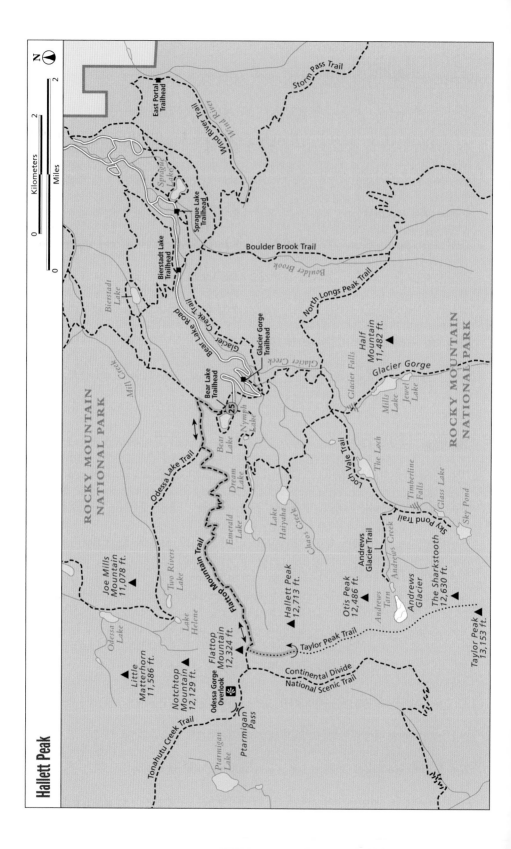

N

Kilometers
0   2

Miles
0   2

ROCKY MOUNTAIN NATIONAL PARK

ROCKY MOUNTAIN NATIONAL PARK

Storm Pass Trail

East Portal Trailhead

Wind River Trail

Wind River

Sprague Lake

Sprague Lake Trailhead

Bierstadt Lake Trailhead

Boulder Brook Trail

Boulder Brook

Bierstadt Lake

North Longs Peak Trail

Bear Lake Road

Glacier Creek Trail

Glacier Gorge Trailhead

Glacier Creek

Half Mountain 11,482 ft.

Mill Creek

Bear Lake Trailhead

25

Nymph Lake

Glacier Falls

Mills Lake

Jewel Lake

Glacier Gorge

Odessa Lake Trail

Bear Lake

Dream Lake

Loch Vale Trail

The Loch

Joe Mills Mountain 11,078 ft.

Two Rivers Lake

Flattop Mountain Trail

Emerald Lake

Lake Haiyaha

Chaos Creek

Timberline Falls

Glass Lake

Sky Pond Trail

Sky Pond

Odessa Lake

Lake Helene

Hallett Peak 12,713 ft.

Andrews Glacier Trail

Otis Peak 12,486 ft.

Andrews Creek

Little Matterhorn 11,586 ft.

Notchtop Mountain 12,129 ft.

Flattop Mountain 12,324 ft.

Taylor Peak Trail

Andrews Tarn

Andrews Glacier

The Sharkstooth 12,630 ft.

Taylor Peak 13,153 ft.

Tonahutu Creek Trail

Odessa Gorge Overlook

Continental Divide

National Scenic Trail

Ptarmigan Lake

Ptarmigan Pass

The low light of dawn colors Hallett Peak reflected in Bear Lake.

Nonetheless, rangers have too often had to remove the bodies of climbers who died on this ascent. Hallett is so attractive, it attracts many potential victims. Some potential victims have become actual victims due to lack of respect for the mountain, poor judgment because of inexperience or youth, fatigue, or just bad luck. Hallett has killed. It should not happen. Likely it will not happen to you (oh, that is why you bought this book). But do not take fog, lightning, snow, or gravity for granted. Carry all the food, warm clothing, and water you might need. Do not imagine shortcuts; the Flattop Mountain Trail is the easiest way down. And do not go alone or leave a companion alone on the mountain.

Miles and Directions

0.0 Start at Bear Lake and go right on the Bear Lake Nature Trail.

0.1 Turn right at the trail up Flattop Mountain.

0.4 The trail divides; head left to Flattop (right leads to Bierstadt Lake).

0.9 Turn left again, away from the trail to Odessa Lake, to ascend Flattop Mountain.

1.9 Pause to look down at most of Dream Lake. Do not descend from here—it looks bad and is really worse.

3.0 Look down 1,300 feet to Emerald Lake. The fact that you can see the entire lake for a good photo op indicates that there is nothing much between you and the lake, which means that the intervening terrain is cliffy steep. Do not be lured into unwise descent and fatal fall.

4.4 From the vaguely defined top of Flattop look past Tyndall Glacier to the top of Hallett Peak; head in that direction. Some cairns have been erected to show the way; they might be correct.

5.0 Reach the top of Hallett. Look to the west for fantastic views—and potential storms. Return by whatever way looks best from the top to the Flattop Mountain Trail to descend to Bear Lake.

10.0 Arrive back at the trailhead and try to dig your car's location from your tired brain.

26 Taylor Peak/Andrews Glacier

There are comparatively few loop hikes in Rocky Mountain National Park. This one is very spectacular.

Start: Bear Lake Trailhead, about 200 yards west of the parking area
Distance: 12.5-mile loop with a shuttle
Hiking time: About 12 hours
Difficulty: Difficult
Trail surface: Dirt, rock, snow/ice
Elevation: Trailhead, 9,475 feet; Taylor Peak, 13,153 feet
Best season: Summer
Other trail users: Human foot traffic only
Canine compatibility: Dogs prohibited
Fees and permits: National park entrance fee

Trail contacts: Rocky Mountain National Park Backcountry Office, 1000 US 36, Estes Park 80517; (970) 586-1242; www.nps.gov/romo
Maps: USGS *McHenrys Peak*; Trails Illustrated *Longs Peak*
Highlights: View of Hallett Peak from Bear Lake, Dream Lake Overlook, Emerald Lake Overlook, Tyndall Glacier, Flattop Mountain, Taylor Peak, Andrews Glacier, Andrews Tarn, The Loch, Alberta Falls
Wildlife: Pikas, yellow-bellied marmots, golden-mantled ground squirrels, chipmunks, mule deer, Clark's nutcrackers, gray jays, Steller's jays, white-tailed ptarmigan, mountain chickadees

Finding the trailhead: From the Beaver Meadows entrance to the national park, take US 36 a short distance west to Bear Lake Road. Turn left and travel 9 miles to the road's end at the large Bear Lake parking lot. **GPS:** N40 18.698' / W105 38.674'

The Hike

A popular hike, likely because it is a loop rather than out-and-back over the same terrain, is to follow the Flattop Mountain Trail from Bear Lake onto the alpine tundra, descend via Andrews Glacier, and hike out through Loch Vale either to the Glacier Gorge Trailhead (preferred) or back to Bear Lake. This makes for an exciting day; but many, if not most, hikers reason that they might as well ascend Hallett and Otis Peaks as long as they are in the neighborhood. And they might as well pick up Taylor Peak on the other side of Andrews Glacier before heading down.

All this is fun, especially if clear skies prevail. But ascending one simple peak after another adds up to considerable weariness before the descent of Andrews Glacier requires a mind working at full capacity. When the mountains take a toll on your stamina, the mind always fails before the body, which can carry on undirected until it collides with a rock at fatal speed.

Andrews Glacier is a popular route of descent from Hallett, Otis, and Taylor peaks to icebergs floating in Andrews Tarn at the head of Loch Vale. ▶

Therefore, if Taylor Peak is the goal, it might be appropriate to bypass Hallett and Otis. Staying level with wherever the top of Flattop seems to be rather than descending the North Inlet Trail, skirt the glacial cirques above Tyndall Gorge and Chaos Canyon, noting where the top of Andrews Glacier is in the next cirque. From Andrews Pass at the glacier, begin slogging up Taylor Peak, which seems deceptively close. Stay clear of precipices to the left above Loch Vale—cliffs that are easy to miss from the lower viewpoint slightly west of the Continental Divide. Picking your way from rock to rock up Taylor is tougher than the same procedure on the lower Hallett and Otis, but the view of Longs Peak and Loch Vale from Taylor's top is marvelous.

Some mountaineers elect to ascend Taylor from the Glacier Gorge Trailhead via Loch Vale and Andrews Glacier. This is shorter than walking the Flattop Trail, but the extra work of gaining altitude by ascending the glacier eats up the advantage of shorter distance and removes the additional interest of a loop hike.

Descending Andrews Glacier for a return via Loch Vale requires care. Taking a rock route alongside the glacier risks a stumble on by now tired legs. Moving over to the seemingly easier and certainly faster glacier ice risks a helpless slide into a fatal crash with rocks. You would not be the first such fatality. Reduce your hazards by switching them: Clamber down the rocks at the top; go with gravity on ice nearer the bottom. Do not willingly submit to an uncontrolled slide.

At the bottom, a rest stop at Andrews Tarn may reveal interesting shapes of bluish icebergs floating in the lake. Do not just trudge on in relief of at last encountering a trail. Turn around to photograph the tarn (a lake created by a mountain glacier) with Andrews Glacier "flowing" into it. Even in these warmer times, perhaps enough snow will continue to blow in from the west and be shaded enough by surrounding peaks for Andrews Glacier to remain a true glacier, defined by its moving ice. Perhaps.

Miles and Directions

0.0   Start at the Bear Lake Trailhead and follow the nature trail along the shore to the right.

0.1   Ascend right from the lakeshore at the Flattop Mountain Trail sign.

0.4   Turn left at the next trail junction, away from Bierstadt Lake, to ascend Flattop Mountain.

0.9   Turn left again, away from the trail to Odessa Lake, to ascend Flattop.

1.9   Pause to look down at most of Dream Lake. Do not descend from here—it looks bad and is really worse.

3.0   Look down 1,300 feet to Emerald Lake. That you can see the entire lake for a good photo op indicates that there is not much between you and the lake, which means that the intervening terrain is cliffy steep. Do not be lured into unwise descent and fatal fall.

4.4   From the vaguely defined top of Flattop look past Tyndall Glacier for a good photo of the true and obvious summit of Hallett. (The dramatic view from Bear Lake is of a false summit.) Do not consider descending via the cliff-hanging Tyndall Glacier; Andrews Glacier is ahead. Bypassing Hallett and Otis peaks will make ascending the higher Taylor Peak easier.

Taylor Peak/Andrews Glacier

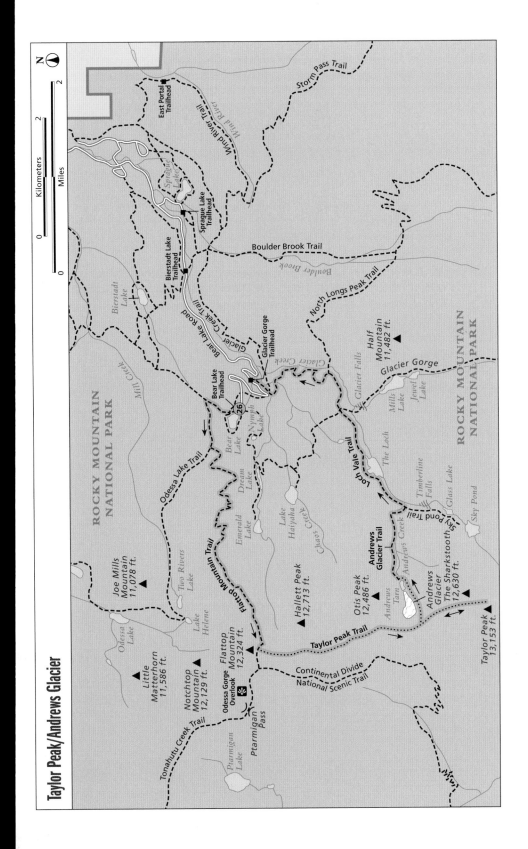

ROCKY MOUNTAIN
NATIONAL PARK

ROCKY MOUNTAIN
NATIONAL PARK

N

Kilometers

Miles

Storm Pass Trail

East Portal Trailhead

Wind River Trail

Wind River

Sprague Lake

Sprague Lake Trailhead

Bierstadt Lake Trailhead

Boulder Brook Trail

Bierstadt Lake

Boulder Brook

Bear Lake Road

Glacier Creek Trail

North Longs Peak Trail

Mill Creek

Glacier Gorge Trailhead

Glacier Creek

Half Mountain 11,482 ft.

Bear Lake Trailhead

Glacier Falls

26

Nymph Lake

Glacier Gorge

Little Matterhorn 11,586 ft.

Odessa Lake

Odessa Lake Trail

Bear Lake

Mills Lake

Jewel Lake

Joe Mills Mountain 11,078 ft.

Dream Lake

The Loch

Loch Vale Trail

Lake Helene

Flattop Mountain Trail

Emerald Lake

Lake Haiyaha

Chaos Creek

Timberline Falls

Two Rivers Lake

Hallett Peak 12,713 ft.

Glass Lake

Andrews Glacier Trail

Notchtop Mountain 12,129 ft.

Sky Pond Trail

Sky Pond

Otis Peak 12,486 ft.

Flattop Mountain 12,324 ft.

Andrews Tarn

Andrews Creek

Odessa Gorge Overlook

Taylor Peak Trail

Andrews Glacier

The Sharkstooth 12,630 ft.

Tonahutu Creek Trail

Ptarmigan Lake

Ptarmigan Pass

Continental Divide National Scenic Trail

Taylor Peak 13,153 ft.

5.25 Arrive at the top of Andrews Glacier at Andrews Pass. Look around so that you can tell where the pass is if you ascend Taylor. Assuming the weather looks clear (storms from the west are the most common; storms from the east are worse), you can follow whatever route looks least steep to the top of Taylor. Stay slightly west of the Continental Divide to avoid east-facing cliffs. Absent fog, you likely can see them and not walk off of them; but they might increase the labor if you end up on a lower bump north of Taylor.

6.24 Arrive at the summit of Taylor Peak. Head back to Andrews Pass by the least-steep route.

7.0 Stumble, slip, and slide (or, better, carefully walk) to the bottom of Andrews Glacier, which enters Andrews Tarn.

7.5 Make your way around to the east end of Andrews Tarn to find a trail that follows Andrews Creek into Loch Vale.

9.0 Reach the west end of The Loch. Continue on the trail to the east end for a photo of Taylor Peak and Taylor Glacier above the lake.

11.6 Arrive at Alberta Falls, named by pioneer innkeeper (and occasional punster) Abner Sprague, who also named The Loch after a guest named Locke. (Alberta was Abner's wife.)

12.3 Come to a trail junction. Glacier Gorge Trailhead is to the right (shorter). Bear Lake is to left in 0.4 mile.

12.5 Reach the Glacier Gorge Trailhead. Catch a free shuttle back to Bear Lake or pick up a car previously placed at Glacier Gorge Trailhead.

27 Bierstadt Lake

After a short climb, this walkway wanders through the woods to a uniquely formed lake.

Start: Bear Lake Trailhead, about 200 yards west of the parking area
Distance: 3.0-mile shuttle
Hiking time: About 4 hours
Difficulty: Moderately easy
Trail surface: Dirt
Elevation: Bear Lake Trailhead, 9,475 feet; Bierstadt Lake Trailhead, 8,850 feet; high point between Bear and Bierstadt Lakes, 9,730 feet
Best season: Fall
Other trail users: Equestrians, except on Bear Lake Nature Trail

Canine compatibility: Dogs prohibited
Fees and permits: National park entrance fee
Trail contacts: Rocky Mountain National Park Backcountry Office; 1000 US 36, Estes Park 80517; (970) 586-1242; www.nps.gov/romo
Maps: USGS *McHenrys Peak*; Trails Illustrated *Longs Peak*
Highlights: Views of Hallett and Longs Peaks from Bear Lake, views of Longs Peak from Bierstadt Lake (1.6 miles), aspen along south side of Bierstadt Moraine
Wildlife: Elk, mule deer, gray jays

Finding the trailhead: From the Beaver Meadows entrance to the national park, take US 36 a short distance west to Bear Lake Road. Turn left and drive 9 miles to the road's end at the large Bear Lake parking lot. **GPS:** N40 18.698' / W105 38.674'

Bierstadt Lake Trailhead, where you park the shuttle car, is 6.4 miles along Bear Lake Road from US 36. **GPS:** N40 19.28' / W105 37.423'

The Hike

Bierstadt Lake sits atop Bierstadt Moraine. Actually, Bierstadt Moraine, a ridge more than 1 mile long between Hollowell Park and Glacier Basin, should be called Bierstadt Moraines, for two lateral moraines dumped along the sides of two glaciers of different ages are jammed parallel to each other. The older moraine is the northerly one, formed by glaciers that flowed from the high peaks from about 127,000 years ago until approximately 87,000 years ago (expert opinions vary). During this time of colder average annual temperature, the first half of Bierstadt Moraine formation began when prevailing east-blowing winds dumped snow to a depth of at least 250 feet on the east side of the Continental Divide, from where precipitation flows either toward the Pacific or Atlantic oceans. Not much flowed at all during the cold spell (called the Bull Lake glaciation). Rather, the precipitation collected as snow, then ice, finally becoming so heavy that it flowed as a river of ice. (Glaciers are accumulations of ice that move; movement is what distinguishes glaciers from permanent ice fields.)

Freezing and thawing of water in cracks in the peaks caused bits and slabs of rock to fall off, leaving pretty much the spectacular skyline of today. The debris from this divine sculpture had to go somewhere. It landed on the glacial ice, which carried it

Aspen leaves in autumn shine from the south side of Bierstadt Moraine.

along the "conveyor belt" edges to dump in the northerly Bierstadt Moraine when the glacier reached a lower, warmer altitude where the ice melted. Eventually, much warmer average annual temperature caused the glacier to melt and retreat completely up the valley, eventually to disappear.

Perhaps 50,000 years later, another cold spell until about 13,000 years ago caused the glaciers to once again form and flow in pretty much the same fashion, but with somewhat less depth than the Bull Lake glaciation. (This most recent widespread glaciation is called Pinedale.) When the Pinedale glaciers melted, they carried less debris than their predecessors, but over 50,000 years the higher Bull Lake moraine had eroded to about the same height as the Pinedale moraine jammed on its northern slope. Both moraines were about 600 to 750 feet above valley floors on either side. In a basin between the older and less-old moraine, at the very tip-top of the ridge, perches Bierstadt Lake.

This story of Bierstadt Lake's unusual formation may seem complex, but it is not nearly as complex as the trails radiating around the lake. Bierstadt Lake is the hub to a pattern of trails in every direction. Fortunately, signs likely will be adequate to prevent complete confusion.

The easiest way to Bierstadt Lake begins at Bear Lake, 15 feet higher than Bierstadt. A short, level walk counterclockwise along Bear Lake leads quickly to the right-hand turn up the Flattop Mountain Trail for a short, easy climb to another right branch and an easy stroll to Bierstadt Lake. After 0.6 mile the confusion begins, probably due to more than century-old lumber operations that preceded the park's establishment and left a web of trails down which logs were hauled to as many as three sawmills in Mill Creek Basin. (Some of these rough timbers may currently hold up the historic Stanley Hotel in Estes Park.) The simplest instruction would be to always go right, which would take you down elaborate switchbacks on the moraine's south side with very pleasant aspen groves. In the afternoon, when you are most likely to arrive, the aspen leaves are backlit like translucent stained-glass windows, framing spectacular mountain silhouettes. You end up at Bierstadt Lake Trailhead along Bear Lake Road, where (during the busy months) you can catch a free shuttle back to Bear Lake.

It is a great hike, especially when the aspen leaves turn yellow in fall. But these instructions give you scant experience with the lake. The best view from Bierstadt Lake itself is from the north shore, looking south toward Longs Peak. To reach the north shore, turn right 0.6 mile after turning right from the Flattop Mountain Trail. Turn right again, continue for another 0.6 mile, then turn left for 0.1 mile before turning right to the lake. Therefore, from the Bear Lake parking lot, make four right turns followed by a short left and then another right. Trails circle the lake, but you have to walk through the forest a bit to get to the north shore for a view of Longs Peak.

ALBERT BIERSTADT

In 1877 Albert Bierstadt, America's foremost landscape artist, traveled around the Estes Park area, scouting the best place for the infamous (in Estes Park history) Lord Dunraven to build a hunting lodge. Bierstadt ultimately chose the valley of Estes Park, but he admired the view from a lake subsequently named for Bierstadt by the Irish noble's local representative. (I doubt they made it all the way to Bear Lake.) Bierstadt's paintings in oil on huge canvases with bold colors and bolder landforms interpreted well the wide vistas of mountains, valleys, and plains of the American West. His 1874 painting of Longs Peak and the surrounding mountains from approximately where US 36 meets Lake Estes today hangs in the Denver Public Library, and a very nice print of that painting decorates my living room.

Though Bierstadt portrayed the peaks as a bit more "alpish" than reality, he captured perfectly the mood as I often experience it, even though today's foreground is jammed with development. I am thankful for the artist's preservation of that pristine scene. I am a Bierstadt fan, as are many geologists, who know his subjects far better than critics who have decried his work, the nearly inevitable result of popularity.

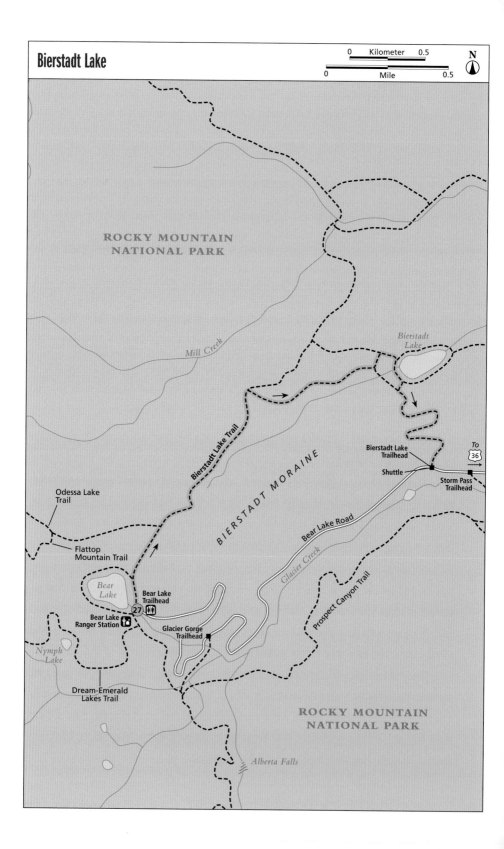

0   Kilometer   0.5

0   Mile   0.5

N

ROCKY MOUNTAIN
NATIONAL PARK

Mill Creek

*Bierstadt
Lake*

Bierstadt Lake Trail

B I E R S T A D T   M O R A I N E

Bierstadt Lake
Trailhead

To
36

Shuttle

Storm Pass
Trailhead

Odessa Lake
Trail

Bear Lake Road

Glacier Creek

Prospect Canyon Trail

Flattop
Mountain Trail

*Bear
Lake*

Bear Lake
Trailhead

27

Bear Lake
Ranger Station

Glacier Gorge
Trailhead

*Nymph
Lake*

Dream-Emerald
Lakes Trail

ROCKY MOUNTAIN
NATIONAL PARK

Alberta Falls

If you are skiing or snowshoeing in winter, backtrack from the lake to the 0.1-mile stretch and keep going west beyond the 0.1-mile junction to link with the trails descending to Mill Creek Basin. This can be a fun run, with much more-reliable north-facing snow cover in these warm times following (or between) glacial advances. You will need prearranged transport in Hollowell Park to return to Bear Lake.

Miles and Directions

0.0 Start at Bear Lake and go right along the Bear Lake Nature Trail.

0.1 Turn right onto the trail up Flattop Mountain.

0.4 The trail divides. The left branch heads up Flattop Mountain; take the right branch toward Bierstadt Lake.

1.0 The trail splits. Left leads down to Mill Creek Basin; take the right branch toward Bierstadt Lake.

1.3 The trail splits again (be thankful for trail marking signs). Left goes to the north side of Bierstadt Lake (after branching almost at once—left down to Mill Creek Basin then right to the lake for photos of Longs Peak). Circle to the south side of Bierstadt Lake for the descent to the Bierstadt Lake Trailhead.

1.6 Reach Bierstadt Lake. The trail circles the lakeshore; the branch at the east end descends to the shuttle parking lot across Bear Lake Road from Glacier Basin Campground.

3.0 Arrive at the Bierstadt Lake Trailhead and pick up your shuttle.

28 Dream Lake

It was not whim or hyperbole that caused a 1913 outing by the Colorado Mountain Club to select the name Dream Lake.

Start: Bear Lake Trailhead, about 200 yards west of the parking area
Distance: 2.2 miles out and back
Hiking time: About 2 hours
Difficulty: Easy
Trail surface: Disintegrating asphalt and dirt
Elevation: Trailhead, 9,475 feet; Dream Lake, 9,900 feet
Best season: Summer
Other trail users: Human foot traffic only
Canine compatibility: Dogs prohibited
Fees and permits: National park entrance fee

Trail contacts: Rocky Mountain National Park Backcountry Office, 1000 US 36, Estes Park 80517; (970) 586-1242; www.nps.gov/romo
Maps: USGS *McHenrys Peak*; Trails Illustrated *Longs Peak*
Highlights: Pondlilies on Nymph Lake, views of Longs Peak above Glacier Gorge, views of Hallett Peak above Dream Lake
Wildlife: Mule deer, red squirrels, golden-mantled ground squirrels, chipmunks, Clark's nutcrackers, gray jays, mountain chickadees

Finding the trailhead: From the Beaver Meadows entrance to the national park, take US 36 a short distance west to Bear Lake Road. Turn left and drive 9 miles to the road's end at the large Bear Lake parking lot. **GPS:** N40 18.698' / W105 38.674'

The Hike

Dream Lake exhibits unsurpassed spectacular beauty. It is the highlight of an easy but authentic hike, and the trip there is similarly beautiful. Of course this is the most popular hike in the national park.

The Dream Lake Trail's initial 0.5 mile of disintegrating asphalt ascends through lodgepole pine forest that grew after a devastating 1900 forest fire begun by picnickers who ignorantly believed that a campfire was an essential part of a visit to the wilds. However, some very interesting limber pines survived around Nymph Lake to stand as fascinating close-up subjects for photographers exploiting fire-accented grain and structure patterns. Nymph was dammed by a receding glacier that dumped its load of debris carved by ice and weather from the Hallett Peak cliffs and spires on the flank of Flattop Mountain above the lake. As the glacier melted back toward the cirque containing Tyndall Glacier, between Hallett and Flattop, it paused for enough years to pile a ridge (moraine) before retreating farther up the valley. As you proceed around the lake, it provides foreground for vistas of Thatchtop Mountain and then of Longs Peak above Glacier Gorge.

Although the crowds of hikers around Nymph Lake may contain some water sprites, it was not named for them. Rather the name is a result of the lake's shallow depth, suitable habitat for the pondlilies whose pads float on its surface. The scientific

The former scientific name of yellow pondlily, Nymphaea polysepala, *gave its name to Nymph Lake below Hallett Peak and Flattop Mountain. The lake was formed by a recessional moraine laid down by a predecessor of Tyndall Glacier, partially visible between Hallett and Flattop.*

name for this large yellow flower used to be *Nymphaea polysepala.* Botanists later renamed it *Nuphar polysepala,* but the original name stuck to Nymph Lake.

When splashed with wildflower color, the grassy hillside above the lake creates a pleasant backdrop for a photo of the trail itself, leading the eye toward Longs Peak and the quaking aspen on a rocky outcrop that in fall provides yellow to replace the wildflower color. After a sharp right bend in the trail, pause to look over your left shoulder again toward the tower of Longs Peak above Glacier Gorge—now revealed as a hanging valley, remaining higher than the deeper Loch Vale coming in from the right. The Loch Vale glacier was larger than that in Glacier Gorge, with more excavation power. The very ragged ridge extending right from blocky Longs Peak to pointy Pagoda Mountain is called Keyboard of the Winds. It is an apt and artful name, although I have never heard the howling wind there to be any more melodic than the nearly continual gales sweeping across all the peaks in winter.

With Tyndall Creek below the ledge of the trail and a cliffy hillside above, the path proceeds past a branch trail to Lake Haiyaha and over another recessional moraine that dams Dream Lake. The lake is long and narrow below the much-photographed wonder of Hallett Peak, named for a nineteenth-century mountaineer who helped organize climbs in Colorado. Limber pines that manage to penetrate the rocky rim of the lake frame the scene and give it the depth of grandeur.

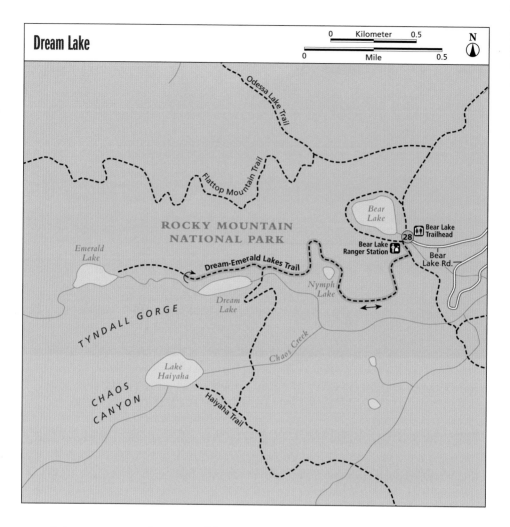

Dream Lake

It is no mystery why many visitors are content to stop here after so little effort yields so much reward. Although there are many other fine goals beyond for only a couple of hours of not much more work, the experience does not get better than this Dream.

Miles and Directions

0.0 Start at the Bear Lake Trailhead, bearing left toward a clearly signed trail to Dream Lake.

0.5 Pass Nymph Lake.

1.0 The trail branches left to Lake Haiyaha.

1.1 Reach Dream Lake. Return the way you came.

2.2 Arrive back at the trailhead.

29 Emerald Lake

Ascending past glacier-carved lakes, the track ends below dramatic cliffs encircling a timberline tarn.

Start: Bear Lake Trailhead, about 200 yards west of the parking area
Distance: 3.6 miles out and back
Hiking time: About 3 hours
Difficulty: Easy
Trail surface: Asphalt to dirt
Elevation: Trailhead, 9,475 feet; Dream Lake, 9,900 feet; Emerald Lake, 10,080 feet
Best season: Summer
Other trail users: Human foot traffic only
Canine compatibility: Dogs prohibited
Fees and permits: National park entrance fee

Trail contacts: Rocky Mountain National Park Backcountry Office, 1000 US 36, Estes Park 80517; (970) 586-1242; www.nps.gov/romo
Maps: USGS *McHenrys Peak*; Trails Illustrated *Longs Peak*
Highlights: Views of Hallett Peak, Flattop Mountain, and Longs Peak with pondlilies at Nymph Lake (0.5 mile); limber pines framing Hallett and Flattop at Dream Lake (1.1 miles), Emerald Lake (1.8 miles)
Wildlife: Mule deer, chipmunks, golden-mantled ground squirrels, gray jays, Clark's nutcrackers

Finding the trailhead: From the Beaver Meadows entrance to the national park, take US 36 a short distance west to Bear Lake Road. Turn left and drive 9 miles to the road's end at the large Bear Lake parking lot. **GPS:** N40 18.698' / W105 38.674'

Hallett Peak and Flattop Mountain rise above Emerald Lake bordered by limber pine.

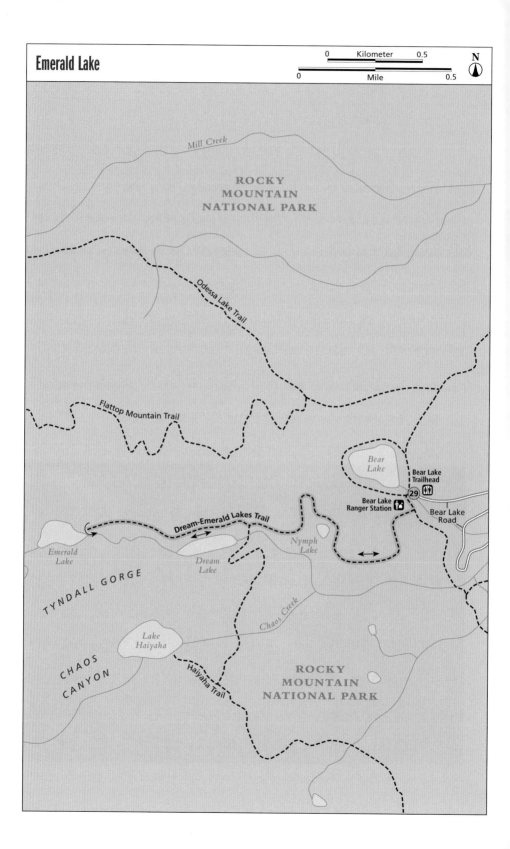

Emerald Lake

Kilometer
0   0.5

Mile
0   0.5

N

Mill Creek

ROCKY
MOUNTAIN
NATIONAL PARK

Odessa Lake Trail

Flattop Mountain Trail

Bear
Lake

Bear Lake
Trailhead

29

Bear Lake
Ranger Station

Bear Lake
Road

Dream-Emerald Lakes Trail

Emerald
Lake

Nymph
Lake

Dream
Lake

TYNDALL GORGE

Chaos Creek

Lake
Haiyaha

CHAOS
CANYON

Haiyaha Trail

ROCKY
MOUNTAIN
NATIONAL PARK

Subalpine flowers border Tyndall Creek cascading below Flattop Mountain along the path to Emerald Lake.

The Hike

Observing that Emerald Lake is a gem is unavoidable. Although that idea surely occurs to many hikers, the lake's color does seem to be greener in hue than other alpine tarns. What is suggested to the mind commonly affects what the eye sees, and perhaps Emerald Lake really is greener because its name declares it to be so.

Of course triumph of the mind does not explain how Emerald Lake originally got its name. Dream Lake—the next lake downstream in the Emerald, Dream, Nymph, Bear Lakes series—used to be called Emerald Lake. Perhaps Emerald got bumped upstream when Dream received its more mystical name. A pond above Emerald is commonly called Pool of Jade, a name that someday will appear on maps.

Tyndall Creek flows from Tyndall Glacier over rock ledges and through well-watered wildflower gardens between Emerald and Dream. Emerald Lake once backed up behind a terminal moraine dumped at its east end by a pause in the recession of a glacier. (Where the end of the moving band of ice melted, rocks it carried from cliffs above accumulated in a natural dam.) However, Emerald Lake eventually ate its way through the moraine barrier, and today the water is contained within a rock basin plucked by glaciers. Limber pines growing from cracks in the basin's rim form a dramatic frame for the lake and the cliffs of Hallett Peak and spires of Flattop Mountain.

Miles and Directions

0.0   Start at the Bear Lake Trailhead and head left on a clearly signed trail for Dream Lake.

0.5   Pass Nymph Lake.

ALPENGLOW

Because the trail to Nymph, Dream, and Emerald (or Haiyaha) Lakes yields so much reward for so little effort, it is the most popular path in the national park. Although the likelihood of encountering nice folks with similar interests along this trail is very high, it may be that a convention of hermits is not your hiking goal.

It is possible, though inconvenient, to rise painfully early to leave Bear Lake an hour before sunrise to savor solitude at Dream Lake. Plan to view and photograph Nymph Lake on the way back. In this way, you may experience alpenglow spreading across the cliffs of Hallett Peak above Dream Lake. Alpenglow is the progression of colorful light on the peaks at sunrise or sunset. John Muir, whose writings in the late nineteenth and early twentieth centuries created the core of the American conservation movement, described alpenglow as "the most impressive of all the terrestrial manifestations of God."

Muir's spiritual terminology seems too grand to be characterized as a description of fun. But the holy, the exciting, the awesome are all enjoyable. We accurately understand them as fun.

Most people in Colorado seek to preserve their fun through photographs, and the constant change created by weather and seasons make alpenglow a popular photo subject. The warm light on Hallett Peak is so far from the photographer's cool position on Dream's shore that alpenglow does not fill the frame with bright color. Happily, the color likely also will be reflected on the hopefully still lake surface, affording the inclusion of interesting silhouettes (pines, fellow hikers, even grass) against lake and sky. If there are clouds in the sky to catch more alpenglow color at sunrise, include them in the photo. The confusing detail the photographer sees in the dark foreground, the camera will record as simple black shadow. This gives visual weight to the bottom of the photograph, providing a foundation and making the alpenglow color even more vivid by contrast.

Be sure to set your camera to record the light at the top of the photo, where the color is, or your camera may try to record everything the same, bleaching the color and cluttering the

1.0 The trail to Lake Haiyaha cuts left. Continue straight to Dream Lake.

1.1 Arrive at Dream Lake. Follow the lakeshore to the right.

1.8 Reach Emerald Lake. Return the way you came.

3.6 Arrive back at the trailhead.

foreground with dull details. If you want to include aesthetically pleasing foreground details, try lighting them with flash or use a graduated neutral density filter, which of course is right at hand in your pack. If you happened to forget this or other filters, fear not; they likely would only mess up the photo anyway. Life provides too few opportunities for easier to be better.

Despite infinite day-to-day variations, alpenglow does not change drastically. There are three phases to this optical phenomenon. The order in which they proceed at sunset (more interesting on the park's western side than on the eastern) is the opposite of the order at dawn. At Dream Lake, alpenglow begins with the purple light stage, also called afterglow when viewed at sunset by folks lacking your early-rising resolve. The sun is not shining directly on the peaks. The purple light, which actually ranges from yellow through purple, results from light reflected off a layer of very fine dust at an altitude of 6 to 12 miles. The light is shining from an angle of approximately 97 degrees to the horizon, which physicists call "zenith 97 degrees." Because the light is indirect, the purple light boundary on Hallett is more diffused than the other two phases of alpenglow, which come next. Although less vibrant, this first stage can start when the sun is as low as zenith 99 degrees or even zenith 101 degrees if there is much particulate impurity in the air, such as from human-caused pollution or volcanic eruption.

The purple light stage may fade to gray before the curtain rises on the next act. Alpenglow proper occurs as Hallett comes into direct sunlight—zenith 90+ degrees. The color is deep, usually rosy. The color is due to the sun's rays hitting the atmosphere at a low angle and thus passing through a greater depth of air. Only those rays toward the red end of the spectrum are strong enough to penetrate so much air. Unsurprisingly, the color begins at the mountain top and spreads down toward the lake.

A bit less dramatic, but still not to be ignored, is the third stage: low light coloration. This takes place when the sun's rays are at an angle of approximately zenith 88 degrees. A series of three photos taken from the same spot with the same composition is worth trying to capture, but much depends on the right atmospheric conditions to provide such a classic example of the three phases of alpenglow.

30 Lake Haiyaha

Careful practice is required to nonchalantly recite the name of this lake. Spelling it is best left to authors of trail guides.

Start: Bear Lake Trailhead, about 200 yards west of the parking area
Distance: 5.2-mile loop
Hiking time: About 4 hours
Difficulty: Easy
Trail surface: A bit of asphalt below Nymph Lake, then dirt
Elevation: Trailhead, 9,475 feet; high point of hike, 10,240 feet
Best season: Summer
Other trail users: Human foot traffic only
Canine compatibility: Dogs prohibited

Fees and permits: National park entrance fee
Trail contacts: Rocky Mountain National Park Backcountry Office, 1000 US 36, Estes Park 80517; (970) 586-1242; www.nps.gov/romo
Maps: USGS *McHenrys Peak*; Trails Illustrated *Longs Peak*
Highlights: Nymph Lake, Dream Lake, Longs Peak/Glacier Gorge views, Lake Haiyaha
Wildlife: Mule deer, chipmunks, yellow-bellied marmots, golden-mantled ground squirrels, Clark's nutcrackers, gray jays, Steller's jays, mountain chickadees

Finding the trailhead: From the Beaver Meadows entrance to the national park, take US 36 a short distance to Bear Lake Road. Turn left and drive 9 miles to the road's end at the large parking lot for Bear Lake. **GPS:** N40 18.698' / W105 38.674'

The Hike

"Haiyaha" evidently is the word for "big rock" or "boulder" in one of the Native American languages. Certainly glaciers did dump large rocks around the lake in numbers extraordinary even for Rocky Mountain National Park. It is a playground for rock scrambling. The chances for mishap, therefore, might seem high, although hiking history does not describe Haiyaha as specifically dangerous.

A few yards before the trail reaches Dream Lake, a branch left crosses Tyndall Creek toward Lake Haiyaha. Be sure to take a very short detour to stand at the outlet of Dream Lake, the best view of the hike. There is a very lovely vista of Dream Lake from above on the way to Haiyaha, but it is vastly inferior to the view from Dream Lake's outlet. This view should be experienced whenever you're in the area, even if you have already stood on Dream's shore a hundred times.

Back at the Lake Haiyaha junction, the trail heads upward soon after crossing the creek. The path climbs through one of the loveliest examples of subalpine forest penetrated by any of the park's trails. Because the slope faces north and is heavily shaded, snow lasts here long into summer. Likely previous hikers will have tramped down a solid surface through the snow, but be sure to keep to the trail, no matter its dampness, to prevent trampling surrounding plants.

A classic limber pine stands guard on the rock rim of Lake Haiyaha.

At the top of the ridge, the trail bends sharply right and a very fine view opens of Longs Peak above Glacier Gorge. It is a convenient place to photograph hiking companions, who will be looking north into the camera, which is pointed south into Glacier Gorge. Their faces will be shadowed and undistorted by squinting. The light granite surface of abundant rocks at this point may reflect pleasing light into faces, but additional light from a camera flash will help greatly.

The trail descends from the view of Glacier Gorge and bears right at another junction toward Haiyaha. (**Option:** Returning to this point to hike toward Glacier Gorge and Loch Vale is a worthwhile alternative way back to Bear Lake, making possible a loop hike with various exciting side trips to Mills Lake or The Loch.) Soon after this junction, the huge rocks for which the lake was named begin to appear.

At the lake, my favorite limber pine adds interest to photos of Hallett above Haiyaha, although the peak is less impressive from this point than from Bear, Nymph, Dream, or Emerald Lakes. Better and less often photographed is the view of Glacier Gorge obtained by a somewhat complicated circumambulation of very many boulders to the opposite side of the lake. If the name Haiyaha indicates the very large number of very large rocks around the lake, the boulders also account for the name Chaos Canyon, in which Haiyaha sits.

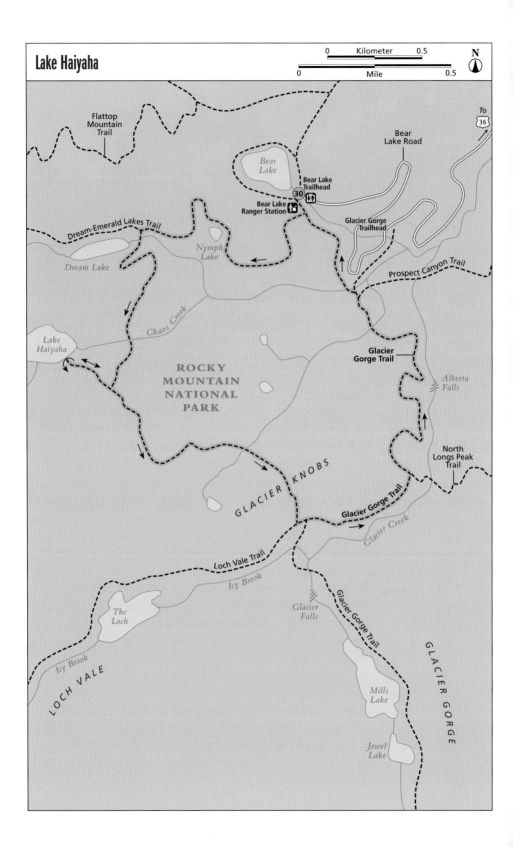

Lake Haiyaha

0	Kilometer	0.5
0	Mile	0.5

N

Flattop
Mountain
Trail

Bear
Lake Road

To
36

Bear
Lake

Bear Lake
Trailhead

30

Bear Lake
Ranger Station

Glacier Gorge
Trailhead

Dream-Emerald Lakes Trail

Nymph
Lake

Prospect Canyon Trail

Dream Lake

Chaos Creek

Lake
Haiyaha

ROCKY
MOUNTAIN
NATIONAL
PARK

Glacier
Gorge Trail

Alberta
Falls

North
Longs Peak
Trail

GLACIER KNOBS

Glacier Gorge Trail

Glacier Creek

Loch Vale Trail

Icy Brook

The
Loch

Glacier
Falls

Glacier Gorge Trail

Icy Brook

LOCH VALE

Mills
Lake

GLACIER GORGE

Jewel
Lake

Miles and Directions

0.0   Start at the Bear Lake Trailhead and head left on the Dream Lake Trail.

0.5   Arrive at Nymph Lake. The trail heads right around the lake.

1.0   The Lake Haiyaha Trail cuts left. Detour for 0.1 mile on trail straight ahead to view Hallett Peak above Dream Lake. Return to the junction.

1.9   The trail to Glacier Gorge and Loch Vale branches left; take the right branch to Lake Haiyaha.

2.1   Arrive at Lake Haiyaha to explore the lakeshore.

2.3   Arrive back at the four-way junction with the trail to Glacier Gorge and Loch Vale.

3.3   Come to a three-way junction with trails to The Loch and Mills Lake. A left turn leads back to Bear Lake.

3.7   North Longs Peak Trail appears below the trail from The Loch, Mills Lake, and Lake Haiyaha before the trail junction is obvious. (**Note:** Some hikers may mistake the North Longs Peak Trail for the trail back to Bear Lake. When they shortcut here, they may become lost and require rescue after a fairly miserable time. Their tribulation seems justified, but it is a bother for the rangers who have to retrieve them.)

4.1   Arrive at Alberta Falls.

4.8   Come to a trail junction. Bear left to Bear Lake.

5.0   At the trail junction, both ways lead back to Bear Lake. The right-hand path leads to the east end of the parking lot. The left path leads back to the Bear Lake Trailhead. Sightings of relatively rare brownie lady's slipper orchids are a bit more likely on the right path.

5.2   Depending on which path you took at the junction, arrive back at the Bear Lake Trailhead or the east end of the parking lot.

Glacier Gorge

31 Mills Lake

Likely the second-most popular hiking trail in Rocky Mountain National Park leads to a rock-rimmed tarn spreading picturesquely below Longs Peak, the ragged Keyboard of the Winds, and Pagoda Mountain.

Start: Glacier Gorge Trailhead
Distance: 5.6 miles out and back
Hiking time: About 4 hours
Difficulty: Easy
Trail surface: Dirt
Elevation: Trailhead, 9,240 feet; Mills Lake, 9,940 feet
Best season: Summer
Other trail users: Equestrians as far as the four-way trail junction 2.2 miles from the trailhead
Canine compatibility: Dogs prohibited

Fees and permits: National park entrance fee
Trail contacts: Rocky Mountain National Park Backcountry Office, 1000 US 36, Estes Park 80517; (970) 586-1242; www.nps.gov/romo
Maps: USGS *McHenrys Peak*; Trails Illustrated *Longs Peak*
Highlights: Alberta Falls, Mills Lake
Wildlife: Mule deer, golden-mantled ground squirrels, chipmunks, yellow-bellied marmots, pikas, gray jays, Steller's jays, Clark's nutcrackers, water ouzels (dippers)

Finding the trailhead: The Glacier Gorge Trailhead is 8 miles along Bear Lake Road, which departs US 36 a short distance west of the Beaver Meadows entrance to the national park. **GPS:** N40 18.671' / W105 38.362'

Note: If the parking lot is full, drive another 0.7 mile to Bear Lake's larger parking area and hike to Glacier Gorge Trailhead via a 0.5-mile horse trail, marked at the east end of the Bear Lake parking area, or via a marked branch from the Dream Lake Trail just south of Bear Lake. Along the trail connecting the Bear Lake and Glacier Gorge parking areas, late-June hikers may encounter very rare brownie lady's slipper orchids.

The Hike

Because beauty is more than a joining of visually appealing elements, the many hikers who praise Mills Lake as the most beautiful in the national park likely are correct. This is an extreme claim, considering Dream, Chasm, Nanita, and many other extraordinary lakes within the park. But when pioneer innkeeper Abner Sprague named Mills Lake for Enos Mills, known since 1915 as the "Father of Rocky Mountain National Park," the lake gained an aura of high regard boosting its beauty to the top spot. Mills Lake should be the most beautiful in the national park—its name memorializes the man responsible for the park's very existence.

Along the first 1.0 mile of trail, Glacier Creek is exciting, especially where it shoots over Alberta Falls. Also along the first part of the trail, notice the weather-etched patterns in the grain of red, gray, and black wood killed by a forest fire in

ENOS MILLS

Enos Mills is known as the "Father of Rocky Mountain National Park" because he led the effort to create the park in 1915 in the area around Longs Peak.

Mills was a sickly 14-year-old in 1884 when he followed relatives to Colorado, which had a reputation for building health. The mountains not only gave Mills health but also inspired him to educate himself through extensive reading about natural history and observation of the mountains around Estes Park. Five years later, while traveling in California, Mills accidentally met John Muir, America's greatest prophet of wilderness protection in the late nineteenth and early twentieth centuries. Well known at age 51, Muir inspired the teenaged Mills to become the John Muir of Colorado.

Enrolling in classes to learn to write as his mentor had done, Mills also added photography to his communication skills. In 1902 he used money saved from work as a miner to buy a lodge at the base of Longs Peak, developing the facility as a nature education base for tourists hiking nearby trails under the leadership of a "nature guide," often Mills himself. In 1904 Mills paid for the publication of his first book, *The Story of Estes Park and a Guide*. It sold well, and his subsequent fourteen books never lacked for a commercial publisher.

Interacting with John Muir made preserving Colorado wilderness Mills's chief goal. In 1909 he began a full-time campaign for creation of Rocky Mountain National Park. Although the idea was not universally popular, Mills persevered with hundreds of lectures across the nation, newspaper and magazine articles, and books. When President Woodrow Wilson signed the bill creating the national park, Mills was widely recognized as the park's father.

Mills died in 1922 at the age 52 from a combination of accidental injury and infection inflicted by civilization. But he had the satisfaction of knowing that his efforts had done much to preserve the wilderness values now protected by Rocky Mountain National Park.

1900. Scrambling over glacier-carved bedrock in Glacier Gorge, you will see several photo-worthy views of Longs Peak, tallest in the park, and the jagged Keyboard of the Winds extending to Pagoda Mountain. The round boulders left isolated on the bedrock by melting glaciers and the twisted shapes of limber pines increase the interest of the scene.

Unlike most lakes on the east side of the park, Mills is prettiest in the afternoon—a welcome change for hikers who usually have to rise before dawn to see the best light on the peaks. Afternoon skies often contain clouds, which either add interesting shapes to an otherwise empty sky or throw the entire landscape into muted shadow.

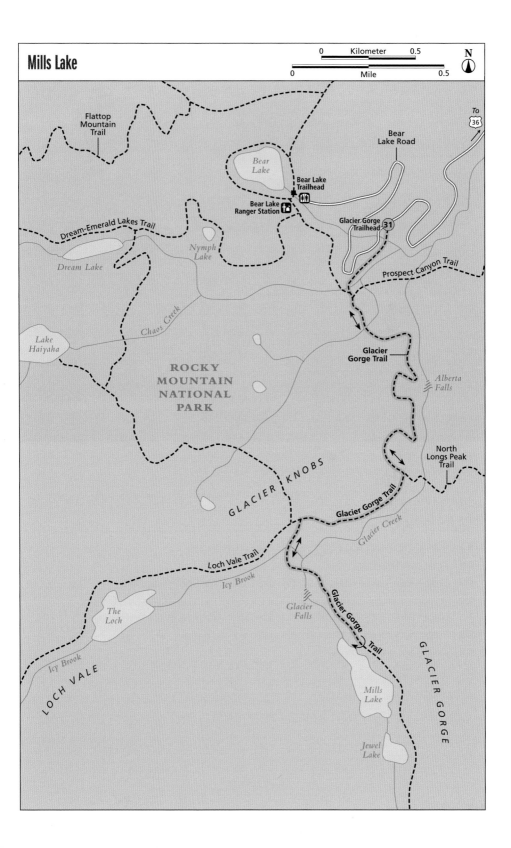

Mills Lake

0 Kilometer 0.5
0 Mile 0.5

N

Flattop
Mountain
Trail

Bear
Lake

Bear Lake
Road

Bear Lake
Trailhead

To
36

Bear Lake
Ranger Station

Glacier Gorge
Trailhead 31

Dream-Emerald Lakes Trail

Nymph
Lake

Prospect Canyon Trail

Dream Lake

Chaos Creek

Glacier
Gorge Trail

Lake
Haiyaha

Alberta
Falls

ROCKY
MOUNTAIN
NATIONAL
PARK

North
Longs Peak
Trail

GLACIER KNOBS

Glacier Gorge Trail

Glacier Creek

Loch Vale Trail

Icy Brook

Glacier
Falls

Glacier Gorge Trail

The
Loch

GLACIER GORGE

Icy Brook

LOCH VALE

Mills
Lake

Jewel
Lake

Longs Peak, Keyboard of the Winds, and Pagoda Mountain dominate the view from Mills Lake, named for Enos Mills, Father of Rocky Mountain National Park.

Miles and Directions

0.0 Start at the Glacier Gorge Trailhead and head down the trail.

0.9 Arrive at Alberta Falls.

1.7 North Longs Peak Trail departs left. Continue right on the Glacier Gorge Trail.

2.2 The trail splits at a four-way junction; turn left on the trail to Black and Mills Lakes in Glacier Gorge. (The middle path goes to Loch Vale; the right goes to Lake Haiyaha.)

2.8 Reach the north end of Mills Lake. Return the way you came.

5.6 Arrive back at the trailhead.

32 Black Lake

Black, Blue, and Green Lakes in the upper end of Glacier Gorge seem to imply that some unlucky nineteenth-century hiker was badly bruised from slipping on glacier-smoothed bedrock in the gorge before Enos Mills published an area map bearing these names in 1905. To me, Black does not appear noticeably darker than other lakes.

Start: Glacier Gorge Trailhead
Distance: 10.0 miles out and back
Hiking time: About 8 hours
Difficulty: Moderate
Trail surface: Dirt
Elevation: Trailhead, 9,176 feet; Black Lake, 10,620 feet
Best season: Summer
Other trail users: Human foot traffic only
Canine compatibility: Dogs prohibited
Fees and permits: National park entrance fee

Trail contacts: Rocky Mountain National Park Backcountry Office, 1000 US 36, Estes Park 80517; (970) 586-1242; www.nps.gov/romo
Maps: USGS *McHenrys Peak*; Trails Illustrated *Longs Peak*
Highlights: Mills Lake, Black Lake
Wildlife: Mule deer, golden-mantled ground squirrels, chipmunks, gray jays, Clark's nut-crackers, Steller's jays, mountain chickadees, ruby-crowned kinglets

Finding the trailhead: The Glacier Gorge Trailhead is on Bear Lake Road, 8 miles from the Beaver Meadows entrance to the national park. Turn left a short way inside the entrance. **GPS:** N40 18.671' / W105 38.362'

Note: If the parking lot is full, drive another 0.7 mile to Bear Lake's larger parking area and hike to Glacier Gorge Trailhead via a 0.5-mile horse trail, marked at the east end of the Bear Lake parking area, or via a marked branch from the Dream Lake Trail just south of Bear Lake. Along the trail connecting the Bear Lake and Glacier Gorge parking areas, late-June hikers may encounter very rare brownie lady's slipper orchids.

The Hike

Glacier Gorge is colorful far beyond some of its lakes' names. Watered by Glacier Creek and its tributaries, meadows between Jewel and Black Lakes display abundant wildflowers with a much greater variety of hues than the surfaces of lakes set among spectacular cliffs.

Where the trail branches 2.2 miles from the Glacier Gorge Trailhead, the forest seems like a surviving remnant of the devastation of the 1900 forest fire that ravaged much of the area. It is easy to spot gray jays and mountain chickadees. With their dull color, ruby-crowned kinglets are less easy to observe (unless you are lucky enough to spot the vivid red stripe atop the males' heads if they raise their feathers), but their cheery call (three high-pitched whistles followed by what sounds to me like "look at me, look at me, look at me") is likely to be even more dominant than

the chickadees' song, which imitates their name. (Of course it is more accurate to say that the chickadees' name imitates their call.) If you are lucky, you might see an orange-crowned warbler.

Beyond the four-way junction to Lake Haiyaha and The Loch, the far left trail leads to bridges over Icy Brook and eventually Glacier Creek. Watch for clumps of blue columbine, the Colorado state flower, in July. The trail zigzags near Glacier Creek through spruce and fir forest until it breaks out onto bedrock, where of course it disappears. Glacial erratics—large boulders dropped by retreating glaciers—perch on the bedrock. It is not difficult to follow the route up the bedrock, but returning is another matter. Pay attention to where the trail enters the bedrock pavement, which is not all the way down to the bottom of the exposed bedrock. If you're not careful on the way down, it is very easy to absent-mindedly walk past the trail until you suddenly realize you're at the bottom of the bedrock. Hikers who have made this error too often cut back to the trail, wearing another path, which creates erosion. If you do walk past the trail on the way down, walk back up to it on the bedrock.

At the top of the bedrock, picturesque limber pines have managed to take root in very little soil in cracks in the rocks. These arboreal heroes make good frames for photos of Longs Peak rising as a blocky tower ahead. Never pass up a good photo, but there will be even better compositions available farther along of Longs Peak above Mills Lake.

After marshes, more bedrock, and stunted trees, you follow cairns to arrive at Mills Lake. There are more limber pine and glacial erratics at the lake to enliven the foreground, but the light likely will be better in the afternoon on your return (assuming you start this adventure fairly early in the day). However, you might be coming back under overcast skies or rain. Therefore, take some blue-sky morning pictures just in case, following up with afternoon shots if the weather cooperates.

Upstream from Mills Lake and almost adjacent, Jewel Lake has trapped sediment flowing down from the peaks above and is almost as marshy as Mills is rocky. Jewel normally is not as photogenic as Mills, but try to jazz it up by including graceful shapes of water grasses at the outlet. Beyond Jewel, the trail traverses bogs that predict what Jewel Lake someday will be. Wet and flowery woods eventually open to reveal Ribbon Falls coursing down a rock slab to water a meadow displaying tall chiming bells, white bistort, and yellow senecios. The falls announce your imminent arrival at Black Lake. Head left over boulders for a few yards and then cut through the woods to the lakeshore. A sheer, glacially cut shelf from which ice flowed to pluck out Black Lake at its base rises above the lake, and a very high, impressive cliff soars above the shelf on McHenrys Peak.

Ribbon Falls waters lush subalpine flowers in Glacier Gorge below Black Lake.

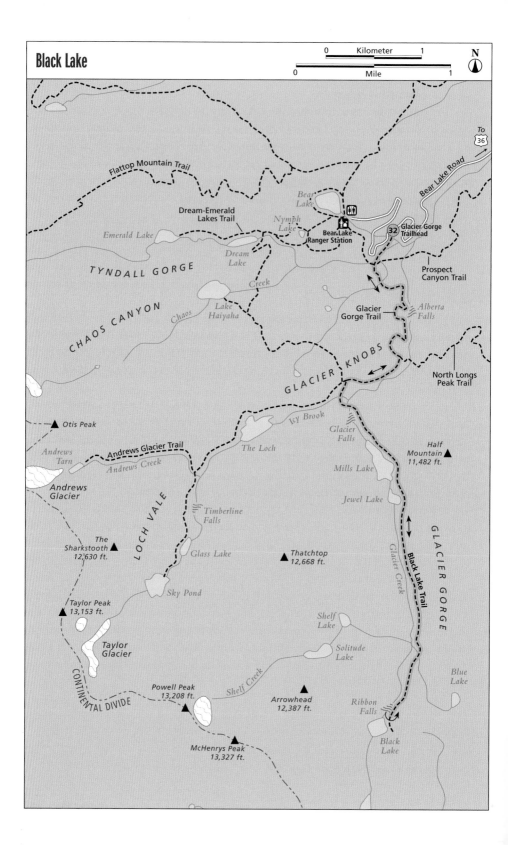

From where you are photographing McHenrys from the lake's eastern shore, a beaten track follows an inlet stream up to the shelf above the lake. This track disappears on more bedrock in the vicinity of Blue and Green Lakes, which are no more bruise-reminiscent than is Black. Rather they are more likely covered by ice, just like the much larger Frozen Lake on the same glacial shelf.

Miles and Directions

0.0   Start at the Glacier Gorge Trailhead and descend on the Glacier Gorge Trail.

0.9   Arrive at Alberta Falls.

1.7   The North Longs Peak Trail heads left. Continue right on the Glacier Gorge Trail to Mills Lake.

2.2   The trail splits; take the far-left path toward Black and Mills Lakes in Glacier Gorge. (The middle trail enters Loch Vale to The Loch; the right-hand trail goes to Lake Haiyaha.)

2.8   Reach Mills Lake. Follow the east shoreline to pick up the trail.

5.0   Compose photos amid trees and tall chiming bells around Black Lake. Return the same way you came.

10.0   Arrive back at the trailhead.

Loch Vale

33 Alberta Falls

The deservedly popular hike to Alberta Falls leads to one of the most frequently photographed waterfalls in Rocky Mountain National Park.

Start: Glacier Gorge Trailhead
Distance: 1.8 miles out and back
Hiking time: About 2 hours
Difficulty: Easy
Trail surface: Dirt
Elevation: Trailhead, 9,176 feet; Alberta Falls, 9,400 feet
Best season: Summer
Other trail users: Equestrians
Canine compatibility: Dogs prohibited

Fees and permits: National park entrance fee
Trail contacts: Rocky Mountain National Park Backcountry Office, 1000 US 36, Estes Park 80517; (970) 586-1242; www.nps.gov/romo
Maps: USGS *McHenrys Peak*; Trails Illustrated *Longs Peak*
Highlights: Alberta Falls (0.9 mile)
Wildlife: Mule deer, red squirrels, golden-mantled ground squirrels, chipmunks

Finding the trailhead: The Glacier Gorge Trailhead is 8 miles along Bear Lake Road, which departs US 36 a short distance west of the Beaver Meadows entrance to the national park. **GPS:** N40 18.671' / W105 38.362'

Note: If the parking lot is full, drive another 1 mile to Bear Lake's larger parking area and hike to Glacier Gorge Trailhead via a 0.5-mile horse trail, marked at the east end of the Bear Lake parking area, or via a marked branch from the Dream Lake Trail just south of Bear Lake. Along the trail connecting the Bear Lake and Glacier Gorge parking areas, late-June hikers may encounter very rare brownie lady's slipper orchids.

The Hike

No one turns off a faucet at Alberta Falls. Winter, however, does much reduce Glacier Creek's glorious gush through a granite chute. Such is human fascination with moving water that easy access on a well-designed trail makes Alberta Falls one of the park's most popular hiking goals.

Apparently humans have been drawn to rushing streams for thousands of years, at least since the author of Ecclesiastes 1:7 wrote, "All streams run to the sea, but the sea is not full; to the places where the streams flow, there they flow again."

The water cycle that Ecclesiastes describes is the main way in which water is distributed among land, ocean, and air. The estimated total volume of water on Earth is 326 million cubic miles (give or take a gallon or two). Although the sea may not be full (depending on how you define the effects of global warming), the sea does contain more than 97 percent of all this water. About 2.2 percent is locked up in ice caps and glaciers (we hope), leaving roughly 0.6 percent as fresh liquid water to flow over Alberta Falls and elsewhere.

Water circulates constantly. Solar energy evaporates huge amounts from ocean and land surfaces. These water molecules float in gaseous form, moved about by winds, until they condense as water droplets or, in subfreezing temperatures at high altitudes, as ice crystals. Very tiny droplets of crystals still float freely, gathering in large quantities to form clouds. Within clouds, droplets join together to produce larger drops, which eventually become so heavy that they fall to earth as rain, snow, or hail. The average time from evaporation to precipitation is nine days.

The sun draws lots of water from the Pacific Ocean, converting salt water to fresh. Prevailing winds from the west carry water-heavy air against the mountains along the West Coast, which force the air to higher, colder altitudes that cannot support as much water as can warmer air. The Pacific ranges, such as California's Sierra Nevadas, get a lot of rain or snow, but not all that the air carries. More is dropped as the air is pushed higher over mountains to the east, such as the Wasatch Mountains in Utah. Then the air hits the very high Rockies in Colorado, which force the air even higher and suck out most of what water is left. Longs Peak, the farthest north of Colorado's 14,000-foot peaks, sends water coursing into Glacier Gorge and Wild Basin. The water in Glacier Creek shoots through Alberta Falls and continues down to the Big Thompson River and then Lake Estes and down the Big Thompson Canyon to the farms and cities on the plains.

As Ecclesiastes points out, this water is headed toward the sea—actually the Gulf of Mexico—via the South Platte, Missouri, and Mississippi Rivers. But very little gets there. Most freshwater re-evaporates or soaks into the ground, where it is used by plants and eventually by animals that eat the plants. Of the water taken up by the aspens growing around Alberta Falls, perhaps 1 percent is used for growth. The rest is transpired or evaporated from the aspens' broad leaves. The needles of pines, spruces, and firs give off less water than do aspen leaves, which is handy, because the needled species tend to grow in areas with less water than the streamside habitat often favored by aspens. Of course the needles stay put and give off some water all year. This water cycle from evaporation to precipitation has been going on since very long before Longs Peak and its neighbors rose to snatch water from the sky—what we can define as forever.

Water passing over Alberta Falls is exposed to more cold air than water remaining within the flow, thus forming ice where the water hits in winter or just slickness on the rocks in summer. Therefore, skipping from rock to rock around the falls can lead to involuntary submersion in Glacier Creek—perhaps cranium-cracking submersion. At least one fatality has occurred here. If you have a good reason to romp from rock to rock, such as recording a unique and gorgeous photo of the water cycle in

◀ *Alberta Falls is a short, interesting, and therefore very popular hike from Glacier Gorge Trailhead.*

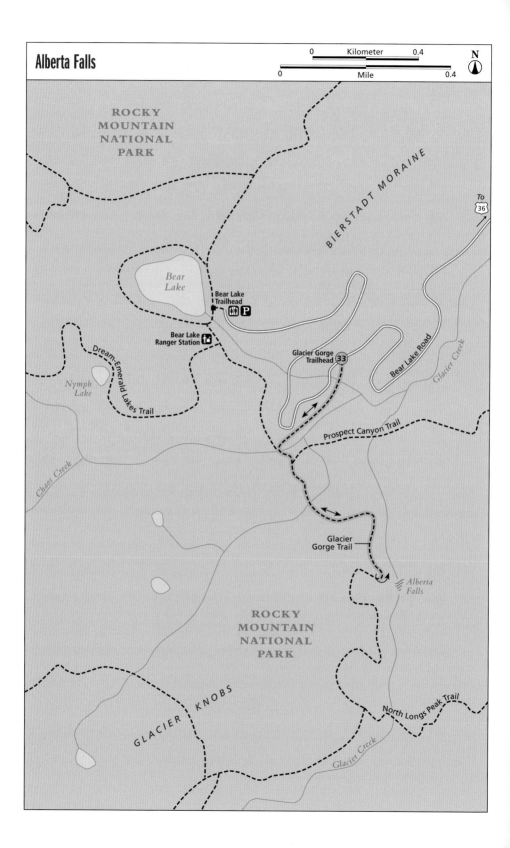

Alberta Falls

Kilometer
0   0.4
0   0.4
Mile

N

ROCKY
MOUNTAIN
NATIONAL
PARK

BIERSTADT MORAINE

To
36

Bear
Lake

Bear Lake
Trailhead

Bear Lake
Ranger Station

Glacier Gorge
Trailhead   33

Bear Lake Road

Glacier Creek

Dream-Emerald Lakes Trail

Nymph
Lake

Prospect Canyon Trail

Chaos Creek

Glacier
Gorge Trail

Alberta
Falls

ROCKY
MOUNTAIN
NATIONAL
PARK

GLACIER KNOBS

North Longs Peak Trail

Glacier Creek

action, be careful. If you want to do it just because you think rock hopping is fun, *don't*. Despite the easy trail to Alberta Falls, the rangers do not relish removing non-respirating hikers from the creek.

Miles and Directions

0.0 Start at the Glacier Gorge Trailhead and head down the trail.

0.9 Arrive at Alberta Falls. Return the way you came.

1.8 Arrive back at the trailhead.

34 The Loch

The name of this lake is a pun dreamed up by pioneer innkeeper Abner Sprague to commemorate a guest of his named Locke. The name is Scottish for "The Lake," and so great are the charms of this lake that many hikers agree that it is appropriate to call it simply The Lake.

Start: Glacier Gorge Trailhead
Distance: 6.0 miles out and back
Hiking time: About 5 hours
Difficulty: Moderately easy
Trail surface: Dirt
Elevation: Trailhead, 9,176 feet; The Loch, 10,180 feet
Best season: Summer
Other trail users: Equestrian as far as three-way trail junction (2.2 miles from trailhead)
Canine compatibility: Dogs prohibited

Fees and permits: National park entrance fee
Trail contacts: Rocky Mountain National Park Backcountry Office, 1000 US 36, Estes Park 80517; (970) 586-1242; www.nps.gov/romo
Maps: USGS *McHenrys Peak*; Trails Illustrated *Longs Peak*
Highlights: Alberta Falls (0.9 mile), The Loch (3.0 miles)
Wildlife: Mule deer, golden-mantled ground squirrels, pikas, yellow-bellied marmots, gray jays, Clark's nutcrackers, water ouzels (dippers)

Finding the trailhead: The Glacier Gorge Trailhead is 8 miles along Bear Lake Road, which departs US 36 a short distance west of the Beaver Meadows entrance to the national park. **GPS:** N40 18.671' / W105 38.362'

Note: If the parking lot is full, drive another 0.7 mile to Bear Lake's larger parking area and hike to Glacier Gorge Trailhead via a 0.5-mile horse trail, marked at the east end of the Bear Lake parking area, or via a marked branch from the Dream Lake Trail just south of Bear Lake. Along the trail connecting the Bear Lake and Glacier Gorge parking areas, late-June hikers may encounter very rare brownie lady's slipper orchids.

The Hike

Abner Sprague affixed some three dozen names to natural features in what would become Rocky Mountain National Park. Of these, Loch Vale may be the most whimsical. Loch Vale is the valley containing The Loch, which Sprague named for one of his lodge guests, who just happened to be named Locke. To non-Gaelic ears Loch and Locke sound identical; Sprague must have thought so too. "Loch" is the Scottish (Gaelic) word for a lake or nearly landlocked inlet of the sea that looks like a lake. Association with the many people of Scottish descent who were his fellow early settlers in Estes Park may have inspired Sprague's pun.

Sprague owned the area of Mills Lake as well as The Loch. He kept them natural and intact despite offers to subdivide them into sites for summer homes, as had been done in Moraine Park. Eventually Sprague traded his core of inspirational hiking destinations to Rocky Mountain National Park for land on which his lodge and lake

Taylor Glacier shines above The Loch along the Loch Vale Trail.

sat, down what now is Bear Lake Road. Today the melodic ring of Loch Vale Trail may attract many hikers to this popular destination. The beauty of the lake, with its fringe of picturesque limber pine surrounded by majestic peaks, is more than enough attraction even without its attractive name.

Abner Sprague also named the first major viewpoint along the trail to Loch Vale, Alberta Falls. Alberta was Sprague's wife, whose meeting Sprague described as "the luckiest thing that ever happened to me." It seems likely that Sprague held in particularly high regard the falls he selected to honor his wife, and a century of subsequent hikers have agreed with his admiration for this often-photographed spot in Glacier Creek.

Perhaps spray from Alberta Falls cools the nearby trail, or maybe hikers just feel cooler looking at the water. But in summer the trail both below and above the falls often is sunny and warm. A 1900 forest fire destroyed shade and opened views along the trail as it climbs around Glacier Knobs. Glaciers flowing from Loch Vale and Glacier Gorge met on the south side of Glacier Knobs, flowed over them, and left behind many signs of their passage—bare rock smoothed by glaciers, grooves cut into rocks,

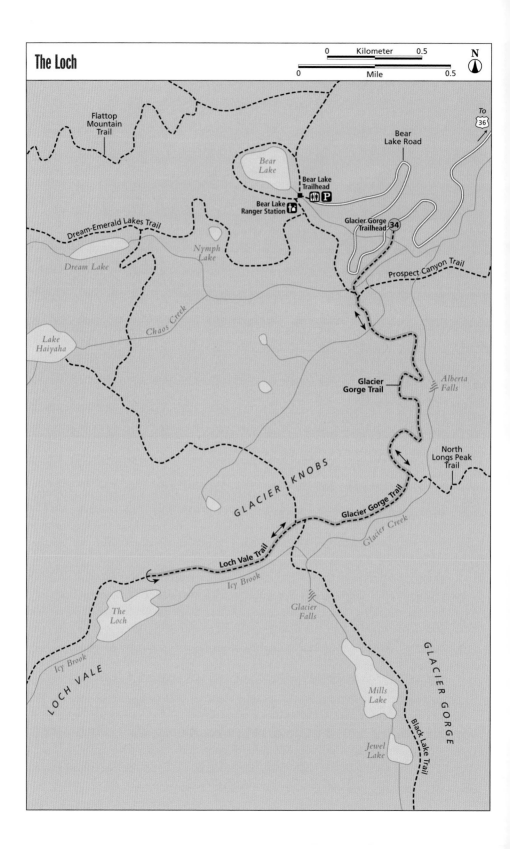

The Loch

0 — Kilometer — 0.5
0 — Mile — 0.5

N

Flattop
Mountain
Trail

Bear
Lake

Bear
Lake Road

Bear Lake
Trailhead

To
36

Bear Lake
Ranger Station

Glacier Gorge
Trailhead — 34

Dream-Emerald Lakes Trail

Prospect Canyon Trail

Dream Lake

Nymph
Lake

Chaos Creek

Lake
Haiyaha

Glacier
Gorge Trail

Alberta
Falls

North
Longs Peak
Trail

GLACIER KNOBS

Glacier Gorge Trail

Glacier Creek

Loch Vale Trail

Icy Brook

The
Loch

Glacier
Falls

GLACIER GORGE

Icy Brook

LOCH VALE

Mills
Lake

Black Lake Trail

Jewel
Lake

and boulders dropped on bedrock, which often protected from weather roughening the smooth glacial polish beneath them. Where the trail bends around the southern side of Glacier Knobs, watch for examples of grooves and scratches gouged by bands of rock-toting ice.

More than 0.5 mile beyond Alberta Falls, the North Longs Peak Trail heads left. Because it is a longer trail to the park's highest point, this trail is not used as much as the trail approaching Longs from the east. Rather unexpectedly, the North Longs Peak Trail goes downhill from the trail that leads to Loch Vale. Slight geographic genius supports hikers' intuition that no trail goes downhill to the top of Longs Peak. This north trail descends only a short way to cross Glacier Creek, beyond which it is all uphill.

On the south side of Glacier Knobs, at a pleasant glade missed by the 1900 fire, three trails branch to their separate goals. The right-hand path goes to Lake Haiyaha and trails radiating from Bear Lake. Left goes to Mills Lake in Glacier Gorge. The middle way rises into Loch Vale along additional south-facing sunny slopes to The Loch. On this ascent, pause to rest and cool off, but claim to be looking south to see how much higher Glacier Gorge hangs than Loch Vale. The glaciers from Glacier Gorge were not as big as those flowing from Loch Vale, which cut more deeply. Even in these warm times, Loch Vale has two actual glaciers (at least they seem to flow downhill a little bit) clinging to cliffs above The Loch. There remain no glaciers in Glacier Gorge, which is named for obvious signs of where glaciers used to be. Loch Vale also is full of such signs. Andrews Glacier is partially hidden from The Loch. Taylor Glacier, which originated only about 4,000 years ago, is the most obvious accumulation of perpetual ice and snow on the skyline above The Loch. The Loch is a rock basin gouged by passing glaciers that long preceded the Taylor and Andrews Glaciers.

Miles and Directions

0.0 Start at the Glacier Gorge Trailhead and head down the trail.

0.9 Arrive at Alberta Falls.

1.7 North Longs Peak Trail descends left. Continue right toward Loch Vale.

2.2 The trail splits at a four-way junction; take the middle path to The Loch in Loch Vale.

3.0 Arrive at The Loch. Return the way you came.

6.0 Arrive back at the trailhead.

35 Timberline Falls

These falls are a gauzy strip of white hanging below ragged crags above The Loch.

Start: Glacier Gorge Trailhead
Distance: 8.0 miles out and back
Hiking time: About 6 hours
Difficulty: Moderate
Trail surface: Dirt, often with stretches of snow until midsummer
Elevation: Trailhead, 9,240 feet; Timberline Falls, 10,450 feet
Best season: Summer
Other trail users: Equestrians as far as the four-way trail junction (2.2 miles from trailhead)
Canine compatibility: Dogs prohibited

Fees and permits: National park entrance fee
Trail contacts: Rocky Mountain National Park Backcountry Office, 1000 US 36, Estes Park 80517; (970) 586-1242; www./nps.gov/romo
Maps: USGS McHenrys Peak; Trails Illustrated Longs Peak
Highlights: Alberta Falls, The Loch, Timberline Falls
Wildlife: Mule deer, golden-mantled ground squirrels, chipmunks, pikas, yellow-bellied marmots, gray jays, Clark's nutcrackers, ruby-crowned kinglets, water ouzels (dippers)

Finding the trailhead: Glacier Gorge Trailhead is 8 miles along Bear Lake Road, which departs US 36 a short distance west of the Beaver Meadows entrance to the national park. **GPS:** N40 18.671' / W105 38.362'

Note: If the parking lot is full, drive another 0.7 mile to Bear Lake's larger parking area and hike to Glacier Gorge Trailhead via a 0.5-mile horse trail, marked at the east end of the Bear Lake parking area, or via a marked branch from the Dream Lake Trail just south of Bear Lake. Along the trail connecting the Bear Lake and Glacier Gorge parking areas, late-June hikers may encounter very rare brownie lady's slipper orchids.

The Hike

Timberline Falls was aptly named by Robert Sterling Yard, a journalist who wrote the first brochure to inform visitors about the newly established Rocky Mountain National Park. Yard was chief of the educational section of the National Park Service.

The demarcation known as timberline wanders up and down at roughly 11,500 feet above sea level (varying according to exposure to wind and sun) in Rocky Mountain National Park. This demarcation between forest and a landscape from which trees are barred by climate is higher farther south and lower farther north due to increasing arboreal tribulation with decreasing latitude.

I once was urged to use the term "tree line" in guidebooks because "timber" is technically an economic term indicating trees that can be cut to saw into lumber. If trees are not permitted to be cut for commercial use in a national park, the reasoning

Parry primrose are watered by the spray of Timberline Falls. ▶

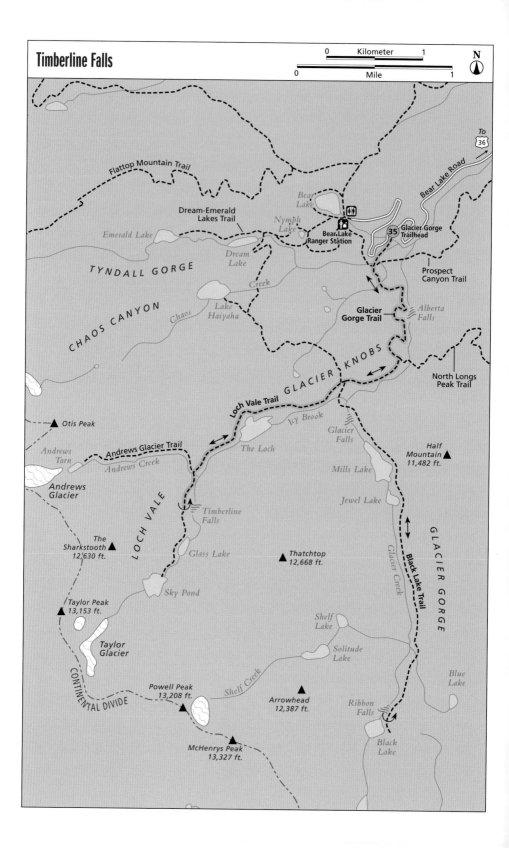

Timberline Falls

Kilometer
0   1

Mile
0   1

N

To 36

Flattop Mountain Trail

Bear Lake Road

Bear Lake

Dream-Emerald Lakes Trail

Nymph Lake

Glacier Gorge Trailhead

Emerald Lake

Bear Lake Ranger Station

35

TYNDALL GORGE

Dream Lake

Prospect Canyon Trail

Creek

CHAOS CANYON

Lake Haiyaha

Chaos

Glacier Gorge Trail

Alberta Falls

GLACIER KNOBS

North Longs Peak Trail

Loch Vale Trail

Icy Brook

Glacier Falls

▲ Otis Peak

Andrews Tarn

Andrews Glacier Trail

The Loch

Half Mountain ▲ 11,482 ft.

Andrews Creek

Mills Lake

Andrews Glacier

Jewel Lake

LOCH VALE

Timberline Falls

Glacier Creek

Black Lake Trail

GLACIER GORGE

The Sharkstooth ▲ 12,630 ft.

Glass Lake

▲ Thatchtop 12,668 ft.

Taylor Peak ▲ 13,153 ft.

Sky Pond

Shelf Lake

Taylor Glacier

Solitude Lake

Blue Lake

CONTINENTAL DIVIDE

Powell Peak 13,208 ft. ▲

Shelf Creek

▲ Arrowhead 12,387 ft.

Ribbon Falls

Black Lake

McHenrys Peak ▲ 13,327 ft.

goes, there is no timber, hence no timberline in a national park. This rather fussy notion, which I find personally appealing, is not widely accepted. Rocky Mountain National Park contains Timberline Falls and Timberline Pass, named by two of the most highly regarded and literate characters in the park's history. (Roger Toll, best known of the park's superintendents, named Timberline Pass.) Timber Creek and, by derivation, Timber Lake, on the park's west side, were named in pre-park days, when trees were viewed in terms of board feet.

Timberline Falls cuts some of the most lovely snow sculpture of any of the park's cascades. It flows over a glacial ledge at a point where wind happens to dump quite a bit of snow in winter. When spring thaw begins, Icy Brook, which starts aptly enough at Taylor Glacier, cuts first through the snow beside the cliff at the north side of the ledge. As the brook splashes into a pool at the base of the ledge, abstract masses of ice remain in constantly evolving beauty beside the flowing file of water. As summer progresses, the sculpture melts to nothing and the brook splashes past clumps of even lovelier Parry's primrose. At the beginning of the process, Icy Brook just disappears into a hole at the top of the ice mass beside which the brook invisibly plunges. But in early July (a guess), luck may favor your arrival at Timberline Falls just when the snow sculpture is at its best.

Miles and Directions

0.0 Start at the Glacier Gorge Trailhead and head downhill.

0.9 Enjoy the cooler temperature at Alberta Falls.

1.7 Head right at the junction with the North Longs Peak Trail.

2.2 Take the middle trail at a four-way junction on the south side of Glacier Knobs.

3.0 Arrive at The Loch. Note Timberline Falls hanging from a ledge above and beyond the far shore.

4.0 Reach Timberline Falls. Retrace your steps to the trailhead.

8.0 Arrive back at the trailhead.

36 Sky Pond

Robert Sterling Yard named Sky Pond when he was guided through newly established Rocky Mountain National Park by Abner Sprague. Yard was researching the park to write an informative brochure for park visitors.

Start: Glacier Gorge Trailhead
Distance: 9.8 miles out and back
Hiking time: About 9 hours
Difficulty: Moderately easy
Trail surface: Rocks and dirt
Elevation: Ute Crossing, 11,440 feet; Sky Pond, 10,900 feet
Best season: Midsummer
Other trail users: Human foot traffic only
Canine compatibility: Dogs prohibited
Fees and permits: National park entrance fee

Trail contacts: Rocky Mountain National Park Backcountry Office, 1000 US 36, Estes Park 80517; (970) 586-1242; www/nps.gov/romo
Maps: USGS *Trail Ridge* and *McHenrys Peak*; Trails Illustrated *Longs Peak*
Highlights: Open vistas, various tundra environments with many wildflower species
Wildlife: Elk, pikas, yellow-bellied marmots, water pipits, horned larks

Finding the trailhead: Glacier Gorge Trailhead is 8 miles along Bear Lake Road, which departs US 36 a short distance west of the Beaver Meadows entrance to the national park. **GPS:** N40 18.671' / W105 38.362'

The Hike

Sky Pond is much bigger than Glass Lake, which lies a short way down Icy Brook. And Glass Lake is usually called a much nicer name: Lake of Glass. But these above–tree line tarns at the head of Loch Vale are much better known for their extreme beauty than for their dubious nomenclature. Robert Sterling Yard named both these lakes while hiking with Abner Sprague researching the first educational pamphlet for park visitors a century ago. Perhaps Yard opted to call the upper lake (which certainly seems near the sky) a pond in order to provide variety from Lake of Glass, which he encountered first. Professional journalists tend to become instantly attached to their own nicely composed words and strive to adjust subsequent words to support those of prior conception. The US Board of Geographic Names overruled Yard in approving the name Glass Lake in 1932, perhaps because a shorter name would fit better on a map. Yard, who died in 1945 after decades of competent public service, may have taken comfort in knowing that local residents follow his lead in calling this body of water Lake of Glass and will correct hikers who enthusiastically praise Glass Lake as part of their descriptions of trips to Sky Pond.

The trail that ends on the rocky shore of Sky Pond begins at the Glacier Gorge Trailhead. It winds through woods, across rocky slopes cleared by forest fire, and

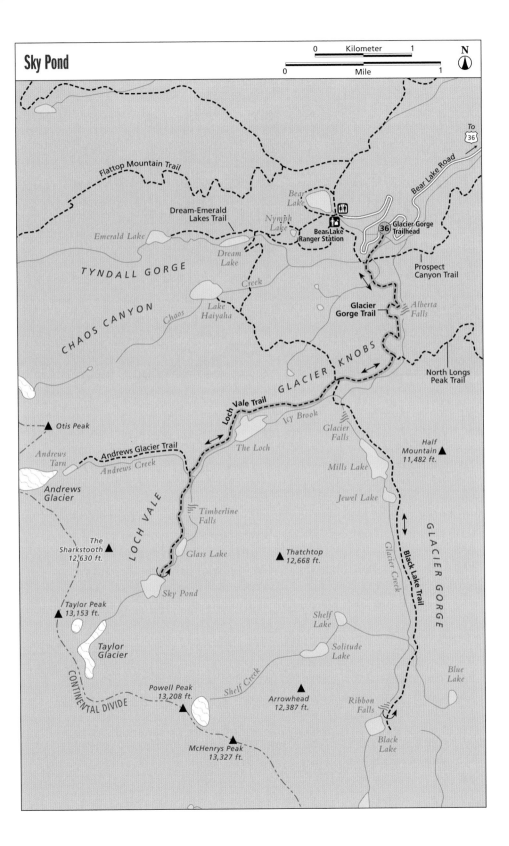

Sky Pond

0 Kilometer 1

0 Mile 1

N

Flattop Mountain Trail

Bear Lake Road

To 36

Dream-Emerald
Lakes Trail

Bear
Lake

Nymph
Lake

36

Glacier Gorge
Trailhead

Emerald Lake

Dream
Lake

Bear Lake
Ranger Station

Prospect
Canyon Trail

TYNDALL GORGE

Creek

CHAOS CANYON

Chaos

Lake
Haiyaha

Glacier
Gorge Trail

Alberta
Falls

GLACIER KNOBS

North Longs
Peak Trail

Loch Vale Trail

Icy Brook

Glacier
Falls

Half
Mountain ▲
11,482 ft.

Otis Peak ▲

Andrews Glacier Trail

The Loch

Andrews
Tarn

Andrews Creek

Mills Lake

Andrews
Glacier

LOCH VALE

Jewel Lake

GLACIER GORGE

The
Sharkstooth ▲
12,630 ft.

Timberline
Falls

Glass Lake

Thatchtop ▲
12,668 ft.

Glacier Creek

Black Lake Trail

Taylor Peak ▲
13,153 ft.

Sky Pond

Shelf
Lake

Taylor
Glacier

Solitude
Lake

Blue
Lake

CONTINENTAL DIVIDE

Powell Peak ▲
13,208 ft.

Shelf Creek

Arrowhead ▲
12,387 ft.

Ribbon
Falls

McHenrys Peak ▲
13,327 ft.

Black
Lake

Lake of Glass is the locally preferred name for what the maps call Glass Lake.

past waterfalls and lakes. At the three-tiered spectacle of Timberline Falls, the way becomes a bit vague, often covered by snowbanks and necessitating climbing up ledges beside Timberline Falls to the level of Lake of Glass. The trail regains informal clarity as it weaves through krummholz—shrubby versions of evergreens made small by battering winter wind.

Lake of Glass may have been unruffled by wind when Yard admired surrounding peaks reflected on its surface. It always is scenic, but smooth water is rare.

More-reliable smoothness is the glacial polish on boulders at the edge of Lake of Glass. An arm of Taylor Glacier reaches down toward Sky Pond. Perhaps the most dramatic evidence of glacial action is the extremely pointy Sharkstooth, rising above Sky Pond adjacent to other pinnacles alluring to rock climbers.

Miles and Directions

0.0 Start at the Glacier Gorge Trailhead.

2.0 Come to Timberline Pass, marked by large tor (hill of rocks).

4.5 Arrive at Lake of Glass after scrambling up ledges beside Timberline Falls. Proceed amid krummholz on the lake's right shore.

4.9 Reach Sky Pond to photograph Taylor Glacier from the shore. It is easy to cross Icy Brook to get a good view of The Sharktooth above Sky Pond. Return by the same route to the Glacier Gorge Trailhead.

9.8 Arrive back at the trailhead.

Bear Lake Road

37 Cub Lake

A wildfire at the end of 2012 demonstrated nature's ability to begin immediate recovery, which nonetheless requires centuries.

Start: Cub Lake Trailhead
Distance: 6.3-mile loop
Hiking time: About 5 hours
Difficulty: Easy
Trail surface: Dirt
Elevation: Trailhead, 8,080 feet; Cub Lake, 8,630 feet
Best season: Summer
Other trail users: Equestrians
Canine compatibility: Dogs prohibited
Fees and permits: National park entrance fee

Trail contacts: Rocky Mountain National Park Backcountry Office, 1000 US Highway 36, Estes Park 80517; (970) 586-1242; www/nps.gov/romo
Maps: USGS *McHenrys Peak* and *Longs Peak*; Trails Illustrated *Longs Peak*
Highlights: Wildflowers, wildlife, Cub Lake (2.2 miles)
Wildlife: Mule deer, marmots, golden-mantled ground squirrels, many bird species (first 0.5 mile), many butterfly species

Finding the trailhead: From the Beaver Meadows entrance to Rocky Mountain National Park on US 36, drive west 0.2 mile and turn left onto Bear Lake Road. Continue 1.2 miles and turn right toward the Moraine Park Campground. Follow the signs for 2.2 miles to the Cub Lake Trailhead and three reasonably convenient parking areas. **GPS: N40 21.399' / W105 36.895'**

The Hike

Unlike Bear Lake, Cub was not named for a wildlife sighting. Pioneer innkeeper and namer of some three dozen points of Rocky Mountain National Park geography Abner Sprague thought Cub Lake was small—a cub of a lake. Perhaps he was comparing it to Sprague Lake, which Abner created by damming Boulder Brook. But among the lakes in the national park, Cub's 10.1 acres make it average in size.

You are as likely to see a cub at Cub Lake as anywhere else in the national park, which is to say not likely at all. But if you are lucky enough to spot one, keep away from it—its mother will "bearly" be patient with any perceived threat to her cub.

Parking is not extensive at the Cub Lake Trailhead, but there is more parking available 0.2 mile down the road. The trailhead also is served by the free park shuttle during heavy hiking months.

The beginning of the trail retains its reputation for blooms and birds along riverside habitat, despite a 2012 wildfire. Due to the most recent glacier in Moraine Park leaving the center of the park slightly higher than the edges, the Big Thompson River flows in branches until reuniting at the east end of Moraine Park.

Birders may flock here to fill various blank spaces on their life lists of birds they have seen. Even more dramatic and much easier to see in July are rare woodlilies, growing from bulbs that survived the 2012 fire. Their large orange blossoms make

The lower part of the Cub Lake Trail is an easy walk for those seeking a wide variety of birds or wildflowers.

these the national park's most spectacular individual wildflowers. Today's park visitors evidently are more cognizant of the sin of flower picking than in previous years, for it is now unusual to see wilted, dead flowers in a pitiful bouquet at trailside.

Beyond the second bridge over the Big Thompson River, watch for glacial erratics—isolated boulders dropped by the last retreating glaciers, approximately 13,000 years ago. The trail half circles one erratic to continue at a slightly lower level. This puts the bottom of the boulder at easy eye level. Reaching underneath the boulder will reveal a granite surface polished almost to countertop smoothness by glacial grinding. The erratic has protected this glacial polish from roughening by weather for thousands of years.

A little more than 0.5 mile from the trailhead, the trail to Cub Lake bends right where a trail along the base of the South Lateral Moraine cuts left. The moraine is a forested ridge about 750 feet high that defines the south edge of Moraine Park. This is a classic example of a moraine that accumulated along the edge of successive glaciers (likely three) where the ice melted. While flowing from high peaks to the west, still snow-accented today, the ice carried rocks plucked from surrounding valley walls or that fell onto successive conveyor belts of ice from cracks in cliffs above the glaciers. Where the ice melted at lower altitude, the rock debris piled on moraine debris left

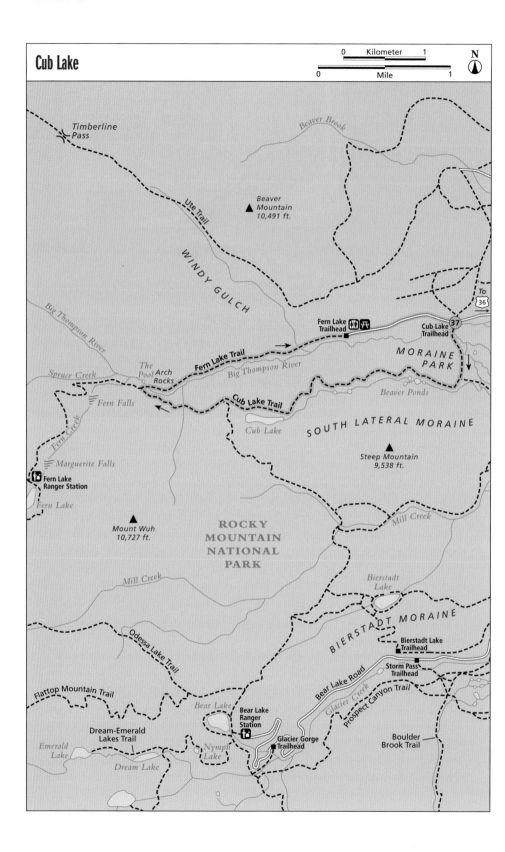

Cub Lake

Kilometer

Mile

N

Timberline Pass

Beaver Brook

Ute Trail

Beaver Mountain 10,491 ft.

WINDY GULCH

Big Thompson River

To 36

Fern Lake Trailhead

Cub Lake Trailhead

MORAINE PARK

Spruce Creek

The Pool

Arch Rocks

Fern Lake Trail

Big Thompson River

Cub Lake Trail

Beaver Ponds

Fern Falls

Fern Creek

Cub Lake

SOUTH LATERAL MORAINE

Marguerite Falls

Fern Lake Ranger Station

Steep Mountain 9,538 ft.

Fern Lake

Mill Creek

Mount Wuh 10,727 ft.

ROCKY MOUNTAIN NATIONAL PARK

Mill Creek

Bierstadt Lake

BIERSTADT MORAINE

Odessa Lake Trail

Bierstadt Lake Trailhead

Storm Pass Trailhead

Flattop Mountain Trail

Bear Lake Road

Glacier Creek

Prospect Canyon Trail

Bear Lake

Bear Lake Ranger Station

Dream-Emerald Lakes Trail

Glacier Gorge Trailhead

Boulder Brook Trail

Emerald Lake

Nymph Lake

Dream Lake

by previous glacial advance and retreat, accounting for the classic height and shape of this moraine.

Although elk may appear anywhere in Moraine Park, this trail junction is a particularly good spot to watch for them. If elk do not appear, about-face to nearby rocky slopes to watch for yellow-bellied marmots, groundhog cousins.

The Cub Lake Trail heads west from the junction along beaver-created marshes. Here is your last chance to look for woodlilies in season. The trail steepens through burned forest to reach a different floral spectacle, yellow pond-lilies on Cub Lake. Stones Peak forms a craggy backdrop west of the lake.

Continuing around the right (north) side of Cub Lake leads to a trail heading left to Mill Creek Basin. Continuing

The Cub Lake Trail is famous for its display of rare woodlilies blooming in early July.

right, the Cub Lake Trail descends through burned woods to a junction with the Fern Lake Trail, which leads left. A few steps to the right, at a bridge across the Big Thompson River, is The Pool. On the north side of the river, the terrain is less damaged by fire but significantly battered by mountain pine beetles.

Boulders line much of the trail, some dropped by a melting glacier, others fallen from cliffs above. These are particularly big at Arch Rocks; you may notice a nearby rockfall from July 1913. An easy, slightly downhill stroll brings you to the Fern Lake Trailhead, where hikers can catch a free shuttle in midsummer or just walk down an aspen-shaded road back to the Cub Lake Trailhead.

Miles and Directions

0.0 Start at the Cub Lake Trailhead and head left (clockwise).

0.5 At the trail junction turn right on the trail to Cub Lake. (The trail to the left is used mainly by horses.)

2.2 From the east end of Cub Lake is a view of Stones Peak rising above the far end of the lake.

2.7 The trail to Mill Creek Basin cuts left. Continue right.

3.7 Come to a junction with the Fern Lake Trail. A left turn leads to Fern Falls; a right turn soon reaches The Pool, in the Big Thompson River at a bridge. Head right on the Fern Lake Trail.

5.4 Reach the Fern Lake Trailhead. Cross a small dirt parking lot to follow an aspen-shaded road back to the Cub Lake Trailhead. (**Option:** In midsummer, take the free shuttle back to the trailhead.)

6.3 Arrive back at the trailhead.

38 The Pool

The trail to The Pool is as flat as any trail is likely to be in this national park, following the Big Thompson River upstream to a point where it shoots between rock buttresses and then slows in a broad pool.

Start: Fern Lake Trailhead
Distance: 3.4 miles out and back
Hiking time: About 3 hours
Difficulty: Easy
Trail surface: Dirt
Elevation: Trailhead, 8,155 feet; The Pool, 8,320 feet
Best season: Summer
Other trail users: Equestrians
Canine compatibility: Dogs prohibited

Fees and permits: National park entrance fee
Trail contacts: Rocky Mountain National Park Backcountry Office, 1000 US 36, Estes Park 80517; (970) 586-1242; www/nps.gov/romo
Maps: USGS *McHenrys Peak*; Trails Illustrated *Longs Peak*
Highlights: Arch Rocks (1.5 miles), The Pool (1.7 miles)
Wildlife: Mule deer, chipmunks, red squirrels, water ouzels (dippers)

Finding the trailhead: From the Beaver Meadows entrance to Rocky Mountain National Park on US 36, drive west 0.2 mile and turn left onto Bear Lake Road. Continue 1.2 miles and turn right toward the Moraine Park Campground. Drive another 0.5 mile and turn left just before reaching the campground. The pavement ends after 1.2 miles; continue 2 miles to the end of the unpaved road. **GPS:** N40 21.294' / W105 37.854'

The Hike

This pool is very different from a home swimming pool. If you jump (or fall) into The Pool, the odds are high that you will hit a rock. If the rock does not kill you, it might conspire with water that was snow the previous day to incapacitate you and then drown you. It has happened before, not far downstream in Moraine Park.

This pool is where the Big Thompson River flows between rock buttresses in a narrower space than the river normally occupies. Because the same amount of water has to pass through less space, it must flow faster. The increased pressure from compression of the stream dissipates beyond the squeeze point at the bridge, and the speed slows in a broader spot downstream called The Pool.

There are countless similar compression points along the streams of Rocky Mountain National Park. This one was distinguished as The Pool in 1889 when Frederick Funston fell into the river at this place during a biological expedition from Kansas. College students on the trip claimed he was startled by a bear (maybe so) and dubbed

The Pool along the Big Thompson River is one of many good places to look for dippers, ▶
birds that dive into white water streams to feed on small aquatic creatures.

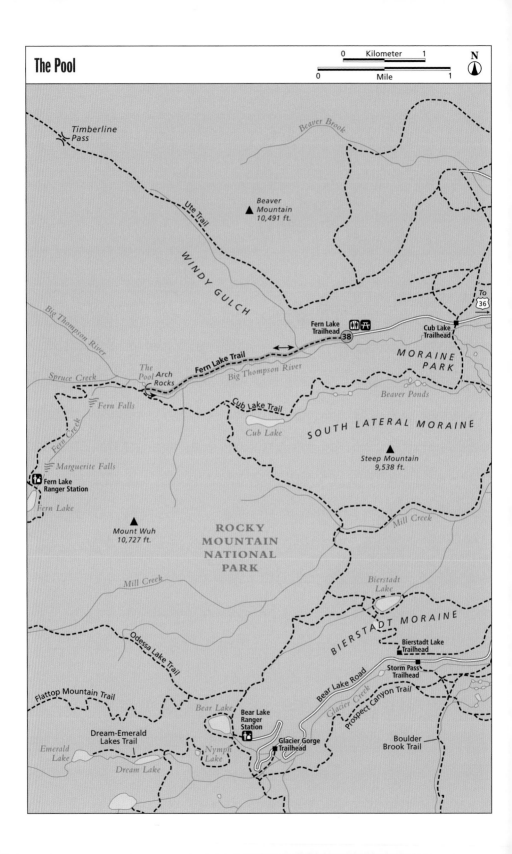

The Pool

0 Kilometer 1
0 Mile 1

N

Timberline Pass

Beaver Brook

Ute Trail

Beaver Mountain 10,491 ft.

WINDY GULCH

Big Thompson River

Fern Lake Trailhead

38

Cub Lake Trailhead

To 36

MORAINE PARK

Spruce Creek

The Pool

Arch Rocks

Fern Lake Trail

Big Thompson River

Beaver Ponds

Fern Falls

Fern Creek

Cub Lake Trail

Cub Lake

SOUTH LATERAL MORAINE

Marguerite Falls

Steep Mountain 9,538 ft.

Fern Lake Ranger Station

Fern Lake

Mount Wuh 10,727 ft.

ROCKY MOUNTAIN NATIONAL PARK

Mill Creek

Mill Creek

Bierstadt Lake

Odessa Lake Trail

BIERSTADT MORAINE

Bierstadt Lake Trailhead

Flattop Mountain Trail

Bear Lake Road

Glacier Creek

Storm Pass Trailhead

Prospect Canyon Trail

Bear Lake

Bear Lake Ranger Station

Dream-Emerald Lakes Trail

Nymph Lake

Glacier Gorge Trailhead

Boulder Brook Trail

Emerald Lake

Dream Lake

the place Funston's Pool. The US Board on Geographic Names shortened the name to The Pool in 1932—tempting addle-headed swimmers thereafter. Unharmed by bear, rocks, or frigid water, Funston went on to become a prominent general in the Philippines during the Spanish-American War. That did not kill him either.

There is a swimmer who evolved to dive into The Pool—the dipper, or water ouzel. This gray wren-shaped bird a little smaller than a robin hunts tiny prey in the water, flies out to a rock, and performs an entertaining bobbing dance, hence the common name dipper. The rock ledges that make The Pool dangerous for humans benefit dippers, which find the ledges ideal for building dome-shaped nests. A natural nesting site, The Pool is an easy, albeit sometimes warm, hike for birders anxious to add this western species to their life lists. These folks also can see dippers nesting under bridges in downtown Estes Park, but The Pool is a more memorable place to sight these birds.

Miles and Directions

0.0 Start at the Fern Lake Trailhead.

1.5 Pass between Arch Rocks, which are actually megaliths beside the trail rather than an arch over it.

1.7 Arrive at the substantial rock-and-timber bridge over the Big Thompson River at The Pool. Return the way you came.

3.4 Arrive back at the trailhead.

39 Sprague Lake

Unlike most other lakes in Rocky Mountain National Park, Sprague is of human construction. Still, it provides abundant natural pleasures to the many park visitors who circumnavigate the lake on a flat trail.

Start: Sprague Lake Picnic Area
Distance: 0.7-mile loop
Hiking time: About 1 hour
Difficulty: Easy
Trail surface: Packed earth
Elevation: Sprague Lake, 8,710 feet
Best season: Summer
Other trail users: Wheelchairs
Canine compatibility: Dogs prohibited

Fees and permits: National park entrance fee
Trail contacts: Rocky Mountain National Park Backcountry Office, 1000 US 36, Estes Park 80517; (970) 586-1242; www/nps.gov/romo
Maps: USGS *Longs Peak*; Trails Illustrated *Longs Peak*
Highlights: Views of Front Range, beaver ponds
Wildlife: Red squirrels, golden-mantled ground squirrels, mallard ducks, gray jay, Steller's jays

Finding the trailhead: From the Beaver Meadows entrance to Rocky Mountain National Park on US 36, drive west 0.2 mile and turn left onto Bear Lake Road. Continue about 6.5 miles to the Sprague Lake Picnic Area. A sign for the picnic area indicates a turn to the left from Bear Lake Road. **GPS:** N40 19.219' / W105 36.525'

The Hike

Abner Sprague dammed Boulder Brook in 1914 to provide fishing for guests at his newly completed lodge built under agreement with the USDA Forest Service, which administered the land prior to the creation of Rocky Mountain National Park in 1915. The National Park Service traded the land on which Sprague Lake and Sprague Lodge sat for the land containing Mills Lake and The Loch, which Sprague owned but had refused to develop as cabin sites. He thus preserved as wilderness the heart of hiking territory in what would become the national park.

Eventually the park service bought back Abner Sprague's lodge and lake. The lodge was torn down in 1958. The 13-acre lake remains, a reminder of Sprague's deep familiarity with where the park's scenic potential was greatest.

Walking clockwise around the lake presents the best series of mountain vistas. From the eastern shore, glacier deposited rocks, bending water grasses, and conifers form foreground for a photo of the Front Range left to right, with Taylor, Otis, and Hallett Peaks and Flattop and Notchtop Mountains (the latter partly hidden by forest) hopefully reflected in the lake. Heading counterclockwise is the easiest route to wheelchair-accessible backcountry campsites.

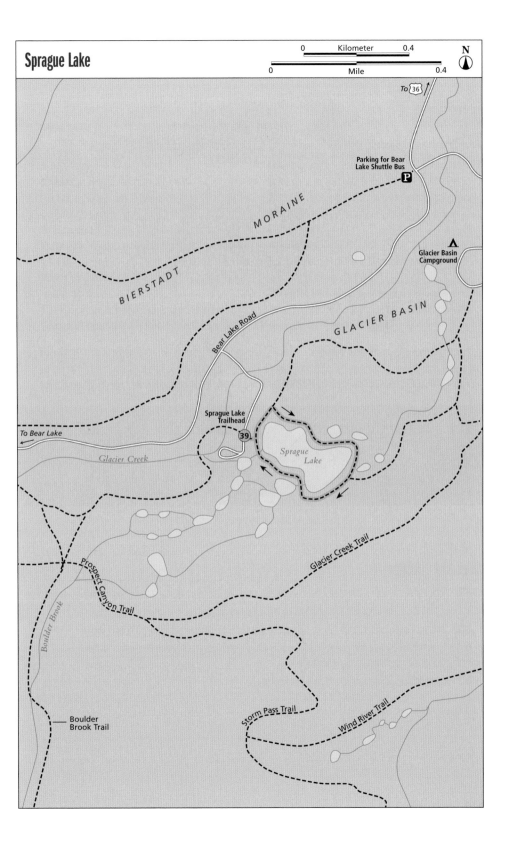

Abner Sprague dammed Sprague Lake with a keen eye for a great view of the Front Range.

Miles and Directions

0.0 Start a short way east of the Sprague Lake Picnic Area. Go left, as described, for the best photo ops; right for easiest surface to the wheelchair-accessible campsite.

0.3 The trail branches left to follow an outlet stream. Continue right along the lakeshore.

0.4 The trail branches left a short way to the wheelchair-accessible backcountry campsite. Continue right along the lakeshore.

0.7 Arrive back at the Sprague Lake Picnic Area.

Trail Ridge East

40 Deer Mountain

Deer Mountain is aptly named, but hikers also enjoy expansive views of many higher mountains.

Start: Deer Mountain Trailhead
Distance: 6.0 miles out and back
Hiking time: About 5 hours
Difficulty: Moderately easy
Trail surface: Dirt
Elevation: Trailhead, 8,930 feet; Deer Mountain, 10,013 feet
Best season: Summer, fall, winter
Other trail users: Equestrians
Canine compatibility: Dogs prohibited
Fees and permits: National park entrance fee

Trail contacts: Rocky Mountain National Park Backcountry Office, 1000 US 36, Estes Park 80517; (970) 586-1242; www.nps.gov/romo
Maps: USGS *Longs Peak*; Trails Illustrated *Longs Peak*
Highlights: Views of Mummy Range and Front Range, picturesque limber pines, uncommon Britton's skullcap wildflower, summit of Deer Mountain
Wildlife: Mule deer, elk, golden-mantled ground squirrels, chipmunks, black-billed magpies, mountain chickadees

Finding the trailhead: Deer Mountain Trailhead is located at the intersection of US 34 and US 36 at the eastern end of Trail Ridge Road. There is no parking lot, but you can park along the highways' broad shoulders. **GPS:** N40 23.25' / W105 36.66'

The Hike

Mule deer do seem to be unusually easy to spot on Deer Mountain, together with red deer, also called elk or wapiti. Red deer, however, is a European name, and elk were not so common on Deer Mountain in the 1880s, when the name appeared in Frederick Chapin's book *Mountaineering in Colorado*. Doubtless, mule deer were the "red deer" named in Chapin's book.

Technically unimposing, Deer Mountain is fortuitously located for views of much higher peaks, from the Mummy Range around the Front Range to Longs Peak. The views and relatively easy access made this so popular a hike that a group of women in Estes Park, later called the Estes Park Women's Club, gathered funds to build a trail to the top of the mountain before the national park was created. A more popular trail (it begins at a higher elevation) now leaves from the junction of US 34 and 36 at Deer Mountain Trailhead, the eastern end of Trail Ridge Road.

Free of snow during much of the year, the trail up Deer Mountain weaves back and forth from one striking vista to another. Shortcutting across these switchbacks encourages unnecessary erosion and may cause you to step on an uncommon wild-flower, the Britton's skullcap, a member of the mint family that grows on a 4- to 6-inch square stem. Each blue-purple bloom has a protruding lip that looks somewhat like a cap.

A mule deer buck grazes on Deer Mountain with Longs Peak and the Front Range in the background.

The grade requires energy to surmount of course, but it is not notably tough. The most striking view is of the deep cirque bowl carved by glaciers on Ypsilon Mountain, obviously marked by the natural Y-shaped snow gullies converging on its face.

Danger on Deer Mountain would seem slight. A high, isolated target for lightning, it receives an above-average number of strikes. But the coming storms are easy to spot, and retreat is easy. I know of no lightning casualties here, although burned trunks on the broad summit speak of past lightning fires. With so many deer, Deer Mountain should attract mountain lions to their main prey. But there are few lions across their very broad range, and they are most likely to prey on the deer. I know of no unpleasant hiker-lion encounters on Deer Mountain.

The mule deer on Deer Mountain attract a steady stream of admirers. Mule deer are about one-half the size of elk, with reddish coats in summer switching to gray in winter. The deer have white rump patches and black-tipped tails. Mule deer inhabit all levels of the park, except perhaps the tallest rockbound summits. They will travel as far as 30 miles a night in search of the 673 plant species they eat. Their wandering ways make them troubling traffic hazards; the number of deer roadkills far exceeds elk kills.

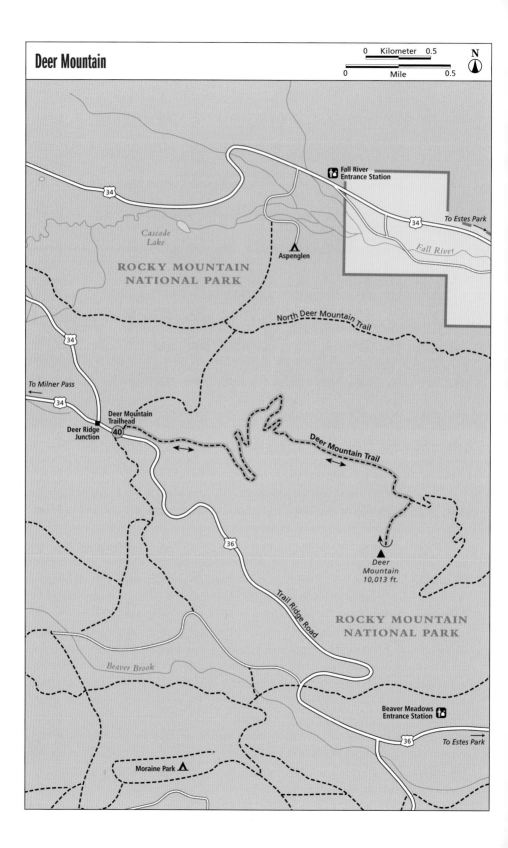

Deer Mountain

0   Kilometer   0.5

0   Mile   0.5

N

Fall River
Entrance Station

To Estes Park

34

Cascade
Lake

Fall River

Aspenglen

ROCKY MOUNTAIN
NATIONAL PARK

North Deer Mountain Trail

34

To Milner Pass

34

Deer Mountain
Trailhead

40

Deer Ridge
Junction

Deer Mountain Trail

36

Deer
Mountain
10,013 ft.

Trail Ridge Road

ROCKY MOUNTAIN
NATIONAL PARK

Beaver Brook

Beaver Meadows
Entrance Station

36

To Estes Park

Moraine Park

Male mule deer grow antlers; females do not. Antlers fall off in spring and regrow with a velvety covering that bucks scrape off prior to autumn rutting battles with other bucks. Fawns, often twins, are born in spring and are covered with light spots that act as camouflage in sun-dappled woods.

Mule deer appear very muscular, although seeming dainty compared to elk. This muscularity enables the deer to retreat in a distinctive four-legged bounce. Yet they seem surprising bold around national park visitors, perhaps considering humans fun to watch. Despite their interest in us, it is illegal for deer to feed people in a national park.

Miles and Directions

0.0 Start at the trailhead on the north side of Deer Ridge Junction.

0.1 Pass the junction with a trail left down to Aspenglen Campground. Continue right.

2.7 Reach a spur right to the summit of Deer Mountain.

3.0 Achieve the summit to enjoy a panoramic view. Return by the same route.

6.0 Arrive back at Deer Ridge Junction.

41 Timberline Pass

The hike to Timberline Pass is the easiest way to experience broad expanses of alpine tundra in Rocky Mountain National Park.

Start: Ute Crossing
Distance: 4.0 miles out and back
Hiking time: About 3 hours
Difficulty: Moderately easy
Trail surface: Rocks and dirt
Elevation: Ute Crossing, 11,440 feet; Timberline Pass, 11,484 feet
Best season: Midsummer
Other trail users: Human foot traffic only
Canine compatibility: Dogs prohibited

Fees and permits: National park entrance fee
Trail contacts: Rocky Mountain National Park Backcountry Office, 1000 US 36, Estes Park 80517; (970) 586-1242; www.nps.gov/romo
Maps: USGS *Trail Ridge* and *McHenrys Peak*; Trails Illustrated *Longs Peak*
Highlights: Open vistas, various tundra environments with many wildflower species
Wildlife: Elk, pikas, yellow-bellied marmots, water pipits, horned larks

Finding the trailhead: Ute Crossing is just above tree line along Trail Ridge Road (US 34), 2 miles above Rainbow Curve and 0.8 mile downhill from Forest Canyon Overlook. There is additional parking a short way up Trail Ridge Road from Ute Crossing. **GPS:** N40 23.60' / W105 41.72'

The Hike

Perhaps the most notable feature of Rocky Mountain National Park is its wide area of easily accessible alpine tundra. "Tundra" is a Russian word for the land without trees covered by carpets of low-growing plants that exist in the vicinity of the Arctic Circle and above tree line. A perfect example of this simple-looking but complex environment completely surrounds the Ute Trail from Trail Ridge Road to Timberline Pass.

According to a semi-familiar Christmas carol:

> Forth they went together,
> Through the rude wind's wild lament
> And the bitter weather.

Evidently, Good King Wenceslas's hiking party was walking the Ute Trail above Timberline Pass, where wind prevents tree survival and plants must grow low to the ground. These tundra plants sometimes are described as delicate, which is not true. Their incredible toughness, though, is tested terribly by wind that often exceeds 100 miles per hour, sucking moisture from all living things and scouring them with sand. They do not need further tribulation from hikers' trampling treads; always stick to the already sacrificed trail and step on rocks whenever possible.

Grazing on these tundra plants are various tundra animals: elk, mule deer, bighorn sheep, and white-tailed ptarmigan. Coyotes and golden eagles prey on pikas and yellow-bellied marmots, which sound alarm calls from the rock piles where

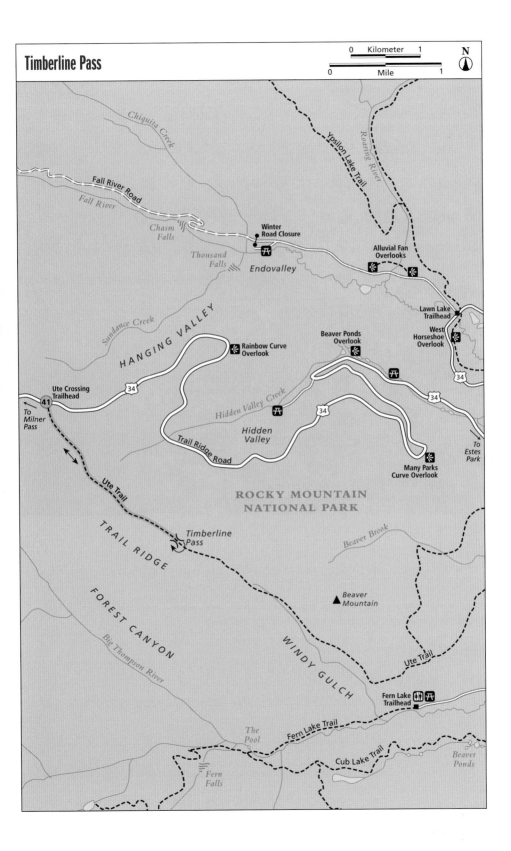

Timberline Pass

0 Kilometer 1
0 Mile 1

N

Chiquita Creek

Fall River Road

Fall River

Chasm Falls

Thousand Falls

Endovalley

Winter Road Closure

Ypsilon Lake Trail

Roaring River

Alluvial Fan Overlooks

Lawn Lake Trailhead

West Horseshoe Overlook

Sundance Creek

HANGING VALLEY

Rainbow Curve Overlook

34

Ute Crossing Trailhead

41

To Milner Pass

Beaver Ponds Overlook

34

34

Hidden Valley Creek

Hidden Valley

Trail Ridge Road

Many Parks Curve Overlook

To Estes Park

Ute Trail

ROCKY MOUNTAIN NATIONAL PARK

TRAIL RIDGE

Timberline Pass

Beaver Brook

FOREST CANYON

▲ Beaver Mountain

Big Thompson River

WINDY GULCH

Ute Trail

Fern Lake Trailhead

The Pool

Fern Lake Trail

Cub Lake Trail

Beaver Ponds

Fern Falls

Mountain sheep rams inhabit the rocks along the Ute Trail on Trail Ridge in summer.

they retreat from their feeding patches, often colorful with wildflowers in July. Hikers descend to the biggest rock pile, which marks Timberline Pass a short way above twisted tree "scouts" advancing a short way above the front line in the constant war between woods and winds for control of the heights.

Miles and Directions

0.0 Start at Ute Crossing.

2.0 Reach Timberline Pass, marked by large tor (hill of rocks). Return the way you came.

4.0 Arrive back at Ute Crossing.

LIGHTNING

In summer 2014 a visitor to Rocky Mountain National Park standing in the small parking area at Ute Crossing was killed by lightning. The next day another visitor was struck and killed a short way down Trail Ridge Road at Rainbow Curve. It is not flippant to observe that these back-to-back tragedies were shocking but not surprising.

Lightning tends to strike the highest point available, which above tree line is likely to be a standing human. Being inside a car along Trail Ridge is safe because of a cocoon of steel, not from rubber tires providing insulating protection. Otherwise, there is no place to hide if you hear thunder. Lightning can strike from as far away as thunder can be heard, about 10 miles.

Away from a car, hikers caught in a lightning storm can scatter to low depressions, trying to stay away from one another so that companions can avoid injury and provide aid to a lightning victim. Also try to stay away from rivulets that can convey current along the ground. Such "step voltage" diffuses in strength through the ground. The degree of damage to victims who survive step voltage depends on the proximity of the lightning strike and the conductivity of the ground.

Direct hits from cloud lightning may also be survivable because the strike partially dissipates in the surrounding air. But there also are upward charges sparking from the ground into the clouds. These are highly likely to kill the conducting hiker hit with temperatures as high as 50,000°F.

Survival of a downstroke or step voltage may depend on the reaction of those nearby. A victim may appear dead because electrical shock can cause the heart and lungs to quit working. CPR (cardiopulmonary resuscitation) may save a life. The heart often restarts on its own; the lungs usually do not. Continued lack of oxygen can cause brain damage, but victims have recovered completely from oxygen deprivation lasting as long as 22 minutes. Additional lightning injuries—shock, cuts, burns, broken bones from falling, internal bleeding—can be serious or fatal if not tended.

Options to avoid being hit, aside from good luck, are limited along the Ute Trail. You will be safer if you retreat below tree line as opposed to huddling under a lone tree, which makes you a likely target for strong step voltage. Despite the old saw, lightning frequently does strike again in the same place. Therefore, if you see a lightning scar down the bark of a tree, avoid that tree. Stay away from step voltage sites such as cliff edges, high rocks, rock debris and vegetation at cliff bases, and cracks or shallow niches in mountainsides. The least-dangerous refuge might be crouched among large flat-topped rocks, but such configurations are uncommon along the Ute Trail.

Respect building storms reverberating with thunder, which at least are easy to spot along the Ute Trail. They usually arrive in the afternoon, coming most often from the west; but the few that do come from the east tend to be worse.

If you are racing a storm back to your car, look down as well as up. Tripping over a rock while rushing down the trail also can inflict serious damage. At Ute Crossing you are not completely safe from a storm until you are inside your car's steel armor.

42 Windy Gulch

If you can place transportation at both ends, this hike is one of the most interesting in the national park, passing through all three plant life zones.

Start: Ute Crossing
Distance: 6.5-mile shuttle
Hiking time: About 5 hours
Difficulty: Moderately easy
Trail surface: Rocks and dirt
Elevation: Ute Crossing, 11,440 feet; Upper Beaver Meadows Trailhead, 8,440 feet
Best season: Summer
Other trail users: Human foot traffic only
Canine compatibility: Dogs prohibited
Fees and permits: National park entrance fee

Trail contacts: Rocky Mountain National Park Backcountry Office, 1000 US 36, Estes Park 80517; (970) 586-1242; www.nps.gov/romo
Maps: USGS *Trail Ridge*, *McHenrys Peak*, and *Longs Peak*; Trails Illustrated *Longs Peak*
Highlights: Open vistas of nearby glaciated peaks, various tundra environments with many wildflower species, tree line, subalpine and montane zone environments, hanging valley
Wildlife: Elk, pikas, yellow-bellied marmots, water pipits, horned larks

Finding the trailheads: Ute Crossing is just above tree line along Trail Ridge Road (US 34), 2 miles above Rainbow Curve and 0.8 mile downhill from Forest Canyon Overlook on Trail Ridge Road. There is additional parking available a short way up the road from Ute Crossing. **GPS:** N40 23.60' / W105 41.72'

The Upper Beaver Meadows Trailhead is at the end of an unpaved road heading west from US 36 at a major bend 0.6 from the Beaver Meadows entrance to Rocky Mountain National Park. **GPS:** N40 22.372' / W105 36.845'

The Hike

Utes with dogs and horses dragging travois (burden platforms) crossed these mountains through Windy Gulch, giving their name to the Ute Trail and, by derivation, Trail Ridge. By 1875 grooves marking their trail had disappeared, to be replaced by treads worn to mines and tourist spots. These too have healed to a single narrow path undulating across the treeless tundra to drop below wind-sculpted limber pines at tree line just below Timberline Pass.

At Ute Crossing on Trail Ridge Road, cushion plants struggle to cover the wear and tear of road construction and hikers' boots. Giving these botanical heroes a chance to do their job means walking gently, stepping from rock to rock when possible. A moderate climb to a low ridge above the road levels to a pleasant meander across windswept alpine tundra, where trees cannot grow to block views of awesome peaks. Glaciers carved the steep-walled Forest Canyon that dramatizes the mountain vistas above to the right of the trail.

The trail through Windy Gulch forest breaks suddenly to an unobstructed view of the Front Range where glaciers descending from the Continental Divide cut off the end of the unglaciated gulch, leaving it suspended hundreds of feet above the Big Thompson River Valley floor as a perfect example of a hanging valley.

Rock piles called tors thrust into the sky to name Tombstone Ridge, part of Trail Ridge. The path descends, likely past elk herds, to a larger tor marking Timberline Pass. The grade steepens considerably below the tor and more steeply yet below tree line.

Unlike most steepness along national park trails, this is caused not by glaciers. Mountain glaciers never filled this valley. After a knee-challenging descent relieved by occasional flatness, the trail passes through meadows and forest to emerge suddenly at the top of a cliff dropping into Spruce Canyon. The glaciers that deepened and steepened Forest and Spruce Canyons sliced off the end of the valley of Windy Gulch, leaving it as a hanging valley. So steep is the fall of Windy Gulch Cascades from this point, they are out of sight below the treeless ledges suspended above the canyon.

The trail winds along the canyon wall, soon enclosed by forest and then by a moraine—a ridge of rock dropped by melting glacial ice against the slope of Beaver Mountain (now blanketed by soil and trees). Branch trails depart from the main path to the top of the ridge for a view into Moraine Park. Bending around Beaver

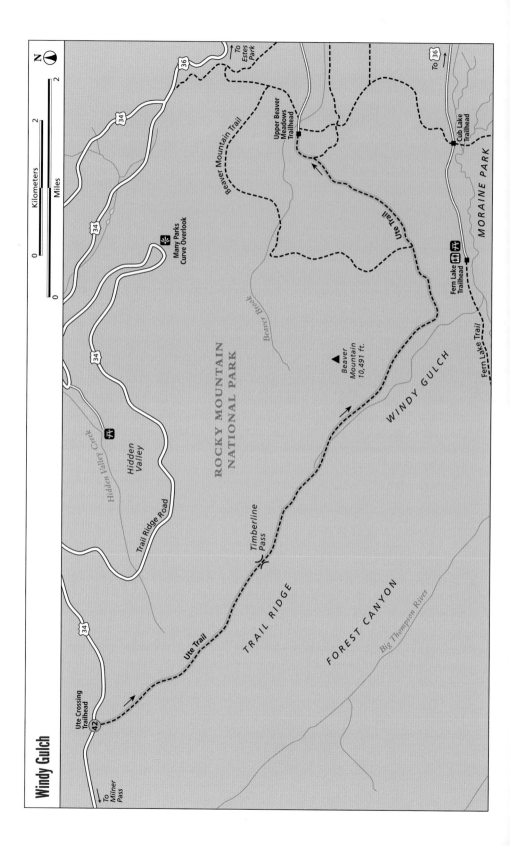

Windy Gulch

N

0 2 Kilometers
0 2 Miles

To Estes Park
36

To 36

To Milner Pass
34
42 Ute Crossing Trailhead

Ute Trail

TRAIL RIDGE

Timberline Pass

FOREST CANYON

Big Thompson River

34
34
34

Hidden Valley Creek

Hidden Valley

Trail Ridge Road

Many Parks Curve Overlook

ROCKY MOUNTAIN NATIONAL PARK

Beaver Brook

Beaver Mountain Trail

Beaver Mountain 10,491 ft.

Ute Trail

WINDY GULCH

Upper Beaver Meadows Trailhead

Cub Lake Trailhead

Fern Lake Trailhead

Fern Lake Trail

MORAINE PARK

Mountain (do not hope to see beaver), the trail leads away from Moraine Park to meadows and aspen groves at the Upper Beaver Meadows Trailhead.

Presumably you have stationed a vehicle or a generous volunteer to drive you back up Trail Ridge Road to pick up the vehicle that carried you to Ute Crossing.

Miles and Directions

0.0   Start at Ute Crossing.

2.0   Descend to Timberline Pass.

3.6   Arrive at flat walking in Ute Meadow.

4.35 Emerge from confining woods to sudden wide open views at a clifftop overlooking Spruce Canyon.

5.8   Pass the junction with the Beaver Mountain Trail.

6.5   Arrive at the Upper Beaver Meadows Trailhead.

43 Toll Memorial

Many folks who start on the short, gentle trail to Toll Memorial fail to get there.

Start: Rock Cut
Distance: 0.8 mile out and back
Hiking time: About 2 hours
Difficulty: Moderately easy
Trail surface: Asphalt
Elevation: Rock Cut, 12,110 feet; Toll Memorial, 12,310 feet
Best season: Midsummer
Other trail users: Wheelchairs
Canine compatibility: Dogs prohibited

Fees and permits: National park entrance fee
Trail contacts: Rocky Mountain National Park Backcountry Office, 1000 US 36, Estes Park 80510; (970) 586-1242; www.nps.gov/romo
Maps: USGS *Trail Ridge*; Trails Illustrated Rocky Mountain National Park
Highlights: Alpine plants, Mushroom Rocks (0.25 mile), Toll Memorial peak finder (0.4 mile)
Wildlife: Yellow-bellied marmots, pikas, chipmunks, ravens, Clark's nutcrackers

Finding the trailhead: The Rock Cut Trailhead is well marked along Trail Ridge Road, 12.5 miles from the junction of US 34 and US 36. **GPS:** N24 24.730' / W105 43.974'

The Hike

Rock Cut is a landmark on Trail Ridge Road, where a slot blasted through a rugged cliff appears rather natural. Ample parking exists on the west side of Rock Cut for those who want to gaze at the glorious view of Gorge Lakes hanging below precipitous peaks on the opposite side of Forest Canyon. Below a wall, amid rocks presumably blasted from Rock Cut and used to bolster the road, is one of the best places in the national park to view pikas, little round-eared rabbit cousins, scurrying busily to gather tundra plants that they store as hay for winter food. Their hay barns are gaps amid the rocks that function as ideal natural rock piles for the pikas, even though the piles are a coincidental result of road building.

These high-altitude hay makers together with the groundhog-like yellow-bellied marmots are so entertaining to watch that many park visitors never cross the road to the excellent paved trail that can introduce them to the alpine tundra. The trail leads to Toll Memorial, a bronze peak identifier. Roger Toll was the third superintendent of Rocky Mountain National Park, whose life of public service and enthusiasm for mountains was cut short at age 53 by a car accident in 1936. To avoid meeting a similar fate, use care when crossing busy Trail Ridge Road between the pika-marmot circus and the Toll Memorial Trailhead.

The trail rises gradually, but the air is oxygen-poor for those who arrive at more than 12,000 feet above sea level the easy way, by car. Informative signs about the tundra environment provide more than adequate excuse for frequent pauses to rest

This peak finder at Toll Memorial atop Trail Ridge honors Roger Toll, third superintendent of the park, who conceived the idea of Trail Ridge Road (seen in the background).

pounding hearts and gasping lungs. So interesting is this outdoor museum of mountaintop ecology that when many folks reach the trail's end and discover that an actual rock scramble is required to reach the peak identifier, they decide that their pleasure has been satisfied without the little climb at the end.

The walk provides interesting, enjoyable visions of somewhat exotic terrain where tiny wonders contrast with grand spectacles. Squinting across the peak identifier (atop the rocks for an unobstructed 360-degree view) adds to visitors' satisfaction by providing names of peaks near and far. But the peak identifier also piques curiosity. What would it be like to stand on that mountain over there? Or on that dim-with-distance peak way over there? Roger Toll would be delighted with his memorial.

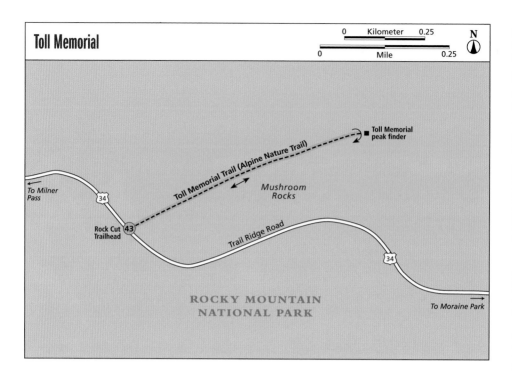

Miles and Directions

0.0 Start at Rock Cut, on north side of Trail Ridge Road.

0.25 A spur path to right leads to Mushroom Rocks.

0.4 Reach Toll Memorial peak finder by scrambling up the rocks. Return the way you came.

0.8 Arrive back at the trailhead.

44 Trail Ridge Road in Winter

Winter wind and snow close the highest continuous paved road in the country to vehicles and thereby open it to foot travel.

Start: Many Parks Curve
Distance: 12.0 miles out and back
Hiking time: About 9 hours
Difficulty: Moderate
Trail surface: Asphalt often covered by snowdrifts
Elevation: Many Parks Curve, 9,620 feet; Ute Crossing, 11,440 feet
Best season: Winter
Other trail users: Human foot traffic only
Canine compatibility: Leashed dogs permitted on Trail Ridge Road after the first Saturday in April, as indicated by signs

Fees and permits: National park entrance fee
Trail contacts: Rocky Mountain National Park Backcountry Office, 1000 US Highway 36, Estes Park 80517; (970) 586-1242; www.nps.gov/romo
Maps: USGS *Trail Ridge*; Trails Illustrated *Longs Peak*
Highlights: Views of the Mummy Range, wind-sculpted snow (4.2 miles), wind- and fire-sculpted trees (4.4 miles)
Wildlife: White-tailed ptarmigan, mountain chickadees, gray jays

Finding the trailhead: From the Beaver Meadow entrance, follow Trail Ridge Road (US 36) to its junction with US 34 and continue straight to its closure at Many Parks Curve. **GPS:** N40 23.28' / W105 37.87'

The Hike

Walking a road may seem unappealing to trail purists, but Trail Ridge Road is inches from wild wonder as it climbs to tree line and beyond to the domain of winter wind. Actually, fearsome wind aids the initial ascent from Many Parks Curve by stripping snow from much of the road. But hikers may do well to carry snowshoes or cross-country skis for those stretches where the wind is not so considerate.

Large Engelmann spruce and subalpine fir in a classic subalpine forest disappear for a short distance where the road crosses an old abandoned ski slope—a verdant, flower-filled meadow in summer. Then the road rises to Rainbow Curve, bends left for a close view of the Mummy Range, and crosses into the kingdom of the wind. Guarding this front line of perpetual war between woods and wind are twisted and squashed trees carved and molded by wind into its self-portrait. Here are krummholz (twisted wood) versions of the mighty pillars of species near the old ski slope.

Seeds of these trees are dropped by the wind, likely laughing at the time, to a place where wind cannot reach behind the shelter of a rock. Snow accumulates there, also now out of the wind's reach. The snow melts to water the seeds, which take root and begin to grow. When they finally peek above the level of the rock, the wind gleefully kills their tops by desiccating their new-growth twigs and blasting them with sand.

A hike up Trail Ridge Road after it is closed by winter may reveal white-tailed ptarmigan in their winter white feathers that disguise them as snow as they eat willow twigs at tree line.

Unable to grow up, the trees grow out—sheltered by their own original growth, by the rocks, and by the fact that friction keeps wind from blowing as fiercely near the ground as it does a few feet higher.

Some trees manage to heed their genes and grow upward a bit. The main new-growth twigs, potential trunks, survive and protect the new branches on the side away from the wind. As these arboreal heroes climb into the air, where the wind is even stronger, all the new branches are blown to death, except for the twigs in the narrow band up the trunk side away from the wind (which usually blows from the west at this latitude). The trunks become poles with branches flung out along one side as defiant banners; hence they're called banner trees. These trees lead the struggle of the forest to capture the heights from the wind.

Gaps in the rocky ridgeline below which the road ascends above Rainbow Curve force the same volume of flowing air to push through a smaller space. When the same volume must pass through a constricted space, it must rush faster. Therefore, wind speed under the increased pressure of this Venturi effect must blow faster, much over 100 miles per hour. Here the forest's storm troopers, flexible limber pines, maintain a picturesque outpost against the wind.

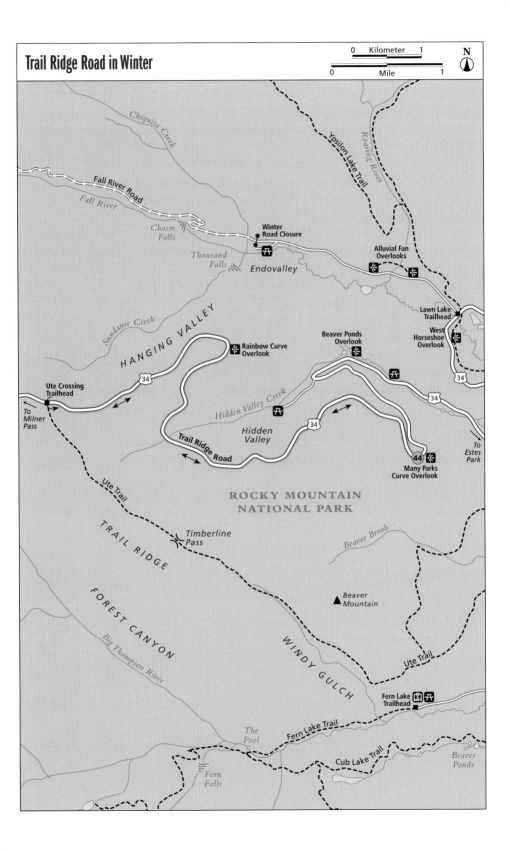

Trail Ridge Road in Winter

0   Kilometer   1

0   Mile   1

N

Chiquita Creek

Ypsilon Lake Trail

Roaring River

Fall River Road

Fall River

Chasm Falls

Winter Road Closure

Thousand Falls

Endovalley

Alluvial Fan Overlooks

Sundance Creek

HANGING VALLEY

Lawn Lake Trailhead

West Horseshoe Overlook

Rainbow Curve Overlook

Beaver Ponds Overlook

34

Ute Crossing Trailhead

To Milner Pass

Hidden Valley Creek

34

34

34

Trail Ridge Road

Hidden Valley

To Estes Park

44

Many Parks Curve Overlook

ROCKY MOUNTAIN NATIONAL PARK

Ute Trail

TRAIL RIDGE

Timberline Pass

Beaver Brook

FOREST CANYON

▲ *Beaver Mountain*

Big Thompson River

Ute Trail

WINDY GULCH

Fern Lake Trailhead

The Pool

Fern Lake Trail

Beaver Ponds

Cub Lake Trail

Fern Falls

At this point, road walkers remember that they too are living beings that stand noticeably taller than the krummholz. Linking arms to increase total weight might be useful as the wind attempts (often successfully) to pin hikers like butterflies against a vertical rock surface. You might be grateful for the road, which provides a broad surface along which to stumble upward without rocks to trip your already uncertain steps.

Of course you already have covered your body with warm clothes, as well as goggles over your eyes. But some skin may be exposed on lips and cheeks. Lift your hands, protected by down mittens, to protect your face from the same frostbite techniques the wind throws against the trees.

As you push beyond the Venturi zone, and the wind decreases to a howling horror, the down you hold over your face may remind you of another mountaineer protected from wind by feathers. White-tailed ptarmigan are small alpine grouse that shed summer's mottled gray and brown feathers for snow white ones that change their appearance from summer rocks to winter lumps of snow. They actually live in this deadly environment year-round, hiding from the wind by burying themselves in the snow. It was to be able to brag that you have seen them in their white feathers that you undertook this trip up Trail Ridge.

But you likely will need to venture from the road if you want to view a ptarmigan. They are most likely to be striding on their snowshoe-like feet, browsing on alpine willow twigs at tree line. Most of these willows are to the right of the road. Also to the right are cliffs. Stepping on perpetual snowbanks can cause the unwary to slip, slide, and shoot over the edge. If you see a white ptarmigan on the way down, you are unlikely to live to boast of the sighting. Be sure to keep willow thickets downhill to protect you from falls.

Back on the road, the way down is much easier on a grade made for cars—the wind mostly at your back, shoving you down where you belong. Henceforth, when you look up at winter plumes of snow streaming from the peaks, you will know how pleasant are the valleys that most people think are windy.

Miles and Directions

0.0 Start at the Many Parks Curve parking area.

6.0 Reach Ute Crossing. Return the way you came.

12.0 Arrive back at the parking area.

Tahosa Valley

45 The Keyhole

The Keyhole opens the door by which thousands of climbers reach the top of Longs Peak. For many, however, The Keyhole itself is an exciting goal.

Start: Longs Peak Trailhead
Distance: 12.5 miles out and back
Hiking time: About 10 hours
Difficulty: Difficult
Trail surface: Dirt and rocks
Elevation: Trailhead, 9,400 feet; The Keyhole, 13,150 feet
Best season: Summer
Other trail users: Equestrians as far as the Boulder Field
Canine compatibility: Dogs prohibited
Fees and permits: No fees or permits required

Trail contacts: Rocky Mountain National Park Backcountry Office, 1000 US 36, Estes Park 80517; (970) 586-1242; www.nps.gov/romo
Maps: USGS *Longs Peak*; Trails Illustrated *Longs Peak*
Highlights: Views of east and north faces of Longs Peak, alpine tundra, the Boulder Field, Agnes Vaille shelter hut, views into Glacier Gorge
Wildlife: Elk, mule deer, pikas, yellow-bellied marmots, white-tailed ptarmigan

Finding the trailhead: The turnoff to Longs Peak Trailhead heads west from CO 7, 7.5 miles south of Estes Park at a sign indicating the Longs Peak Area. A mile from CO 7, a left turn leads to the Longs Peak Ranger Station and parking for the trailhead. **GPS:** N40 16.325' / W105 33.394'

The Hike

A web of unmarked routes to the top covers Longs Peak. All but a tiny percentage of climbers who make it to the top ascend along a way that has been called The Keyhole for nearly a century and a half. Though not as obvious as the distinctive notch on the east face of Longs, the much smaller Keyhole is just as distinctive and nearly as easy to see in the ridge between Longs and Storm Peaks. This Keyhole ridge separates the north and west faces of Longs Peak—so popular a mountaineering goal that every assemblage of rocks seems to be named.

As with summit climbs, an early start is best when The Keyhole is the goal. Early means predawn, perhaps 3 a.m., for three reasons. For aesthetics, such an early start allows hikers to reach the most memorable points of the journey when the morning light is most beautiful. For safety, it is best to have enough time to retreat from lightning-generating clouds that are most likely to assemble in the afternoon. For logistics, leaving the trailhead in the deep dark increases the likelihood of finding a parking place somewhere west of Kansas, and thus closer to The Keyhole.

While walking in your sleep up the well-beaten East Longs Peak Trail, you miss uniform lodgepole pine woods, wake up occasionally at approaches to or crossings of noisy Alpine Brook and Larkspur Creek, and pass unaware through interesting stands

The Agnes Vaille Memorial Shelter just below The Keyhole offers protection to climbers caught by storms on Longs Peak.

of limber pine, subalpine fir, and Engelmann spruce. You can experience all these sights on your way back.

Happily, somnambulism ceases at tree line amid bent and bold krummholz trees, reduced to shrubs by weather. Beyond these distorted specimens of several conifer species opens the broad and treeless tundra. Now begins a thin-air race with dawn's early light to reach good photo sites just before the sun gets there. The nearest, and arguably the best, photo spot is atop Mills Moraine. The trail heads right to circle Mount Lady Washington. To the left, the sudden drop into the valley of Roaring Fork punctuated by Peacock Pool would look awesome except that the whole glorious vista ends at the huge vertical wall of the east face of Longs Peak, which grabs all the attention. This scene is unexcelled, and weather at dawn likely will favor photogenic light.

However, if you heed reasonable urgings for speed, 2.0 miles ahead, the view of the north face with the curving trail from Granite Pass leading into the Boulder Field might be just as rewarding. The Diamond, the particularly massive part of the east face, grabs your eyes on the left. The hike's goal, The Keyhole, is relatively tiny but clear on the right.

In the middle are rocks gaining in size as hikers gain in altitude toward Longs. When you reach the Boulder Field, there technically are no boulders. There *are*

The Keyhole

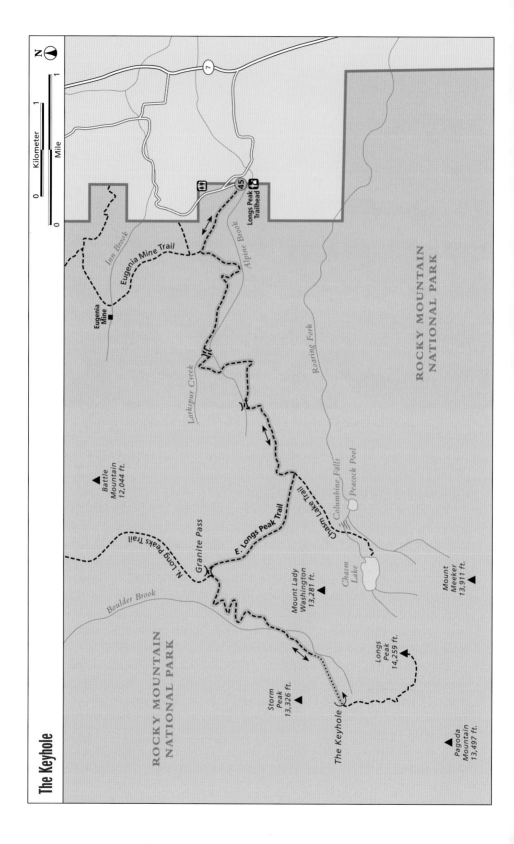

innumerable big (though not necessarily stable) rocks, a sea of rocks, the definition of *felsenmeer* (*felsen* means "rock"; *meer* means "sea"). The earliest reference to the Boulder Field is in an 1873 travel account, which implies that a then-current name of "lava beds" was incorrect, which it was. Boulders, of which there are more than plenty in this national park, are rocks more than 8 inches in diameter. Thinking of this definition in the Boulder Field, where many rocks exceed 20 feet may inspire smirks. But boulders also are supposed to be rounded by water (rivers or glaciers) or general weathering. The word "boulder" even *sounds* round. But the rocks in the Boulder Field tend to be angular, separated along cracks by expansion of freezing water then tilted by the same freezing-thawing cycle.

Such a surface frustrates trail development, and the path seems to just quit trying to proceed in the middle of the Boulder Field. From there a wave of *felsenmeer* leads your eye apprehensively up to The Keyhole, formed by rocks being levered away from the ridge by freezing and thawing. Theoretically, there must be an ideal way up the tilting rock slabs to The Keyhole. It seems unlikely, though, that even those mighty mountaineers who have passed through The Keyhole many dozens of times have ever found the best route. Point your face toward the gap in the ridge, and do your best exploring.

As you approach The Keyhole, a stone shelter hut becomes less inconspicuous below and to the left of the gap. It was built as a memorial to Agnes Vaille, who died nearby after an exhausting first winter ascent of the east face (in 1925), and to Herbert Sortland, who attempted her rescue but had to turn back in the face of January storms, broke his hip, and died near the Tahosa Valley floor.

Although the interior of the shelter seems somewhat grim, its virtue becomes evident when bitter wind shrieks through The Keyhole. Often, however, the wind is moderate, and the view beyond The Keyhole into the upper reaches of Glacier Gorge is beyond wondrous. West of Longs Peak, three 13,000-foot peaks—Pagoda Mountain and Chiefs Head and McHenrys Peaks—form a gigantic bowl at the head of Glacier Gorge, glittering with streams and lakes. Most of the lakes strung along the drainage of Glacier Creek are in the shadow of Longs Peak until midmorning.

Miles and Directions

- **0.0** Start at the Longs Peak Trailhead and begin your "sleepwalk."
- **0.5** Ignore a trail heading right to Eugenia Mine.
- **0.9** Listen for Alpine Brook.
- **1.6** Cross a bridge over Larkspur Creek.
- **2.1** Cross Alpine Brook at a higher altitude.
- **3.5** Put off a 0.7-mile side trip to Chasm Lake for another day and head right, around Mount Lady Washington, on the East Longs Peak Trail.
- **4.5** Arrive at Granite Pass and a junction with the North Longs Peak Trail. Turn left.
- **5.9** The trail dies in the Boulder Field. Imagine the best route to The Keyhole, above to the right.
- **6.25** Celebrate your arrival at The Keyhole. Make your way back to the trailhead.
- **12.5** Celebrate your arrival back at the trailhead.

46 Longs Peak

Many of the climbers who aspire to ascend all of Colorado's fifty-plus "fourteeners" (mountains more than 14,000 feet tall) put off Longs Peak until last, reasonably assuming it will be the best.

Start: Longs Peak Trailhead

Distance: 15.4 miles out and back

Hiking time: About 14 hours

Difficulty: Difficult

Trail surface: Dirt and rock

Elevation: Trailhead, 9,400 feet; Longs Peak, 14,259 feet

Best season: Summer

Other trail users: Equestrians as far as the Boulder Field

Canine compatibility: Dogs prohibited

Fees and permits: No fees or permits required

Trail contacts: Rocky Mountain National Park Backcountry Office, 1000 US 36, Estes Park 80517; (970) 586-1242; www.nps.gov/romo

Maps: USGS Long Peak; Trails Illustrated *Longs Peak*

Highlights: Stunning views in all directions from the highest point in Rocky Mountain National Park

Wildlife: Elk, mule deer, yellow-bellied marmots, pikas, white-tailed ptarmigan

Finding the trailhead: The turnoff to Longs Peak Trailhead leaves west from CO 7, 7.5 miles south of Estes Park at a sign indicating the Longs Peak Area. A mile from CO 7, a left turn leads to the Longs Peak Ranger Station and trailhead parking. **GPS:** N40 16.325' / W105 33.394'

The Hike

First of all, "The Keyhole Route is NOT a hike!" according to a National Park Service brochure using bold face type. "It is a climb that crosses enormous sheer vertical rock faces, often with falling rocks, requiring scrambling, where an unroped fall likely would be fatal. The route has narrow ledges, loose rock, and steep cliffs. The terrain requires good route-finding and scrambling skills. Use caution, as injuries requiring rescue are very dangerous and take many hours, if not days, to evacuate."

If this emphatic NPS warning does not inspire you with a longing to climb Longs Peak, make a gift of this book to a very good friend, because you do not really want to use it. At 14,259 feet in altitude, Longs Peak dominates the western horizon seen from Denver north to the Wyoming border. Not only its height but also its distinctive shape adjacent to 13,911-foot Mount Meeker make Longs Peak an alluring goal for approximately 15,000 Colorado residents and visitors each year. This pair of peaks, called "the two ears" by the Arapaho, each day serve as a reminder for hundreds of thousands of people of why they live in Colorado.

Puffy clouds west of Longs Peak viewed from the top of The Homestretch may turn into dangerous storms as the day progresses. ▶

Longs is such a horizon definer that it is the subject of the oldest picture of the Rocky Mountains. In 1821 Samuel Seymour, an artist accompanying Stephen Long's federal expedition of explorers, painted Longs Peak from the approximate location of today's Greeley. The Long expedition at last reached the mountains south of the prominent peak and turned left. Three members of the party climbed another four-teener made famous by the alliterative name of an earlier western explorer: Pikes Peak. On July 19 Long and his men turned their backs on the Colorado Rockies and returned east with emotions similar to those of modern travelers who must leave the mountains. In his official report, Long labeled the 600 miles of plains east of the Rockies "the great American desert," which was "uninhabitable by a people depend-ing on agriculture for their subsistence." Climbers gazing into the rising sun from well above tree line on Longs Peak can forgive the explorer for not foreseeing the many reservoirs that glitter red on the plains.

The caution strongly urged for Longs Peak climbers by the National Park Service is achieved mainly by allotting enough time for the climb. This includes taking days to climb other fun peaks of successively higher altitude, ranging from 11,000 through 13,000 feet, in order to condition yourself for a fourteener. Start up Longs very early, and do not plan to do anything else on the day of the climb.

Early means well before sunrise, such as 3 a.m. Begin the climb by following flash-light beams up the trail from the Longs Peak Trailhead. Many hikers are sleepwalking through dark pine forest, briefly awakened occasionally by the sound of Alpine Brook or Larkspur Creek.

Watching the alpenglow turn the east face of Longs Peak a warm reddish pink from Mills Moraine (trail built in 1921) is very spectacular but not particularly wise. Better would be to already have curved in the gloom around the base of Mount Lady Washington to the right of Longs Peak and be approaching the peak's north face when alpenglow seems to be shining from within the mountain. This timing likely will place hikers in the center of the Boulder Field—a bowl surrounded by Lady Washington, Longs, and Storm Peak—in time to reach the top of Longs before storms threaten. Such storms usually are hidden at a distance by surrounding high peaks, giving scant warning of their advance until climbers are nearly on top. Allow-ing time to compensate for a meteorological surprise is prudent.

The least-difficult route to the summit is through The Keyhole, an obvious open-ing in the ridge to the right between Longs and Storm Peaks. Somewhat inconspicu-ous below The Keyhole is a conical stone hut built in 1925. The shelter is a memorial to Agnes Vaille, who died nearby from exhaustion and cold after making the first win-ter ascent of the east face, and to Herbert Sortland, who died attempting to rescue her.

Beyond The Keyhole, the route to the top of Longs crosses very narrow ledges following red-and-yellow targets painted on rocks, passing two iron bars drilled into rock at a slot along the route. After climbing above these bars, the way descends to The Trough. Note carefully where you reach this rock-filled gully, because it is easy to miss when you're tired on your descent. Cutting up to a ridgeline gap called the False

Longs Peak

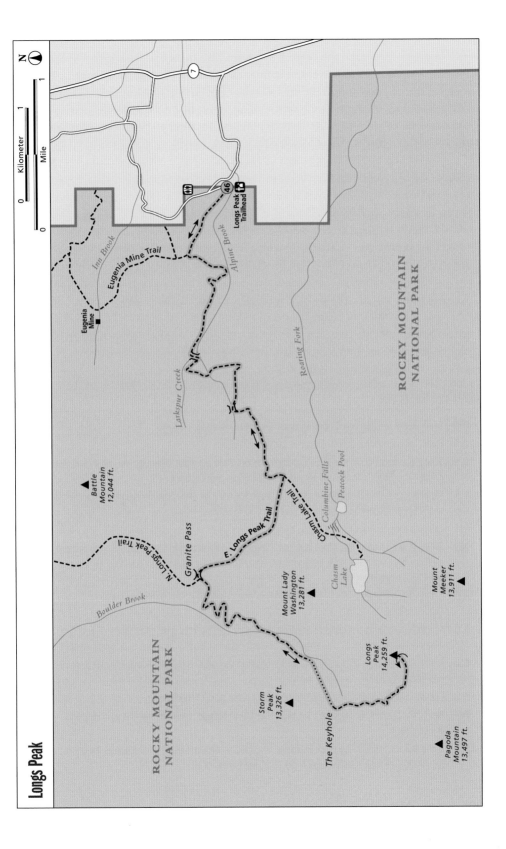

N

Kilometer
0   1

Mile
0   1

Longs Peak Trailhead

Eugenia Mine Trail

Eugenia Mine

Inn Brook

Alpine Brook

Larkspur Creek

Roaring Fork

Columbine Falls

Peacock Pool

Battle Mountain
12,044 ft.

Boulder Brook

N. Longs Peak Trail

Granite Pass

E. Longs Peak Trail

Chasm Lake Trail

Chasm Lake

Mount Lady Washington
13,281 ft.

Mount Meeker
13,911 ft.

Storm Peak
13,326 ft.

The Keyhole

Longs Peak
14,259 ft.

Pagoda Mountain
13,497 ft.

ROCKY MOUNTAIN
NATIONAL PARK

ROCKY MOUNTAIN
NATIONAL PARK

7

46

Keyhole before you reach the correct exit from The Trough is dangerous. Descending below the correct exit is very irritating. Uncertain footing in loose rock in The Trough is tiring, inspiring climbers to sit while pretending to admire the extremely spectacular views plunging from surrounding summits into the depths of Glacier Gorge. Beware of sending loose rocks to pummel the climbers below you; beware of loose rocks that other climbers may send your way.

Finally, the top of The Trough ends in a scramble onto the less-steep ledges leading across the west face of Longs. Crossing the dramatic Narrows is made less scary by secure footing and convenient handholds as far as the bottom of The Homestretch—a length of steep, sometimes slick granite. The top of The Homestretch is the top of Longs Peak.

The summit is several acres large. There is lots of meander room, but most climbers end up looking over the stomach-clenching edge of the east face down the dizzying 2,500-foot cliff to Chasm Lake. Even for climbers normally unaffected by heights, this drop is sufficiently intimidating to make a warning about taking care seem superfluous.

Less evident, and thereby perhaps more dangerous, are the clouds that often build in the west across ranks of ragged ranges. Watching skies to the east is also a good idea, together with remembering that the descent to the Vaille shelter hut is a long and shaky retreat, with an even longer retreat past boot-tripping rocks to tree line. Most accidents on Longs happen on the descent.

Miles and Directions

0.0 Start at the Longs Peak Trailhead and follow your flashlight beam.

0.5 Head left where the trail to Eugenia Mine goes right.

0.95 When you come to Alpine Brook, do not put on more clothing, although you likely will need it later. The drop in temperature beside the stream will be brief.

1.6 Carefully cross a bridge over Larkspur Creek. It would be very embarrassing to experience a climb-ending fall so soon.

2.1 Cross Alpine Brook with the same care.

3.5 Arrive at the Chasm Lake Trail junction. (There is no finer trail in the national park, but put it off for another day.) Bear right to push around the base of Mount Lady Washington on the East Longs Peak Trail.

4.5 Arrive at Granite Pass and meet the North Longs Peak Trail. Head left toward the Boulder Field.

5.9 The trail quits in the middle of the Boulder Field. Turn right to gaze past discouraging flat slabs up to The Keyhole. The most direct route you find to The Keyhole is as good as any.

6.2 Reach The Keyhole and decide that the view on the other side into Glacier Gorge is worth any effort.

6.5 Enter the base of The Trough, perhaps the hardest part of the climb.

7.7 Pause for prayer: "Thank God. The top." Mindful of fatigue, carefully retrace your route to the trailhead.

15.4 Arrive back at the Longs Peak Trailhead and begin contemplating your reasons for climbing mountains—a task much longer than climbing Longs Peak.

47 Chasm Lake

The journey to Chasm Lake can be a life-changing experience, infecting national park visitors with a perpetual passion for hiking.

Start: Longs Peak Trailhead
Distance: 8.4 miles out and back
Hiking time: About 7 hours
Difficulty: Moderate
Trail surface: Dirt
Elevation: Trailhead, 9,400 feet; Chasm Lake, 11,760 feet
Other trail users: Equestrians to Chasm Lake Trail Junction
Canine compatibility: Dogs prohibited
Fees and permits: No fees or permits required

Trail contacts: Rocky Mountain National Park Backcountry Office, 1000 US 36, Estes Park 80517; (970) 586-1242; www.nps.gov/romo
Maps: USGS *Longs Peak*; Trails Illustrated *Longs Peak*
Highlights: Alpine tundra, view into Peacock Pool, Columbine Falls, Chasm Lake, view of east face of Longs Peak
Wildlife: Elk, mule deer, yellow-bellied marmots, pikas, red squirrels, mountain chickadees, white-tailed ptarmigan

Finding the trailhead: The turnoff to Longs Peak Trailhead leaves west from CO 7, 7.5 miles south of Estes Park at a sign indicating the Longs Peak Area. A mile from CO 7, a left turn leads to the Longs Peak Ranger Station and trailhead parking. **GPS:** N40 16.325' / W105 33.394'

The Hike

Most of the hike to Chasm Lake follows the same trail that leads to The Keyhole and Longs Peak but at a much less odious time of day. I do not believe that I can convince you to start for Chasm Lake at the same intimidating time you must leave for Longs Peak. I do, however, believe that such an early start would be a good idea, putting you on the lakeshore as alpenglow spreads down the peak's overwhelming east face. This wondrous experience would cause you to forget the pain of early rising should you actually bring yourself to do it.

If you can manage it, starting for Chasm Lake at least before sunrise takes you through unexciting lodgepole pine forest in the dark, when you are half asleep. If you wake up at tree line near dawn, long shadows thrown by twisted trees and alpine tundra in the rising sun begin the part of the hike you'll remember with considerable excitement that will last through the rest of the hike. Compared with reaching the top of Longs, Chasm Lake is a relatively (an important adverb) easy hike, mostly across exquisite alpine tundra bounded by exciting scenery, culminating in a stone amphitheater of unexcelled drama.

The Chasm Lake route is very popular. And its hikers use the same parking area as the throng headed up Longs—more encouragement for an early start. The Chasm Lake Trail branches left where the Longs Peak Trail bends right at the base of Mount Lady Washington. If light already fills the scene, with the steep-sided valley of Roaring

Columbine Falls tumble below Chasm Lake and the East Face of Longs Peak.

Fork below and the absolutely vertical east face of Longs Peak above, hikers can be forgiven for turning around at this point, believing the view cannot get better. But it can—and without much more effort.

When looking at a park map speckled by lakes named for native birds such as bluebird, chickadee, and ptarmigan, the name Peacock Pool below the trail may seem puzzling. But actually standing on the trail and looking down at the lake instantly erases any confusion, for the lake obviously looks like the "eye" at the end of a peacock's tail feather. Above, Columbine Falls drops dramatically from a shelf below the east face precipice. Most of the Chasm Lake Trail is very easy except where it crosses a steep snowbank present during much of the summer, a site of slips and bone-breaking falls. Do not become distracted from caution by the abundance of blue columbine, the state flower, among the surrounding rocks.

The trail ends in a high alpine meadow; Chasm Lake is hidden a short scramble above. The lakeshore spectacle is so overwhelming that first-time visitors should

Chasm Lake

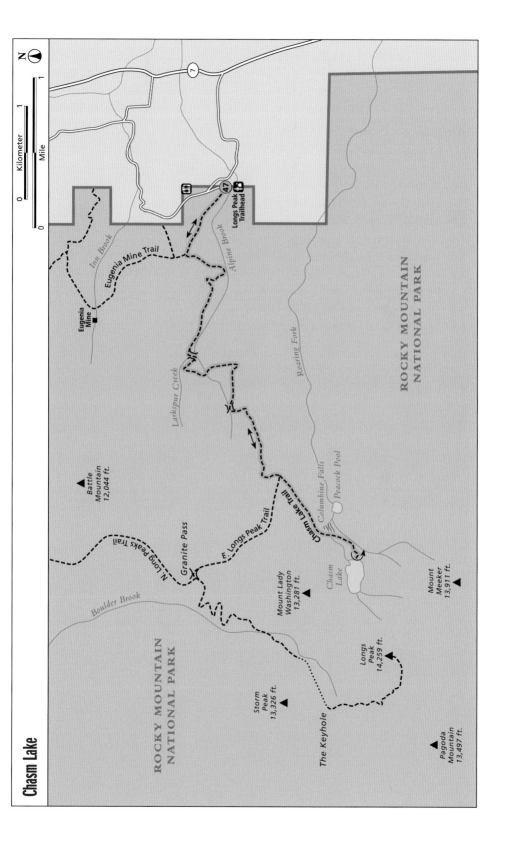

immediately sit down on a handy rock before gazing up. The huge scale is difficult to realize until you may notice tiny climbers looking down 2,500 feet from the summit. This sudden revelation of how high the cliff is can induce dizziness in even experienced first-time visitors—and provides a good excuse for transferring weight from your feet to higher up your anatomy.

Miles and Directions

0.0 Start at the Longs Peak Trailhead.

0.5 Climb left where the trail to Eugenia Mine goes right.

0.95 Approach Alpine Brook; the trail cuts away before reaching the water.

1.6 Cross a bridge over Larkspur Creek.

2.1 Now cross a bridge over Alpine Brook.

3.5 Reach the top of Mills Moraine and a junction where Chasm Lake Trail heads left above the valley of Roaring Fork.

4.2 Arrive at Chasm Lake. Return by the same route.

8.4 Celebrate a great hike back at the trailhead.

48 Twin Sisters Peaks

Hikers have long regarded Twin Sisters Peaks on the east side of the Tahosa Valley as a high platform from which to view higher wonders.

Start: Twin Sisters Trailhead
Distance: 7.4 miles out and back
Hiking time: About 6 hours
Difficulty: Moderate
Trail surface: Dirt
Elevation: Trailhead, 9,148 feet; Twin Sisters Peaks, 11,428 feet
Best season: Summer
Other trail users: Equestrians
Canine compatibility: Dogs prohibited
Fees and permits: No fees or permits required

Trail contacts: Rocky Mountain National Park Backcountry Office, 1000 US 36, Estes Park 80517; (970) 586-2141; www.nps.gov/romo
Maps: USGS *Longs Peak* and *Allens Park*; Trails Illustrated *Longs Peak*
Highlights: Twisted limber pines at tree line, rare dwarf columbine, outstanding views of Longs and nearby peaks
Wildlife: Mule deer, yellow-bellied marmots, mountain chickadees, pygmy nuthatches, Steller's jays

Finding the trailhead: From Estes Park, drive 6.3 miles south on CO 7 to a parking area across the road from Lily Lake. From Lily Lake parking area, drive through lodgepole pine forest up 0.4 mile of unpaved road to the Twin Sisters Trailhead. In winter, the unpaved road is closed and you must walk to the trailhead. **GPS:** N40 18.176' / W105 32.209'

The Hike

On the eastern edge of Rocky Mountain National Park, Twin Sisters is (are) a ridge of confusing plurals. On the same map you'll see the name Twin Sisters Peaks at three high points along a whole ridge named Twin Sisters Mountain. Travelers along the Tahosa Valley may care little about exactly what to call Twin Sisters when visual attention naturally pivots west to the gigantic glory of Longs Peak. Hikers, though, wind back and forth up Twin Sisters to surmount a viewing platform from which to admire higher hiking goals. Having dropped drastically along roughly parallel fractures in the earth's surface, the floor of the Tahosa Valley is out of the way, isolating the mighty 14,259-foot Longs Peak flanked by thirteener Mounts Meeker and Lady Washington. Thus the view from Twin Sisters appears to be from an aircraft.

Because of its strategic viewpoint, Twin Sisters was the site of a forest fire lookout tower reached by an elaborate switchbacked trail. Twin Sisters was added to the national park in 1917, just two years after the park's creation. But the trail weaves back and forth between Rocky Mountain National Park and Roosevelt National Forest. The fire tower was removed in 1977, having outlived its usefulness as a firefighting tool. Two years later, I noticed that its boxy silhouette had disappeared, so I quit pointing it out to hikers from below.

Twin Sisters Peaks

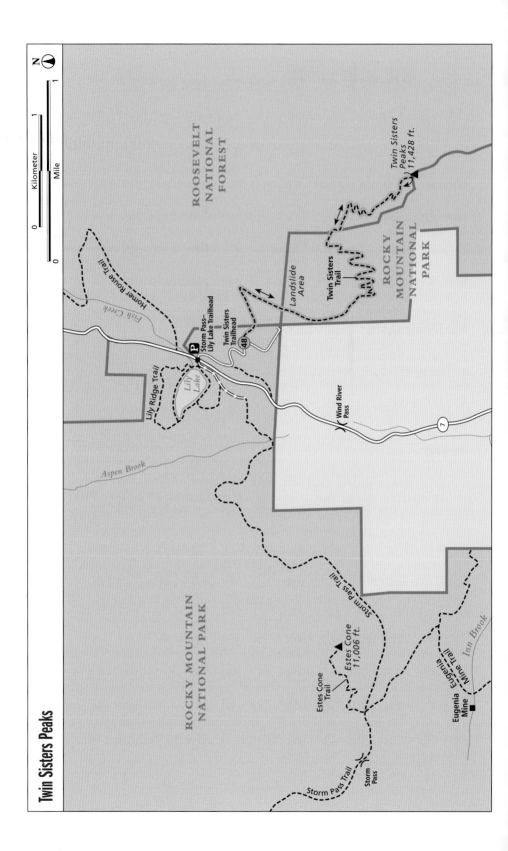

Sunset clouds reflect color above Twin Sisters.

Another change occurred when the National Park Service closed the lower part of the trail and substituted a new trailhead to avoid an ever-growing number of hikers crossing private land. A section of the new trail was obliterated by a landslide resulting from a gigantic rain/flood event in September 2013. Unwilling to surrender views from the top, hikers have pioneered various routes around and across the landslide. Below the popular western summit where the lookout tower once stood, a radio repeater uses the strategic location to facilitate communications for various government agencies.

Miles and Directions

0.0 Start at the Twin Sisters Trailhead.

1.0 Views west to Longs and other peaks begin to open through gaps in the forest.

1.3 Encounter an area disrupted by the landslide of September 2013.

1.6 After detouring around or across the landslide area, arrive back on the trail.

2.9 The trail rises above tree line.

3.7 The trail reaches the most popular of three summits. Return by the same route.

7.4 Arrive back at the trailhead.

49 Lily Lake

Lily Lake's level loop trail may be the easiest place in Rocky Mountain National Park to see a variety of woody plants—but no pondlilies.

Start: Lily Lake Trailhead
Distance: 0.8-mile loop (1.2-mile loop with detour along the Lily Ridge Trail)
Hiking time: About 0.5 hour
Difficulty: Easy
Trail surface: Packed gravel
Elevation: Trailhead, 8,927 feet; trail highpoint, 8,937 feet (9,030 feet for Lily Ridge loop)
Best season: Summer and fall
Other trail users: Wheelchairs
Canine compatibility: Dogs prohibited
Fees and permits: No fees or permits required

Trail contacts: Rocky Mountain National Park Backcountry Office, 1000 US 36, Estes Park 80517; (970) 586-1242; www.nps.gov/romo
Maps: USGS *Longs Peak*; Trails Illustrated *Longs Peak*
Highlights: Views of Mummy Range and Longs Peak, above-normal variety of woody plants
Wildlife: Elk, mule deer, beavers, muskrats, yellow-bellied marmots, chipmunks, mallard and ring-necked ducks, red-winged blackbirds, paedomorphic tiger salamanders

Finding the trailhead: From Estes Park, drive 6.3 miles south on CO 7 to Lily Lake. There are parking areas on both sides of the highway. **GPS:** N40 18.403' / W105 32.279'

The Hike

Lily Lake, or Lake of the Lilies, was smaller and shallower when tourist Isabella Bird mentioned it in her travel book, *A Lady's Life in the Rockies*, in 1873. A dam to enlarge the lake into a reservoir in 1915 made it too deep to support pondlilies. Before its acquisition by the national park in 1992, Lily Lake served as a movie set for the epic television miniseries *Centennial*, based on James A. Michener's novel of Colorado history.

Rocky Mountain National Park built a wheelchair-accessible trail at the lake, as well as a spur trail called the Lily Ridge Trail, which takes rock climbers closer to cliffs above the lake. The NPS also bolstered the strength of the dam it inherited with the lake just in time to survive the huge flood that occurred along the Front Range in September 2013. The popularity of this easily accessible enlarged lake exploded with park acquisition.

Lily Lake

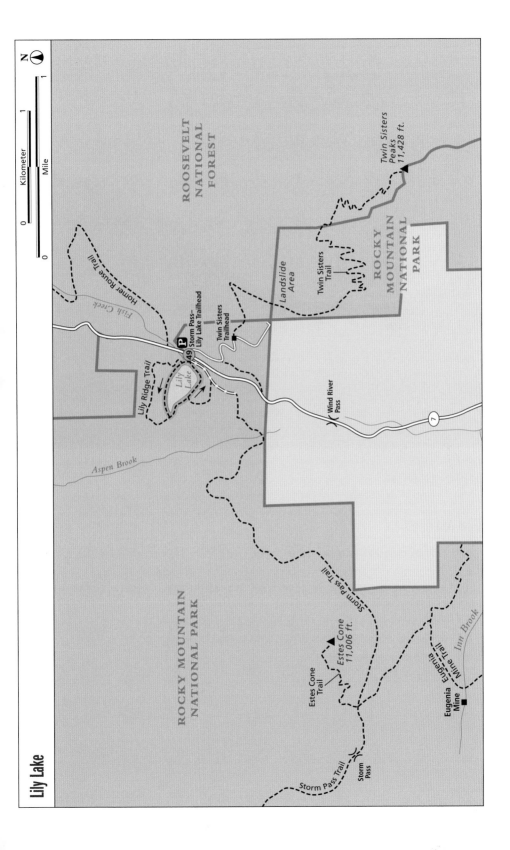

Lily Lake provides an easy-to-view variety of animals and plants in a wetlands environment, but no yellow pondlilies.

Miles and Directions

0.0 Start counterclockwise at the east end of Lily Lake.

0.1 Come to the east junction with detour up the Lily Ridge Trail. (**Note:** The Lily Ridge Trail, which is not wheelchair accessible, adds 100 feet elevation gain, 0.4 mile, and considerable variety to the loop.)

0.3 Reach the west end of Lily Lake; the Lily Ridge Trail climbs back east.

0.5 Trail junction connects with Storm Pass Trail and Estes Cone.

0.8 Arrive back at the trailhead.

50 Estes Cone

Estes Cone has several approaches. The shortest on public land begins at Longs Peak Trailhead. This approach also presents the most conical view of Estes Cone.

Start: Longs Peak Trailhead
Distance: 6.6 miles out and back
Hiking time: About 4 hours
Difficulty: Moderate
Trail surface: Dirt
Elevation: Trailhead, 9,400 feet; Estes Cone, 11,006 feet
Best season: Summer
Other trail users: Equestrians on Storm Pass Trail
Canine compatibility: Dogs prohibited

Fees and permits: No fees or permits required
Trail contacts: Rocky Mountain National Park Backcountry Office, 1000 US 36, Estes Park 80517; (970) 586-1242; www.nps.gov/romo
Maps: USGS *Longs Peak*; Trails Illustrated *Longs Peak*
Highlights: Eugenia Mine remnants, limber pines at Storm Pass, excellent view from summit, dwarf columbine
Wildlife: Mule deer, chipmunks, golden-mantled ground squirrels, mountain chickadees

Finding the trailhead: The turnoff to Longs Peak Trailhead leaves west from CO 7, 7.5 miles south of Estes Park at a sign indicating Longs Peak Area. A mile from CO 7, a left turn leads to the Longs Peak Ranger Station and trailhead parking. **GPS:** N40 16.325' / W105 33.394'

The Hike

Dating from at least as far back as the 1870s, the name Estes Cone has described the conical shape of the ninety-first highest peak in Rocky Mountain National Park. The Arapaho lumped it with nearby prominences as Three Buttes.

If it did not have such a distinctive shape (caused by erosion of an isolated mountain) when seen from the Tahosa Valley, Estes Cone, at only 11,006 feet, likely would have no name. But if well located, even the small can be important. Estes Cone is strategically positioned to provide excellent views of dramatic and interesting vistas in all directions.

There are several approaches to Estes Cone, but it appears conical mainly when viewed from the south. The most conical appearance is also from the shortest trail—the path from Longs Peak Trailhead, past Eugenia Mine, through Moore Park, and on to Storm Pass. From the trailhead, the initial part of the hike is a stroll through lodgepole pine woods to Eugenia Mine. At the mine site, a few miscellaneous remnants indicate where a 1905 mine sought wealth much too far north of the Colorado mineral belt exploited during the last part of the nineteenth century. Rocky Mountain National Park is a national treasure partly because so little mineral treasure turned up within the future park boundaries. Many people find the hike to Eugenia Mine dull because they are comparing it to Chasm Lake and Longs Peak, which are as far removed from dull as anyone is likely to experience.

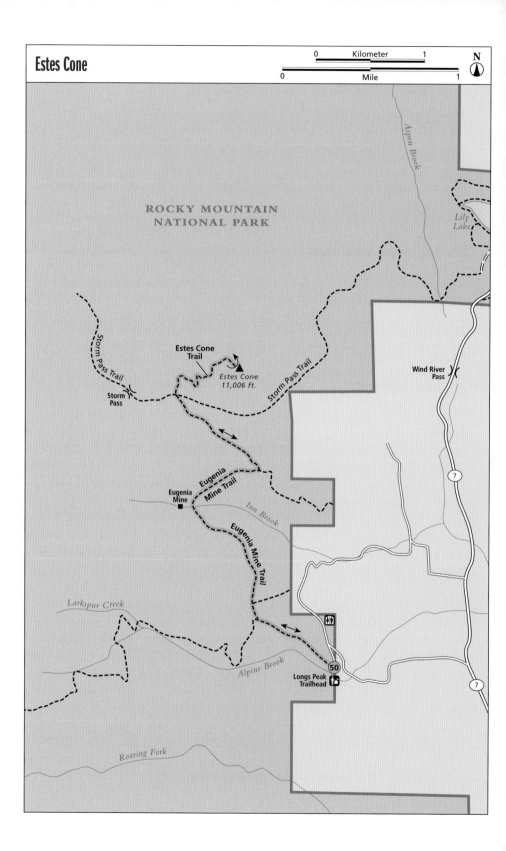

ROCKY MOUNTAIN
NATIONAL PARK

Aspen Brook

Lily Lake

Storm Pass Trail

Estes Cone
Trail

Storm Pass Trail

Estes Cone
11,006 ft.

Storm
Pass

Wind River
Pass

Eugenia Mine Trail

Eugenia
Mine

Inn Brook

Eugenia Mine Trail

7

Larkspur Creek

Alpine Brook

50

Longs Peak
Trailhead

7

Roaring Fork

0   Kilometer   1

0   Mile   1

N

Estes Cone derived its conical shape from erosion of a relatively low, isolated mountain.

After however long it takes to satisfy your curiosity at Eugenia Mine, continue north to a pleasant meadow, Moore Park. The floral display here can be very memorable. Aspen and deciduous shrubs replace lodgepole pines for a short distance. A left turn at a trail junction leads up to the Storm Pass Trail. Grand limber pines take over from lodgepoles. A large cairn (some *Homo constructus* was bored and busy) marks a clear right turn across the Storm Pass Trail to ascend Estes Cone. The path at first is gentle and clear, rising to a less-clear path on steeper terrain. The last stretch is a rock scramble to the top. The benefits of the distant view have become clearer than the path. But look down as well as out, careful not to tread on rare dwarf columbine near the top.

Miles and Directions

0.0   Start at the Longs Peak Trailhead, and begin the hike to the park's ninety-first highest peak among the throng headed for its highest. Early arrival will help ease the parking dilemma.

0.5   Leave nearly all other hikers behind when you turn right for Eugenia Mine.

1.3   Arrive at the Eugenia Mine site.

1.9   Enter the meadow at Moore Park.

2.5   Cross the Storm Pass Trail to climb Estes Cone. (So many hikers complain about the toughness of this part of the trail that I am about to believe them, although I may hold the record for most ascents of this particular peak.)

3.3   Scramble to the top of Estes Cone. Return the same way to Longs Peak Trailhead.

6.6   Arrive back at the trailhead.

Wild Basin

51 Allens Park Trail to Calypso Cascades

Lovely Calypso Cascades are named for the equally lovely calypso orchids that bloom nearby in July.

Start: Allens Park Trailhead
Distance: 6.2 miles out and back
Hiking time: About 5 hours
Difficulty: Moderately easy
Trail surface: Dirt
Elevation: Trailhead, 8,520 feet; Calypso Cascades, 9,200 feet
Best season: Summer
Other trail users: Equestrians
Canine compatibility: Dogs prohibited
Fees and permits: No fees or permits required

Trail contacts: Rocky Mountain National Park Backcountry Office, 1000 US 36, Estes Park 80517; (970) 586-1242; www.nps.gov/romo
Map: USGS *Allens Park*
Highlights: Area burned by the forest fire of 1978, interesting trail building, views of Longs Peak, Calypso Cascades (3.1 miles)
Wildlife: Mule deer, red squirrels, chipmunks, golden-mantled ground squirrels, mountain chickadees, Steller's jays, gray jays

Finding the trailhead: From CO 7, turn south on Business 7 (Washington Street) into the town of Allenspark. Drive 1 block and turn right onto unpaved CR 90. After 0.7 mile, bear left (uphill) on South Skinner Road. After 0.5 mile turn right on Meadow Mountain Drive and continue a short distance to the Allens Park Trailhead parking area, on the right. **GPS:** N40 09.924' / W105 11.180'

The Hike

According to ancient Greek legend as recorded in *The Odyssey* Calypso was a nymph who bewitched the voyager Odysseus into staying on her island for seven years while he was trying to get home from the Trojan War to his wife, Penelope. Modern travelers on Wild Basin trails likely do not face this hazard. If you are gone for seven years, something else is amiss.

However, in summer 1917 a leopard skin–clad nymph was reputedly roaming Wild Basin. A Michigan college student named Agnes Lowe evidently wanted to prove that she, as a representative of modern womanhood, could survive in the wilds. The *Denver Post* dubbed her "the Modern Eve" while publishing numerous photos of her bold, for that era, attire. This publicity stunt to gain attention for the new national park continued for months, with no one, understandably, anxious to take credit for it. National Park Service officials in Washington, DC, did not find the incident amusing—not a suitable event for holy ground. In a photo of Enos Mills shaking hands with Eve in her leopard skin, the "Father of Rocky Mountain National Park" looks embarrassed, as though he would rather be atop Longs Peak. If the Modern Eve spent time, as claimed, deep in Wild Basin at Thunder Lake, she surely would have passed Calypso Cascades, too gorgeous to miss.

Calypso Cascades tumble through a classic, mature subalpine forest that survived the Ouzel Fire.

Wild Basin really did not need publicity stunts to gain popularity, as indicated by crowds on the streamside trail to Calypso Cascades. The trail from the Allens Park Trailhead is much less heavily used, perhaps because few hikers can remember whether the trail is spelled as one word or two. The US Postal Service uses the one-word spelling; the United States Geological Survey uses two. I sometimes have trouble keeping the spellings straight, a problem I am certain I share with other Wild Basin fans. Alonso Allen started this problem by showing up to do some unsuccessful prospecting for gold in 1859.

Much of the upper trail from Allenspark (post office spelling, I am pretty sure) passes through country renewing itself after a fire generated by lightning in 1978. Sweeping east along the side of Meadow Mountain from Ouzel Lake, the fire stopped just inside the park boundary after causing predictable anxiety among homeowners in the Allenspark community. The fire opened views of high peaks surrounding Wild Basin. The sunny areas provide good grazing for elk and deer. The small pink calypso orchids, though, require damp shade, still preserved where fire skipped over the deep woods at Calypso Cascades.

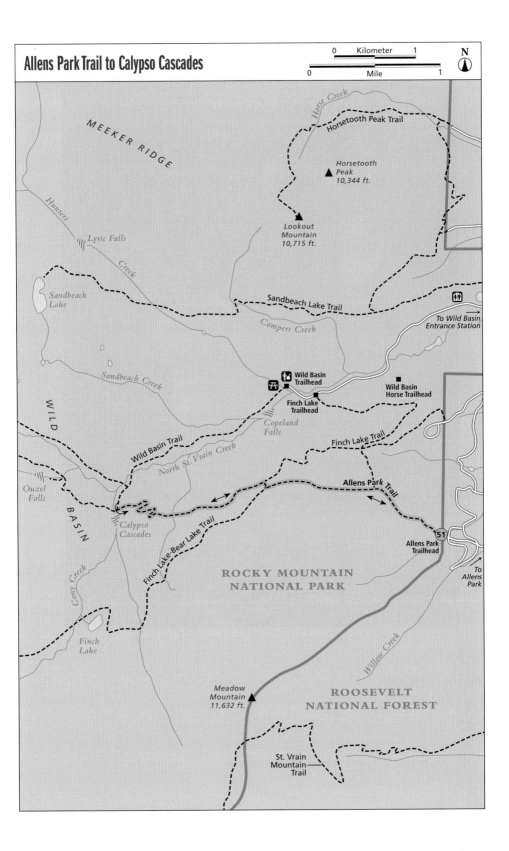

Allens Park Trail to Calypso Cascades

0   Kilometer   1

0   Mile   1

N

MEEKER RIDGE

Horse Creek

Horsetooth Peak Trail

▲ Horsetooth
Peak
10,344 ft.

▲ Lookout
Mountain
10,715 ft.

Hunters

Lyric Falls

Creek

Sandbeach
Lake

Sandbeach Lake Trail

Campers Creek

To Wild Basin
Entrance Station

Sandbeach Creek

Wild Basin
Trailhead

Wild Basin
Horse Trailhead

Finch Lake
Trailhead

W I L D

*Copeland
Falls*

Wild Basin Trail

Finch Lake Trail

North St. Vrain Creek

Ouzel
Falls

Allens Park Trail

B A S I N

*Calypso
Cascades*

Finch Lake–Bear Lake Trail

51

Allens Park
Trailhead

Cony Creek

ROCKY MOUNTAIN
NATIONAL PARK

To
Allens
Park

Finch
Lake

Willow Creek

Meadow
Mountain ▲
11,632 ft.

ROOSEVELT
NATIONAL FOREST

St. Vrain
Mountain
Trail

Calypso Cascades are named for small calypso orchids that bloom nearby in early July.

Miles and Directions

0.0 Start at the Allens Park Trailhead.

0.7 The trail drops right; continue ascending Allens Park Trail to the left.

1.6 Come to aptly named Confusion Junction; continue straight across the Finch Lake Trail.

3.1 Reach Calypso Cascades. Return the way you came.

6.2 Arrive back at the trailhead.

52 Finch Lake

This is one of the many hiking destinations in Wild Basin named for wildlife.

Start: Allens Park Trailhead
Distance: 7.6 miles out and back
Hiking time: About 6 hours
Difficulty: Moderate
Trail surface: Dirt
Elevation: Trailhead, 8,520 feet; Finch Lake, 9,912 feet
Other trail users: Equestrians
Canine compatibility: Dogs prohibited
Fees and permits: No fees or permits required

Trail contacts: Rocky Mountain National Park Backcountry Office, 1000 US 36, Estes Park 80517; (970) 586-1242; www.nps.gov/romo
Maps: USGS *Allens Park*; Trails Illustrated *Longs Peak*
Highlights: Forest fire of 1978, interesting trail building, views of Longs Peak, Mount Copeland
Wildlife: Red squirrel, chipmunk, mountain chickadee, Steller's jay, gray jay, mule deer

Finding the trailhead: From CO 7, turn south on Business 7 (Washington Street) into the town of Allenspark. Drive 1 block and turn right onto unpaved CR 90. After 0.7 mile, bear left uphill onto South Skinner Road. After 0.5 mile turn right onto Meadow Mountain Drive and continue a short distance to the Allens Park Trailhead parking area on the right. (No, I did not make a mistake in spelling.) **GPS:** N40 09.924' / W105 11.180'

The Hike

Wild Basin has been splashed with many bird names in seemingly random fashion. The presence of a bird name does not necessarily mean that hikers will see that particular creature near that named point. At Finch Lake, the chances of seeing Cassin's finches are good, less so house finches and nil for brown-capped rosy finches in summer, but maybe in winter. Finches by other names—pine grosbeak, red crossbill, or pine siskin—also may turn up at Finch Lake. The main feature of finches is that they have bills particularly suited to open whatever seeds they are adapted to eat. Obviously there are many different species of finches, because there are many different types of seeds.

Particular habitats rather than particular names predict success in spotting particular wildlife species. Wild Basin bird names on maps mean nothing except perhaps that prior to the national park's creation in 1915, mapmakers assumed that filling up blank spaces might improve chances of the wild in Wild Basin being preserved.

The easiest trail to Finch Lake is not from the Finch Lake Trailhead, near the road's end in Wild Basin. The Allens Park Trail is 0.7 mile shorter and requires 56 feet less elevation gain than the Finch Lake Trail. On the other hand, spelling can be a problem when identifying photos from this hike. The National Park Service and United States Geological Survey call it the Allens Park Trail (two words) because it departs from Allenspark (one word according to the US Postal Service). The sign

marking the Allens Park Trailhead is in the national park, whereas the parking for the trailhead is a few feet away in dedicated open space in a residential subdivision. (If the small parking lot is full, do not park anywhere that blocks driveways or access to the subdivision water system.) Unsurprisingly, the second trail junction on the way to Finch Lake has been informally dubbed Confusion Junction by NPS rangers.

The first trail junction, 0.8 mile from the trailhead, is not confusing. It departs the Allens Park Trail downhill to the right where it intersects with the Finch Lake Trail climbing up from the Finch Lake Trailhead. Going down this appealing trail will increase your distance to Finch Lake by 0.3 mile, and of course you will need to regain altitude. You know that you are unlikely to go down to get up to Finch Lake, so the temptation to go wrong at this point is slight. Moreover, the correct path to the left is gentle of grade at this first junction.

The next junction is Confusion, where the confusion is rather mysterious. The way up to Finch Lake seems as though it should be clear; go left, hard left. Do not meander straight ahead to Calypso Cascades. Definitely do not cut hard right, which leads down to the Finch Lake Trailhead. In all likelihood, the only thing you will find confusing about Confusion Junction is why some people have found it confusing.

Now that you are at last on the Finch Lake Trail, after 0.25 mile you will encounter a forest fire corridor that extends for approximately another 0.25 mile. This fire, started by lightning in 1978, burned through a broad band of forest on the flank of Meadow Mountain, the name of which now is much more accurate than it was prior to 1978. Much to the relief of homeowners in Allenspark, just outside the park boundary, the fire finally was contained within the national park. Some wildlife species did lose their homes, hence their lives. For instance, the fire was not good for most finches. On the other hand, it did open more feeding habitat for deer and elk.

Thus the fire was said to be good for wildlife. This is true only if you define wildlife as species that are legal to shoot after obtaining a license. By this definition, there is no wildlife in Rocky Mountain National Park—a revelation that no doubt would startle the park superintendent, who noticed some nice wildlife through the office window a few minutes ago. Fire can benefit elk and deer while seriously harming ruby-crowned kinglets, northern three-toed woodpeckers, and red-backed voles. In the wilds, as everywhere else, change is constant, harming some and helping others.

After crossing small streams, the Finch Lake Trail leads over a small ridge and descends to Finch Lake. Finch often is calm enough to reflect massive Copeland Mountain (13,176 feet high). The forest surrounding the lake is mainly Engelmann spruce and subalpine fir, home to pine grosbeaks and pine siskins. (I told you the names mean nothing.)

◀ *The red crossbill has the most remarkable beak of the various finches that may be seen along the trail to Finch Lake.*

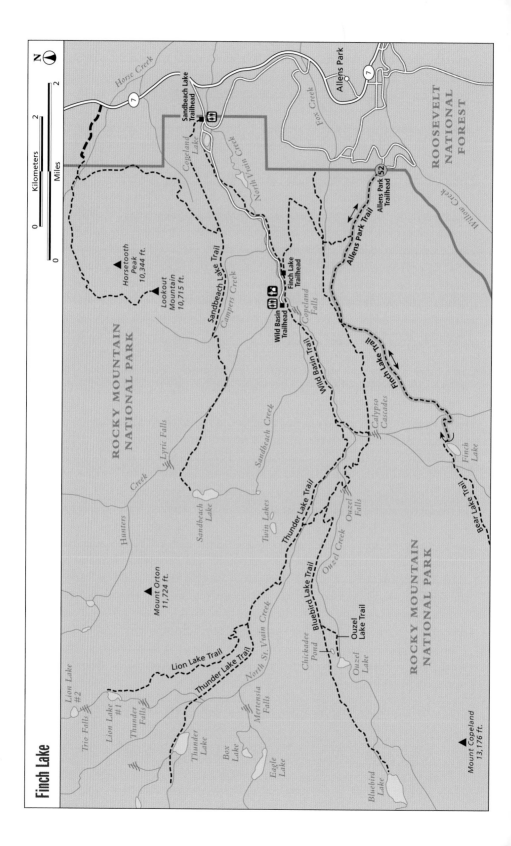

Finch Lake

N

Kilometers
0 — 1 — 2

Miles
0 — 1 — 2

ROCKY MOUNTAIN NATIONAL PARK

ROOSEVELT NATIONAL FOREST

Horse Creek

Allens Park

7

Sandbeach Lake Trailhead

Copeland Lake

Fox Creek

North Vain Creek

Sandbeach Lake Trail

Campers Creek

Horsetooth Peak 10,344 ft.

Lookout Mountain 10,715 ft.

Wild Basin Trailhead

Finch Lake Trailhead

Allens Park Trail

Allens Park Trailhead

52

Willow Creek

Lyric Falls

Hunters Creek

Sandbeach Lake

Mount Orton 11,724 ft.

Sandbeach Creek

Wild Basin Trail

Copeland Falls

Finch Lake Trail

Twin Lakes

Thunder Lake Trail

Calypso Cascades

Lion Lake Trail

Thunder Lake Trail

North St. Vrain Creek

Bluebird Lake Trail

Chickadee Pond

Ouzel Creek

Ouzel Falls

Finch Lake

Bear Lake Trail

Lion Lake #2

Lion Lake #1

Trio Falls

Thunder Falls

Thunder Lake

Box Lake

Eagle Lake

Mertensia Falls

Ouzel Lake Trail

Ouzel Lake

ROCKY MOUNTAIN NATIONAL PARK

Mount Copeland 13,176 ft.

Bluebird Lake

Miles and Directions

0.0 Start at the Allens Park Trailhead and begin hiking among the pines.

0.9 Continue left past the trail that heads down to the right.

1.7 Do not be confused by Confusion Junction. Take the trail farthest to the left, toward Finch Lake.

3.8 Reach Finch Lake, where the best photo point likely is where you first encounter the lake, reflecting (if unruffled by wind) Mount Copeland. Return the way you came.

7.6 Arrive back at the trailhead.

53 Ouzel Falls

A popular hike in all seasons or weather situations, the trail to Ouzel Falls follows whitewater streams most of the way.

Start: Wild Basin Trailhead
Distance: 5.4 miles out and back
Hiking time: About 5 hours
Difficulty: Moderately easy
Trail surface: Dirt
Elevation: Trailhead, 8,500 feet; Calypso Cascades, 9,200 feet; Ouzel Falls, 9,450 feet
Best season: Summer
Other trail users: Equestrians
Canine compatibility: Dogs prohibited
Fees and permits: National park entrance fee

Trail contacts: Rocky Mountain National Park Backcountry Office, 1000 US 36, Estes Park 80517; (970) 586-1242; www.nps.gov/romo
Maps: USGS *Allens Park*; Trails Illustrated *Longs Peak*
Highlights: Abundant wildflowers (first 0.5 mile), noisy whitewater stream (first 1.3 miles), Calypso Cascades (1.8 miles), regrowth after 1978 forest fire (2.0 miles), Ouzel Falls (2.7 miles)
Wildlife: Mule deer, red squirrels, chipmunks, yellow-bellied marmots, golden-mantled ground squirrels, water ouzels (dippers)

Finding the trailhead: From Estes Park follow CO 7 south more than 11 miles and turn right onto a well-marked road into Wild Basin (2.3 miles are unpaved and narrow). **GPS:** N40 12.513' / W105 33.658'

The Hike

Ouzel seems an odd name for a creek, falls, lake, and peak in Wild Basin. But to wild bird enthusiasts the word labels a chunky gray bird somewhat smaller than a robin and shaped something like a wren. The odd but fun word (OO z'l) is derived from an Anglo-Saxon word for a blackbird, which makes no sense to anyone with any notion of what a blackbird of any species looks like. However, the European ring ouzel is a black bird that vaguely resembles another bird species the English call a water ouzel. Following the English precedent, as American birders once did slavishly, the gray bird common to whitewater streams in the West was called a water ouzel—as it still often is called as an alternative to its very descriptive name of dipper.

Because of its entertaining behavior of flying into fierce currents to hunt for tiny aquatic creatures to eat and then landing on a rock protruding from the water to do a dipping, bobbing dance, the water ouzel was the favorite bird of John Muir, America's most famous exponent of wilderness preservation in the late nineteenth and early twentieth centuries. Muir was the inspiration and mentor for Enos Mills,

Ouzel Falls is an exciting place to view water ouzels, although these remarkably entertaining birds are common in all whitewater streams in Wild Basin. ▶

Dipper or water ouzel (Cinclus mexicanus).

"Father of Rocky Mountain National Park." (For more information on Mills, see the Enos Mills sidebar in Hike 31.) While hiking in California with Muir, Mills doubtless heard much about this marvelous water bird and applied its name to water features in Wild Basin. The dramatic peak above Ouzel Lake came to be called Ouzel Lake Peak, later shortened to Ouzel Peak.

Climbers will find no ouzels on Ouzel Peak, because dippers never leave the area above or immediately adjacent to streams or sometimes mountain lakes. Ouzel Falls perhaps is the most exciting place to see ouzels in this national park. But you're likely to see them anywhere along whitewater streams that define hiking in Wild Basin, while walking along the Big Thompson or Fall Rivers in downtown Estes Park (dippers sometimes nest on bridge girders instead of on streamside rock ledges), or while driving down the Big Thompson Canyon (where of course you are paying close attention to the curving road).

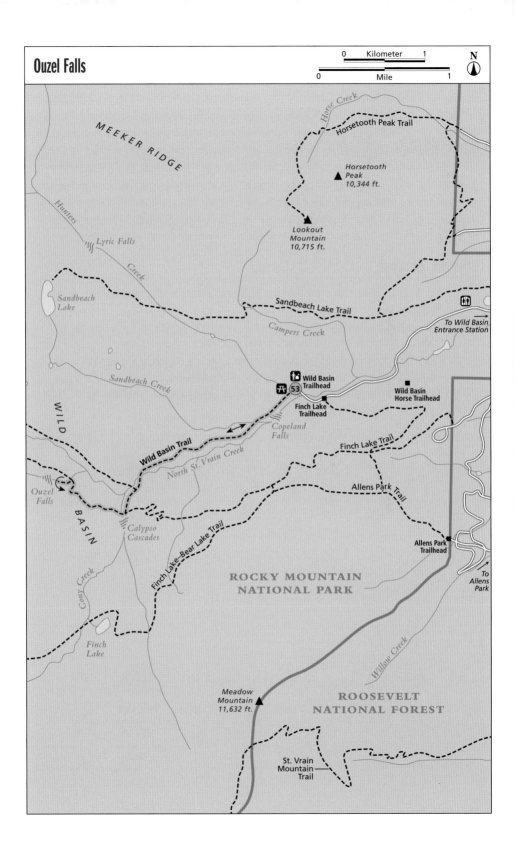

Ouzel Falls

0 Kilometer 1
0 Mile 1

N

MEEKER RIDGE

Horse Creek

Horsetooth Peak Trail

Horsetooth Peak
10,344 ft.

Lookout Mountain
10,715 ft.

Hunters Creek

Lyric Falls

Sandbeach Lake

Sandbeach Lake Trail

Campers Creek

To Wild Basin Entrance Station

Sandbeach Creek

WILD

Wild Basin Trailhead

53

Finch Lake Trailhead

Wild Basin Horse Trailhead

BASIN

Wild Basin Trail

Copeland Falls

North St. Vrain Creek

Finch Lake Trail

Ouzel Falls

Allens Park Trail

Calypso Cascades

Finch Lake–Bear Lake Trail

Allens Park Trailhead

To Allens Park

Cony Creek

ROCKY MOUNTAIN
NATIONAL PARK

Finch Lake

Willow Creek

Meadow Mountain
11,632 ft.

ROOSEVELT
NATIONAL FOREST

St. Vrain Mountain Trail

John Muir's ecstatic 1894 account of the water ouzel might be the most famous writing about any American bird. I find Muir's ending a puzzle, however, because it reflects an attitude toward ouzel habitat—whitewater streams—that is totally unfamiliar to my experience. Today such streams are extremely popular; people literally will risk their lives to be near such watercourses to watch their action and listen to their turbulence. It is possible that Muir and Mills, and others with similar aesthetic sensibilities, reversed society's negative attitude toward wilderness as particularly represented by wild water inhabited by ouzels. Muir doubtless would claim that the entertaining ouzels have helped change our perceptions "... throughout the whole of their beautiful lives interpreting all that we in our unbelief call terrible in the utterances of torrents and storms as only varied expressions of God's eternal love."

Miles and Directions

0.0 Start from the south side of the Wild Basin Trailhead parking lot and cross bridge onto the Wild Basin Trail.

1.8 Arrive at Calypso Cascades. The trail from the Allens Park Trailhead comes in from the left; follow the bridges and trail to the right toward Ouzel Falls.

2.7 Reach Ouzel Creek crossing. The falls are visible to the left, but the view obtained by climbing up to the base of the falls is definitely worth the effort. Retrace your path to the trailhead.

5.4 Arrive back at the trailhead.

54 Lion Lake #1

Lion Lake is a fun pun transitioning from valuing mountain lakes as reservoirs to appreciating their scenic and spiritual values.

Start: Wild Basin Trailhead
Distance: 13.4 miles out and back
Hiking time: About 12 hours
Difficulty: Moderately difficult
Trail surface: Dirt
Elevation: Trailhead, 8,500 feet; Lion Lake #1, 11,065 feet
Fees and permits: National park entrance fee
Trail contacts: Rocky Mountain National Park Backcountry Office; 1000 US 36, Estes Park 80517; (970) 586-1242; www.nps.gov/romo

Maps: USGS *Allens Park*; Trails Illustrated *Longs Peak*
Highlights: Abundant wildflowers, noisy whitewater streams, Copeland Falls, Calypso Cascades, regrowth after 1978 forest fire, Ouzel Falls, Lion Lake #1
Wildlife: Mule deer, red squirrels, chipmunks, yellow-bellied marmots, golden-mantled ground squirrels, water ouzels (dippers), mountain chickadees, ruby-crowned kinglets

Finding the trailhead: From Estes Park, follow CO 7 south more than 11 miles and turn onto a well-marked road into Wild Basin (2.3 miles are unpaved and narrow).
GPS: N40 12.513' / W105 33.658'

The Hike

Perhaps a mountain lion will appear at Lion Lake #1, or a bear at Bear Lake, or a cub at Cub Lake, but don't count on it. On the other hand, if you have a long telephoto lens, lug it along just in case. There are two Lion Lakes. The trail stops at #1, which is the prettier, with a dramatic view of pointy Mount Alice.

In 1923 park superintendent Roger Toll decided that the former label designating these lakes as reservoirs for Lyons, a town on the plains, was not appropriate. Evidently, superintendents at that time could change names, and he did. With a clever play on words, Lyons Reservoirs became Lion Lakes.

Mountain lions originally ranged throughout the Western Hemisphere more broadly than any other mammal except humans. That does not mean, however, that lions (cougars, catamounts, pumas, and thirty-some other names) are commonly seen, which may be just as well because humans are approximately the same size as this long-tailed cat's favorite prey—deer. The opening of Wild Basin woods by the lightning-caused, 1,000-plus-acre Ouzel Fire of 1978 may have increased lion habitat by providing lions with more deer to eat in the burned areas. These areas became more bushy and grassy, hence better feeding ground for deer than are thick woods. Lions travel so far that they can turn up just about anywhere in natural settings. But actually sighting one of these rare symbols of wilderness is very unusual.

Mountain lion cubs are very unlikely to feed on people at Lion Lake #1 or anywhere else.

Do not be overly concerned; it is certain that many more people have been observed unaware by lions than lions have been observed by people. Do not allow children to run ahead or lag behind out of sight on any trail. The two people killed in Colorado by mountain lions in recent memory were both children left temporarily alone. Adults have been attacked but, as of this writing, have managed to fight off the lions and survive. Standard advice if you encounter a lion that looks hungry (they *all* look hungry) are to talk firmly to the beast, make yourself look as big as possible (for instance, by spreading a jacket wide with outstretched arms), back slowly away (do *not* turn and run), and fight viciously if attacked. (Do *not* "play dead" or you soon will not be playing.) Throwing rocks or large sticks might help, if you can grab them without bending over.

Lion Lake #1

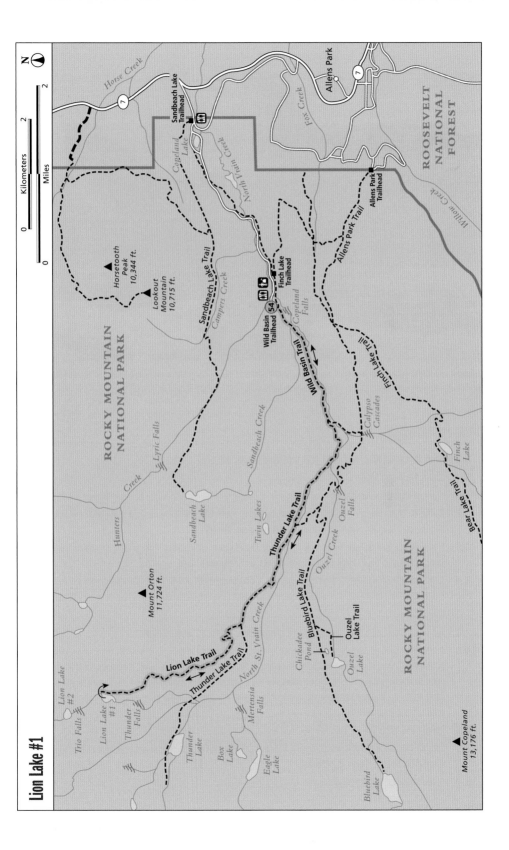

Mountain lions like this mother and her nearly grown cub provided a substitute name for lakes once identified as water sources for the town of Lyons down on the plains.

Miles and Directions

0.0   Start this long hike early at the Wild Basin Trailhead.

1.5   Cross North St. Vrain Creek on a bridge.

1.9   View of Calypso Cascades.

2.7   Come to a crossing of Ouzel Creek below Ouzel Falls. The falls are visible from the crossing but much more impressive from a short walk up the hill.

3.2   The trail splits. The left-hand trail heads to Ouzel Lake, Chickadee Pond, and Bluebird Lake. The right-hand trail leads to the Lion Lakes and Thunder Lake.

3.6   A shortcut trail comes in from the right at a crossing of North St. Vrain Creek; continue left.

4.9   The trail splits. Thunder Lake Trail heads left. Lion Lakes Trail (hikers only) goes right on an easy grade.

7.1   Arrive at Lion Lake #1. Return to the bridge over North St. Vrain Creek.

10.6   Arrive at a bridge over North St. Vrain Creek. Do not cross it unless you wish to revisit Ouzel Falls and Calypso Cascades (light for photos at the falls and cascades might be better than in the morning due to afternoon overcast skies). Otherwise bear left on a shortcut past several backcountry campsites to rejoin the Wild Basin Trail. (The shortcut cuts 0.8 mile off the return trip.)

11.9   Rejoin the Wild Basin Trail.

13.1   Detour toward North St. Vrain Creek to view Copeland Falls, which likely will be prettier in afternoon than in morning light.

13.4   Arrive back at the trailhead.

55 Bluebird Lake

Ouzels, chickadees, bluebirds—it's a wonder that Wild Basin was not named Bird Basin.

Start: Wild Basin Trailhead
Distance: 13.0 miles out and back
Hiking time: About 12 hours
Difficulty: Moderately difficult
Trail surface: Dirt
Elevation: Trailhead, 8,500 feet; Bluebird Lake, 10,978 feet
Best season: Summer
Other trail users: Equestrian until final haul up to Bluebird Lake
Canine compatibility: Dogs prohibited
Fees and permits: National park entrance fee

Trail contacts: Rocky Mountain National Park Backcountry Office, 1000 US 36, Estes Park 80517; (970) 586-1242; www.nps.gov/romo
Maps: USGS *Allens Park*; Trails Illustrated *Longs Peak*
Highlights: Abundant wildflowers, noisy white-water streams, Calypso Cascades, Ouzel Falls, Ouzel Lake, Chickadee Pond, Bluebird Lake
Wildlife: Mule deer, red squirrels, chipmunks, yellow-bellied marmots, golden-mantled ground squirrels, water ouzels (dippers)

Finding the trailhead: From Estes Park, follow CO 7 south more than 11 miles and turn right onto a well-marked road into Wild Basin (2.3 miles are unpaved and narrow) **GPS:** N40 12.513' / W105 33.658'

The Hike

Since likely the 1870s, the valley drained by North St. Vrain Creek appropriately has been called Wild Basin. Notable early Estes Park resident Joe Mills drew a map of Wild Basin from the top of Longs Peak and called it "Land of Many Waters." His more notable brother Enos called one of these waters Ouzel Lake. In 1911 botanist William Cooper published a map that, no surprise, applied flower names to scenic features, such as Calypso Cascades, but added even more bird names to the landscape. Although Wild Basin is no more watery or birdy than other areas of the national park, the labeling of its aqueous features with bird names seems a pleasant system.

A ladybird beetle crawls across a snow or glacier lily between Ouzel and Bluebird Lakes.

Yellow pondlilies cover Ouzel Lake below Ouzel and Mahana peaks.

Above the noise of Ouzel Falls and Ouzel Creek, hikers are almost certain to hear the raspy *chick-a-dee-dee-dee* call of the mountain chickadee. Black-capped chickadees are around too, but much less common. Along the long trail to Bluebird Lake, a 0.5-mile spur leads to Ouzel Lake, with its pondlilies and views of Ouzel and Mahana Peaks—definitely worth the detour. Beyond the spur to Ouzel Lake, the Bluebird Lake Trail passes Chickadee Pond, where you're likely to encounter the popular and friendly little bird with a black cap and black line through its eye.

Beyond yet more remnants of the 1978 Ouzel Fire, pause from looking for birds to watch for spectacular yellow glacier lilies emerging near melting snowbanks. The maintained trail ends at Bluebird Lake, large now but once even larger behind a concrete dam removed by the National Park Service in a mighty engineering effort in 1988. Rock-rimmed Bluebird Lake's appearance was not much marred by the lowering of the lake level, which has left a "bathtub ring" around other park lakes rescued from reservoir status. Neither the uncommon western bluebird, with its rusty breast and back, nor the very common mountain bluebird is likely to fly by Bluebird Lake. Both are birds of lower altitude. Around Estes Park, the magnificent mountain

Bluebird Lake

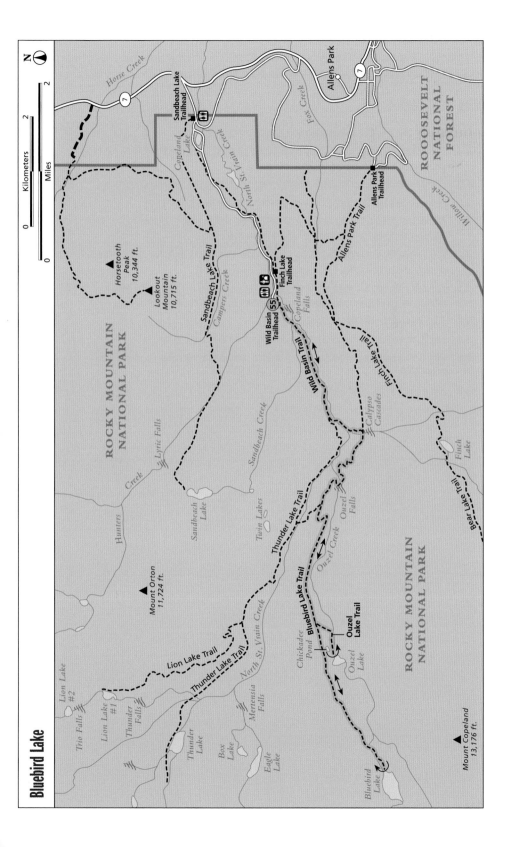

N

Kilometers
0   2

Miles
0   2

Horse Creek

7

Sandbeach Lake Trailhead

Copeland Lake

Allens Park

7

ROOOSEVELT NATIONAL FOREST

Allens Park Trailhead

Willow Creek

Fox Creek

North St. Vrain Creek

ROCKY MOUNTAIN NATIONAL PARK

Horsetooth Peak
10,344 ft.

Lookout Mountain
10,715 ft.

Sandbeach Lake Trail

Campers Creek

Finch Lake Trailhead

Wild Basin Trailhead

55

Copeland Falls

Wild Basin Trail

Finch Lake Trail

Allens Park Trail

Calypso Cascades

Finch Lake

Bear Lake Trail

Sandbeach Creek

Sandbeach Lake

Twin Lakes

Thunder Lake Trail

Ouzel Falls

Ouzel Creek

Ouzel Lake

Ouzel Lake Trail

Bluebird Lake Trail

Chickadee Pond

Lyric Falls

Hunters Creek

Mount Orton
11,724 ft.

Lion Lake Trail

Thunder Lake Trail

North St. Vrain Creek

ROCKY MOUNTAIN NATIONAL PARK

Mount Copeland
13,176 ft.

Lion Lake #2

Trio Falls

Lion Lake #1

Thunder Falls

Mertensia Falls

Thunder Lake

Box Lake

Eagle Lake

Bluebird Lake

bluebird is a common resident of bird boxes where natural holes in tree trunks are not available. These birds are tough to miss.

Miles and Directions

0.0   Start at the Wild Basin Trailhead and begin a long hike.

0.3   Detour toward North St. Vrain Creek to view Copeland Falls, which will likely be more photogenic under overcast skies on the return trip.

1.5   Cross North St. Vrain Creek on a bridge. Head uphill toward Calypso Cascades.

1.9   Arrive at Calypso Cascades; look for pink calypso orchids in early July.

2.7   Come to a crossing of Ouzel Creek. Ouzel Falls is visible from the crossing but much more spectacular from the base of the falls, a short way uphill.

3.2   The trail splits. The right branch goes to Thunder Lake and Lion Lakes. Follow the left branch to Bluebird Lake.

4.6   Turn left onto the 0.5-mile spur trail (1.0 mile round-trip) to Ouzel Lake, boasting pondlilies and views of Ouzel and Mahana Peaks. Return to the Bluebird Lake Trail.

5.6   Continue up the Bluebird Lake Trail.

6.1   Pass Chickadee Pond and an area heavily burned in the 1978 fire.

7.0   Reach Bluebird Lake after final steep stretch limited to hikers. Return to the Wild Basin Trailhead.

13.0   Arrive back at the trailhead.

Hike Index

About the Author

Guidebooks by Kent Dannen are the standard reference for the trails of Rocky Mountain National Park. He has hiked every trail in the park and those in this guide many times. Nonetheless, these trails never get old or fail to offer something new each time he travels them. He began his professional guiding activities as hike master and naturalist for the YMCA of the Rockies and has led hundreds of hikes covering thousands of miles.

A former contributing editor of *Backpacker Magazine*, Kent freelances as a writer and photographer. He has taught classes in nature photography, bird identification, and the history of wildlife in America for the National Wildlife Federation and Canadian Wildlife Federation from coast to coast. He also is a recipient of the US Department of Agriculture Certificate of Appreciation for his outstanding volunteer services in developing educational materials that help manage and protect the Indian Peaks Wilderness.

Kent has written four other guidebooks: *Short Hikes in Rocky Mountain National Park, Best Easy Day Hikes Rocky Mountain National Park, Hiking Rocky Mountain National Park* (10th edition), and *Rocky Mountain Wildflowers*. He lives near Allenspark, Colorado.

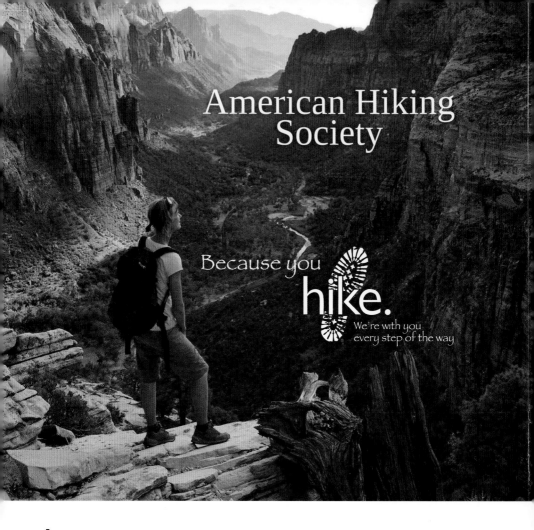

American Hiking Society

Because you

hike.

We're with you every step of the way

As a national voice for hikers, **American Hiking Society** works every day:

- Building and maintaining hiking trails
- Educating and supporting hikers by providing information and resources
- Supporting hiking and trail organizations nationwide
- Speaking for hikers in the halls of Congress and with federal land managers

Whether you're a casual hiker or a seasoned backpacker, become a member of American Hiking Society and join the national hiking community! You'll enjoy great member benefits and help preserve the nation's hiking trails, so tomorrow's hike is even better than today's. We invite you to join us now!

American Hiking Society

Take to the Trails

"FalconGuides point the compass to the best spots to play, climb, hike, fish, and be."—CNN.com

Best Hikes Rocky Mountain National Park features fifty-five of the best hikes throughout one of America's most popular national parks. Detailed maps and trail descriptions make navigating these wonderful trails easy, from family-friendly strolls to popular vistas to hillier wooded pathways. FalconGuides have set the standard for outdoor guidebooks for more than thirty-five years. Written by top experts, each guide invites you to experience the adventure and beauty of the outdoors.

Look inside to find:

- Hikes suited to every ability
- Mile-by-mile directional cues
- Difficulty ratings, trail contacts, fees/permits, and best hiking seasons
- An index of hikes by category—from easy day hikes to waterfalls
- Full-color photos throughout
- GPS coordinates

Kent Dannen, a former contributing editor for *Backpacker* magazine, is a guide, naturalist, and master outdoorsman who has been leading hiking trips in Rocky Mountain National Park for more than forty years.

Front and back cover photos by Kent Dannen

An imprint of Rowman & Littlefield
falcon.com

Distributed by NATIONAL BOOK NETWORK
800-462-6420

Join our community

$22.95
ISBN 978-1-4930-0813-1

9 781493 008131

0 2295

Best Hikes
Rocky Mountain
National Park

A Guide to the Park's Greatest Hiking Adventures

KENT DANNEN

American
Hiking
Society

Best Hikes Rocky Mountain National Park